THE ART
OF
LOGICAL REASONING

THE ART OF LOGICAL REASONING

Thomas Schwartz
University of Texas

Random House  New York

First Edition

9 8 7 6 5 4 3 2 1

Copyright © 1980 by Thomas Schwartz

Library of Congress Cataloging in Publication Data

Schwartz, Thomas,
  The art of logical reasoning.

  Bibliography: p.
  Includes index.
  1. Reasoning. I. Title.
BC177.S35   160   79-28378
ISBN 0-394-32267-3

Manufactured in the United States of America

Cover Design: Ivan Paslavsky

To
Ellie

PREFACE

My subject is how to articulate and evaluate arguments according to logical standards broadly conceived. As rigorous as any up-to-date introduction to formal logic, as practical as any of the fashionable treatments of informal logic, my approach is neither of these. It is a sophisticated introduction to applied logic, a rigorous approach to critical thinking.

This is a textbook, but not just a textbook. It is written for students, but written no less for a general audience: for speakers and writers, for editors and critics, for lawyers, teachers, policy-evaluators, and others who wish to improve their logical skills, or who simply enjoy argument, language, and intellectual challenge.

Writers of logic texts typically begin with a body of theory (first-order predicate logic, a taxonomy of fallacies), whence they extract principles and techniques whose mastery, they assure us, aids one in some important (if largely unspecified) modes of reasoning and criticism. Having found scant cause for such assurance, I took the opposite approach. Instead of beginning with a body of theory and extracting principles and techniques whose mastery might serve some hazy skill objective, I began with a skill objective—an unquestionably important one—then worked back to such theory-related principles and techniques as seemed useful in achieving that objective. Because studying this book involves practicing the skill objective itself, the notorious problem of educational transfer is largely overcome.

What is this objective? In rough terms, it is the ability to pick apart, reconstruct, and criticize pieces of reasoning in the careful, rigorous, sharply focused way philosophers typically do. This skill is by no means peculiar to philosophy; philosophers are just peculiarly explicit and self-conscious about it. It is best described, perhaps, as *the art of composing a closely reasoned critical or argumentative essay*.

After identifying this skill objective in a rough way, I analyzed it, more fully and precisely, as a series of steps. These are briefly summarized in § 7.1, summarized in greater detail in Appendix One, elaborated in Chapters 7 to 9, extended in Chapter 10, and given sustained illustration in Chapters 11 and 12. Working back to basics, I then identified some concepts and techniques that are essential to this objective and some that help one fulfill it. These are explained in Chapters 1 to 6.

Courses and textbooks devoted to formal or symbolic or mathematical logic have their place. Especially when presented in a theoretical rather than mechanical way, the subject is interesting on its own account, it helps one use and understand formal theories, and it is good background for studies in philosophy, artificial intelligence, structural linguistics, and other subjects. But it does not equip one with most of the tools one needs to analyze and evaluate real reasoning couched in ordinary language.

Standard treatments of so-called informal logic trade logical rigor for offhand applicability. Containing more informality than logic, they provide tools that are wanting in temper and sharpness. We expect well-educated people to construct and criticize pieces of reasoning with an uncommon degree of rigor, subtlety, and precision—just the qualities that are downgraded by many informal-logic texts.

Although I ignore symbolic logic, I dwell on *deductive validity*. I try to equip students with a firm grasp of the general concept and real skill at applying it—skill that outlives memory of algorithmic routines. The reason is not that evaluating an argument is mainly a matter of deciding whether a given conclusion is a valid consequence of given premises; rarely does argumentative discourse display premises and a conclusion related this way. The reason rather is that analyzing an argument is largely a matter of *reconstructing* it so that the conclusion is a valid consequence of the premises. This in turn is partly a matter of formulating validating tacit premises (I spell out the details in Chapter 7). Validity is less a trait to be found in argumentative discourse than a constraint on the way one reconstructs such discourse. There lies its importance.

In Part Two (Chapters 4 to 6) I explain and illustrate the use of Venn diagrams for ascertaining validity. Simple, natural, and pictorial, the Venn-diagram technique is easier to learn, harder to forget, more efficient to use, and more likely to be internalized than comparable symbolic methods. What is more, it gives a "yes" or "no" answer to questions of validity; it does not involve the translation of English into another, mathematical-looking language; it can be mastered without memorizing rules; it enables one, not only to ascertain validity, but to identify validating tacit premises; and it draws upon geometric skills to enhance less-developed logical skills. As they are standardly presented, of course, Venn diagrams apply only to a small class of arguments. But this is a limitation of standard presentations, not of the diagrams themselves. The Venn-diagram technique presented here fully accommodates singly quantified monadic predicate logic; it also handles singular terms, predicate modifiers, certain relational locutions (not all, of course), and non-truth-functional sentential connectives.

While I do not adopt the fallacy-label approach (or even use the word "fallacy"), I share many concerns with partisans of that approach. In effect (though usually not in quite these terms), I discuss non sequitur in Chapters 1 to 6, fallacies of ambiguity in Chapter 8, fallacies of false cause in Chapter 10, the fallacies of composition and division in §§ 8.3 and 12.3, inconsistency in §§ 3.4 and 9.3, question-begging also in § 9.3, and hasty generalization in §§ 9.4 and 10.3. I do not explicitly discuss the traditional formal fallacies, because I give a sustained treatment of deductive validity in Parts One and Two. Neither do I explicitly discuss certain traditional fallacies of relevance, because when arguments that commit these fallacies are reconstructed according to the method of

Chapter 7, their irrelevant appeals (to authority, to force, to the people, or whatever) are transformed into distinct, blatantly unacceptable premises.

I explain and illustrate my procedure for analyzing and criticizing arguments in Chapters 7 to 9. Chapters 10 extends the procedure to explanations and reverse-explanation arguments. Chapters 11 and 12 contain sustained applications of the procedure. Any of Chapters 10, 11 and 12 can be omitted from a course to satisfy a time constraint. Chapters 1 and 2 and § 3.4 are essential in understanding the rest of the book. The remainder of Chapter 3 and Chapters 4 to 6 are not strictly essential. I think they are important, naturally; I know they help students master the procedure of Chapters 7 to 9. But depending on your priorities and constraints, you might properly find a good deal of Chapters 3 to 6 to be dispensable. I hope you will be able at least to cover Chapter 4—the first of the three Venn-diagram chapters: even a week's study of Venn diagrams makes a great improvement in one's ability to ascertain validity and to identify validating tacit premises. But I must emphasize that instructors who do not share my enthusiasm for Venn diagrams can skip most if not all of the Venn-diagram material and read around the few diagrams used in Chapters 7 and 8.

All or part of this text is easily combined with all or part of a short text on symbolic logic, informal fallacies, rhetoric, statistical fallacies, probability, scientific method, or philosophic analysis. It also is easily combined with a text on some substantive subject, such as practical ethics, current social issues, or problems of philosophy. Even apart from my judgment of what is important, I saw no reason to take up topics ably covered elsewhere. Among textbook writers, too many owe too much to too few.

Each chapter contains a large number of illustrative examples and exercises. Solutions to exercises marked with a star—about half the total—are given in Appendix Four.

I have used successive incarnations of this book in a course that fulfills a general requirement at the University of Texas, which has a relatively noncompetitive admissions policy. A majority of the students who have taken the course have been freshmen and sophomores. Some were urged to take the course by other professors, some by fellow students who had taken it before. Many took it as preparation for the LSAT (Law Boards), having been told by other students who had taken both the course and the LSAT that the course helped. Some students took the course because they thought they were particularly logical, more because they thought they were particularly deficient in logic. Some students took it because they appreciated the fraud perpetrated by curricula that stress topical coverage rather than skill enhancement. Surprisingly many took it for logical self-defense against roommates, friends, and paramours who had taken it. Perhaps the largest single group comprised those who found the course the most convenient way (or the only convenient way) to fulfill the general requirement. A perfectly representative sample of American college students this is not. But it is a diverse group, whose average ability should not be much above or below that of introductory-logic students at any respectable college or university.

Using this book, it is possible to teach a course students find easy. I hope you will not do so. Although I did not write the book for an elite audience, I intended it to be intellectually challenging. Education is struggle: to improve one's competence at anything, one must strive to exceed it. It takes a hard stone to hone a good tool to a nice edge, and a lot of grinding if the tool was dull.

Not that studying this book is all a dull grind. A gratifying number of students have told me they enjoyed the examples and exercises. The intellectual challenge, combined with occasional whimsey and topicality, makes the work fun for some.

This book reflects my experience teaching the art of logical reasoning. I hope future editions will reflect yours. Please share with me your reactions, good and bad, and any suggestions you have for improvements.

My academic creditors are too numerous for a fair accounting. But I must mention Susan Gragg, who helped me teach this material for several years; Dennis Packard, from whose own approach to teaching logic I have borrowed liberally; and especially Preston Covey, with whom I jointly conceived my general approach. I shall not minimize their contributions by denying them any responsibility for remaining deficiencies. Marguerite Ponder flawlessly typed difficult manuscript on short notice, correcting errors of mine in the process. My greatest single debt is to Jane Cullen of Random House. She saw the oak in the acorn, often more clearly than I.

Austin, Texas
October 1979

CONTENTS

PART THREE: EVALUATIONS

THE ART
OF
LOGICAL REASONING

PART · 1
CONCEPTS

Arguments

1.1. SOMETHING YOU GIVE

Much of what we shall do, you and I—much of what you doubtless do already—is construct arguments, evaluate arguments, argue about them even.

In my sense, an argument is something you give rather than something you have. It is a piece of reasoning, not a dispute, although a disputant might use it. When you say something and defend it—when you offer reasons to support it—your words constitute an argument. *An argument is any piece of discourse that gives reasons (good or bad) to support some statement.*

Examples of arguments, good and bad:

Example 1   Socrates is a man, and all men are mortal, so Socrates is mortal.

Example 2   Communists admire Marx. So do some faculty members. Therefore, some faculty members are Communists.

Example 3   We had best allow gas prices to rise to meet demand, else there will be a shortage, with long lines at gas pumps and stranded motorists.

Example 4   Because standard IQ tests are culturally biased, they are discriminatory. That makes it unconstitutional to use them in public schools.

3

Example 5   Without itches, we wouldn't enjoy scratching. Consequently, evil sometimes is necessary for the existence of good.

Example 6   A thousand balls have been drawn from the urn. All are blue. It is reasonable to expect the next ball drawn from the urn to be blue.

Example 7   It evidently rained, because the streets are wet.

Example 8   If it is wrong to kill a one-month-old infant but not a six-month fetus, there has to be a difference between them—not just some difference or other, but a *morally relevant* difference: there has to be something true of the six-month fetus but not of the one-month-old infant that makes it permissible to kill the former. Surely, though, there is no significant developmental difference, somatic or psychological. True, the six-month fetus is dependent on its mother for its life. But so, normally, is the one-month-old infant—in a different way, of course, but to no less a degree. Apparently there is no morally relevant difference. Therefore, if it is not wrong to kill a six-month fetus, it is not wrong to kill a one-month-old infant. But the latter *is* wrong. Hence, so is the former.

Example 9   My walking on your lawn doesn't violate your right that I not do so unless you don't want me to walk there. My driving your car doesn't violate your right that I not drive it unless you don't want me to drive it. My doing something doesn't violate any right of yours unless you desire that the thing not be done. But a fetus has no desires, hence no desire not to be killed. So even if a fetus has a right not to be killed, killing it would not violate that right.

Example 10   If capital punishment deterred crime, it would be justified. It doesn't. So it isn't.

Example 11   Homosexual acts involving only consenting adults have no victims. So how can you call them crimes?

Example 12   THEOREM: If x + y is odd, then x or y is even.
Proof: If x and y are both odd, then $x-1$ and $y-1$ are even, and thus, since a sum of even numbers must itself be even, $(x-1) + (y-1) + 2$ is even. But $(x-1) +$

$(y-1) + 2 = x + y$. So if x and y are both odd, $x + y$ is even. Hence, if $x + y$ is odd, either x or y must be even, q. e. d.

1.2. THE GROSS ANATOMY OF ARGUMENTS

The statements constituting an argument, called the *steps* of the argument, come in three varieties:

(i) A *conclusion*   This is the statement the argument is designed to support or defend.
Here are the conclusions of Examples 1−4:

Socrates is mortal.

Some faculty members are Communists.

We had best allow gas prices to rise to meet demand.

It is unconstitutional to use standard IQ tests in public schools.

of Examples 7 and 8:

It rained.

It is wrong to kill a six-month fetus.

and of Example 11:

Homosexual acts involving only consenting adults are not crimes.

Instead of slavishly copying the relevant sentence from each argument, I formulated each conclusion as a fully explicit declarative sentence devoid of extraneous matter. But *you* need not be so fussy at this stage. Asked for the conclusion of an argument, you may adhere as closely as you like, consistent with intelligibility, to the original text of the argument. The important thing is to distinguish the conclusion from the rest of the argument.
What are the conclusions of Examples 5, 6, 9, 10, and 12? (Do not proceed till you have answered this question!)

(ii) *Premises*   In most arguments, at least one statement is affirmed without any defense.* An argumentative starting point, it is used to defend the conclusion but is not itself defended in the argument in question, although it could be the conclusion of another argument. Such

*The exceptions, for the record, are arguments whose conclusions are so-called *logical truths*, e.g.: "Either all swans are white or not all swans are white."

a statement is one of the *ultimate reasons* given by the argument to support its conclusion: it is one of the argument's *premises*.

Example 2 has two premises:

> Communists admire Marx.
>
> Some faculty members admire Marx.
>
> (*or*: So do some faculty members.)

Here are the premises of Example 6:

> A thousand balls have been drawn from the urn.
>
> All the balls drawn from the urn are blue.
>
> (*or*: All are blue.)

Asked for the premises of Example 1, you could say this argument has one premise, "Socrates is a man, and all men are mortal," or two, "Socrates is a man" and "All men are mortal." I prefer the second answer. Either is correct.

Example 10 has two premises. What are they? (Do not proceed till you have answered this question!)

Extracting premises from surrounding text can be tricky. Look at Example 3:

> We had best allow gas prices to rise to meet demand, else there will be a shortage, with long lines at gas pumps and stranded motorists.

The first clause, "We had best allow gas prices to rise to meet demand," is the conclusion, not a premise. But "there will be a shortage, with long lines . . ." is not a premise either. Why? Because the author of Example 3 is not saying that a shortage *will occur*. He evidently hopes his recommendation is followed and thinks no shortage will occur in that case. He is just saying that a shortage will occur *if* his recommendation is *not* followed. His premise, in other words, is the following:

> Either we allow gas prices to rise to meet demand, or else there will be a shortage, with long lines at gas pumps and stranded motorists.

The clause "else there will be a shortage . . ." is elliptical for this premise. That means the "else" clause is an incomplete sentence whose missing part, "either we allow gas prices to rise to meet demand," is understood from context.

Identifying the premises of the remaining examples raises special difficulties, which I discuss shortly.

An argument is no better, in a way, than its premises. Although impeccably reasoned, it will not enhance the credibility of its conclusion if its premises are implausible. Thanks to an implausible premise, this argument lends no support to its conclusion:

> Queen Elizabeth II is a vampiress. Therefore, she is not a strict vegetarian.

(iii) *Intermediate steps*   Even when the premises of an argument would, if plausible, support the conclusion, this connection between premises and conclusion might not be obvious. To make it obvious, one adds further steps to the argument—not additional premises, but assertions designed to *bring out the connection* between premises and conclusion. These I call *intermediate steps*.

Like most arguments commonly encountered, Examples 1–3 and 5–7 contain no intermediate steps. Example 4 contains one:

> Standard IQ tests are discriminatory.

Because this step is offered as a reason for believing the conclusion, it must be a premise or an intermediate step. But because the premise, "Standard IQ tests are culturally biased," is offered as a reason for believing this step, this step is not offered as an *ultimate* reason for believing the conclusion. That is, it is not a premise. So it must be an intermediate step. Example 8 contains two intermediate steps:

> There is no morally relevant difference (between a one-month-old infant and a six-month fetus).
>
> If it is not wrong to kill a six-month fetus, it is not wrong to kill a one-month-old infant.

Do Examples 10 and 11 contain intermediate steps? (Do not proceed till you have answered this question!)

Sometimes it is hard to decide whether a step is a premise or an intermediate step. Take another look at Example 9:

> My walking on your lawn doesn't violate your right that I not do so unless you don't want me to walk there.
>
> My driving your car doesn't violate your right that I not drive it unless you don't want me to drive it.
>
> My doing something doesn't violate any right of yours unless you desire that the thing not be done.
>
> A fetus has no desires, hence no desire not to be killed.

So even if a fetus has a right not to be killed, killing it would not violate that right.

The third sentence states a general principle, of which the first two sentences give examples. If the examples are supposed merely to clarify the principle, then the third sentence is a premise and the first two are not steps of any sort—not really parts of the argument. But if the examples are supposed to support the principle—to enhance its credibility—then the first two sentences are premises and the third is an intermediate step.

In Example 12, distinguishing premises from intermediate steps is problematic for a reason I discuss in the next section.

1.3. MISSING PIECES

Sometimes an argument's *conclusion is unstated.* Suppose I say:

I oppose the death penalty because it has not been shown to be an effective deterrent.

Then I have given an argument against the death penalty. Its conclusion is not: "I oppose the death penalty." Its conclusion, unstated, is something like: "The death penalty is unjust." What I am trying to convince my audience is not that I oppose the death penalty (they can take my word for that), but that the death penalty merits opposition.

Often an argument contains *unstated premises*—premises implicitly used in the argument but assumed to be so obvious to the likely audience that it would be gratuitous to mention them. Unstated premises often are called *assumptions.*

Consider this argument:

Capital punishment must be unjust, because it has not been shown to be an effective deterrent.

The conclusion is:

Capital punishment is unjust.

The single *stated* premise is:

Capital punishment has not been shown to be an effective deterrent.

Something like the following seems to function as an *un*stated premise:

A punishment is unjust if it has not been shown to be an effective deterrent.

To be sure, the author of the argument might insist that *this* really is not his tacit premise. He might say, for example, that what he tacitly assumed were these two statements:

> A *severe* punishment is unjust if it has not been shown to be an effective deterrent.
>
> Capital punishment is severe.

It is hard to tell with absolute certainty what an argument's tacit premises are.

Examples 1 and 2 do not seem to rest on any tacit premises. Here are Examples 3, 4, and 8, with tacit premises made explicit:

Example   3   Either we allow gas prices to rise to meet demand, or else there will be a shortage, with long lines at gas pumps and stranded motorists. (express premise)

Allowing gas prices to rise to meet demand is better than there being a shortage, with long lines at gas pumps and stranded motorists. (tacit premise)

If doing something is better than not doing it, we had best do it. (tacit premise)

We had best allow gas prices to rise to meet demand. (conclusion)

Example   4   Standard IQ tests are culturally biased. (express premise)

Whatever is culturally biased is discriminatory. (tacit premise)

Standard IQ tests are discriminatory. (intermediate step)

It is unconstitutional to use anything discriminatory in public schools. (tacit premise)

It is unconstitutional to use standard IQ tests in public schools. (conclusion)

Example   8   If it is wrong to kill a one-month-old infant but not a six-month fetus, there has to be a morally relevant difference between them (that makes it permissible to kill the latter). (express premise)

There is no significant developmental difference, somatic or psychological, between a one-month-old infant and a six-month fetus. (express premise)

A one-month-old infant is no less dependent on its mother for its life than is a six-month fetus. (express premise)

Any morally relevant difference between a one-month-old infant and a six-month fetus (that makes it permissible to kill the latter) is either a significant developmental difference, somatic or psychological, or else a difference consisting in the infant being less dependent on its mother for its life than is the fetus. (tacit premise)

There is no morally relevant difference between a one-month-old infant and a six-month fetus (that makes it permissible to kill the latter). (intermediate step)

If it is not wrong to kill a six-month fetus, it is not wrong to kill a one-month-old infant. (intermediate step)

It *is* wrong to kill a one-month-old infant. (express premise)

It is wrong to kill a six-month fetus. (conclusion)

Sometimes it is not clear whether a step is a stated premise, or an intermediate step supported by a tacit premise. In Example 12, the step:

If x and y are both odd, then x−1 and y−1 are even

could be either a premise or an intermediate step justified by this tacit premise:

For any n, if n is odd, then n−1 is even.

Do Examples 5, 6, 7, 8, 10, and 11 have tacit premises? (Do not proceed till you have answered this question!)

An argument with tacit premises or a tacit conclusion is called an *enthymeme*. Most everyday arguments are enthymemes.

1.4. DEDUCTIVE ARGUMENTS

So-called *deductive* arguments constitute the most widely studied, best-understood class of arguments. Among the arguments we shall play with, deductive ones are of supreme importance. Mathematical proofs are deductive arguments. It is the business of the science of logic (as opposed to the *art* of logic, which is our present concern) to theorize mathematically about correct and incorrect deductive arguments.

The author of any argument makes, or at least commits himself to accepting, three contentions:

(i)   The premises are true.

(ii) The conclusion is true.

(iii) Truth of the premises would enhance the credibility of the conclusion.

What makes an argument *deductive* is that its author goes beyond (iii), contending:

> Supposing the premises to be true, it would be *impossible* for the conclusion not to be true as well. One who affirms the premises but denies the conclusion contradicts oneself.

All arguments purport to show that their premises, if true, would provide some support for their conclusions. A deductive argument purports to show more: that the evidentiary connection between premises and conclusion is the strongest it could possibly be. One who gives a deductive argument holds that truth of the premises would not only support but *necessitate* truth of the conclusion—that the premises could not possibly be true without the conclusion being true.

Another way to say that an argument is deductive is to say that it is an attempt to *deduce* its conclusion *from* its premises, or to show, to prove, to demonstrate that the conclusion *follows from* or is *logically implied by* or is *entailed by* or is a *logical consequence of* its premises.

Example 1 pretty clearly is a deductive argument. Because truth of the premises, "Socrates is a man" and "All men are mortal," would so obviously necessitate that of the conclusion, "Socrates is mortal," the author of this argument doubtless meant to maintain as much.

Let us suppose that Example 6 has no tacit premises—a reasonable enough supposition. Then this argument clearly is not deductive. Although unlikely, it is *possible* for all thousand balls drawn from the urn to be blue without the next one being blue. Truth of the stated premise would merely support, not necessitate, that of the conclusion. Because this is so obvious, the argument's author doubtless meant to maintain no more.

It would be wrong to characterize all deductive arguments as *conclusive* arguments, or even *purportedly* conclusive ones. An argument, deductive or not, is only as good as its premises. Insofar as there is doubt about the truth of any essential premise, the conclusion is left somewhat in doubt. And insofar as an argument leaves its conclusion in doubt, it does not conclusively support the conclusion. The author of a deductive argument holds that his conclusion could not possibly be false *if his premises be true*. That is not the same as holding that his conclusion could not possibly be false.

The author of Example 1 could conceivably have been a logical milk-toast, who meant merely that the premises enhanced the likelihood of the conclusion. And the author of Example 6 could conceivably have been a logical daredevil, who meant that truth of the stated premise would necessitate that of the conclusion. In the first case, Example 1 would not be a deductive argument after all. In the second, Example 6 would be a deductive argument. It would be a bad one, though, because the purported necessary connection between premise and conclusion obviously does not obtain. Rarely can one tell *with complete certainty* whether an argument is deductive. It depends on the author's contention regarding the premise-conclusion relationship, and rarely is that contention fully explicit.

Actually, putting it this way understates the problem of classification. We have been supposing that Example 6 has no tacit premises. Suppose we now allow it this tacit premise:

> If a thousand balls have been drawn from the urn and all are blue, then the next ball drawn from the urn will be blue.

Then we can reasonably construe Example 6 as a *pretty good* deductive argument. For truth of its two premises would not merely support but necessitate that of its conclusion. What is more, to assert or accept the original argument is to assert or accept, among other things and without further defense, that the conclusion is true if the premises are true. So it is perforce to assert or accept, without further defense, the new premise. Therefore, even if the new premise is false or otherwise objectionable, adding it to the premises cannot impair the argument: although not a premise, it already was an undefended part of the argument.

To be sure, Example 6 with the tacit premise is no better *as an argument* than Example 6 without the tacit premise. Adding that premise adds no support to the conclusion. It just enables us to treat the argument as deductive.

As this illustrates, *any argument can be construed as deductive without impairment*—though often without improvement. For this reason, although I expect you to understand the special contention that makes an argument deductive (truth of premises would necessitate truth of conclusion), I do not expect you to be able to sort garden-variety arguments into deductive and nondeductive display cases.

We shall study deductive arguments for the most part. Or rather, we shall construe the arguments we study as deductive for the most part, not much caring (because it does not much matter) whether their authors intended this construction.

1.5. INDUCTIVE ARGUMENTS

If an argument is not deductive, what is it? *Inductive,* perhaps. Custom ordains that every elementary discussion of *de*ductive arguments shall contrast these with so-called *in*ductive arguments. Custom is less instructive about the meaning of "inductive."

In a *wide sense,* an *inductive argument* is any *nondeductive* one—any argument whose premises purport merely to support, not to necessitate, its conclusion.

In a *narrow sense,* an inductive argument is an attempt to *generalize:* its conclusion generalizes the information contained in its premises.

Among inductive arguments in the narrow sense, the simplest reason from premises of this (or a similar) form:

(i)   Every A examined so far is B,

to the corresponding conclusion:

(ii)   Every A is B.

Example:

All swans examined so far are white.

Therefore, all swans are white.

Less simple inductive arguments, still in the narrow sense, can have weaker premises (affirming that most As examined so far, or a certain relatively large proportion of the As examined so far, are B) or additional premises concerning the distribution of the sample of As examined so far. They also can have weaker conclusions (affirming that most As are B) or probabilistic conclusions (affirming the probability that a randomly selected A will be a B).

Every inductive argument in the narrow sense obviously is inductive in the wide sense, too. Is any argument inductive in the wide sense but not in the narrow sense? Construed as nondeductive, the following two arguments are of course inductive in the wide sense:

Some swans have been examined so far, and all are white. Therefore, the next swan to be examined is white.

Boris is Russian. But relatively few Russians are Baptist. And Boris is not known to belong to any category containing relatively many Baptists. Therefore, Boris is not Baptist.

Yet these arguments are not inductive in the narrow sense: their conclusions do not generalize the information contained in their premises. To be sure, one might fairly contend that the first argument involves an implicit generalization of the information contained in the premise—that the premise supports the conclusion only because it supports the generalization: "All swans are white." But that cannot be said of the "Boris" example.

Even in the narrow sense, some inductive arguments are bad arguments, despite unimpeachable premises. Sometimes (i) is unquestionably true yet fails to provide *any* support for (ii); it might even support the falsity of (ii). This is brought out by the following example, which we owe to the distinguished American philosopher Nelson Goodman.

You are familiar, of course, with the adjectives "blue" and "green." Here is a new one: "grue." To call something *grue* is to say that it is either *green (all over) and examined so far or blue (all over) and not yet examined.* Every emerald examined so far is green, hence grue. In other words, this premise, which has the form of (i), is true:

Every emerald so-far examined is grue.

Probably every emerald not yet examined also is green, hence not blue, hence not grue. Therefore, the corresponding conclusion of the form (ii), namely:

Every emerald is grue,

almost certainly is false; at any rate, it is unsupported by the premise. If anything, the premise supports the *falsity* of the conclusion. Sometimes, then, a premise of the form (i) provides no support for the corresponding conclusion of the form (ii).

For deductive arguments, logicians have developed fairly clear and complete criteria of correctness, which I discuss in subsequent chapters. We lack comparable criteria of inductive correctness. Sometimes (i) supports (ii); sometimes it does not. Students of inductive reasoning have not agreed on any rule for distinguishing the good cases from the bad.

EXERCISES

Identify the stated premises and conclusions of the following three arguments:

* 1. All conservatives are Republicans. But no Democrat is Republican. So no Democrat is conservative.

* 2. No worker is rich. But some Democrats are workers. So some Democrats are not rich.

3. Someone is a politician. And someone is greedy. Thus, someone is a greedy politician.

4. List the premises and intermediate steps (if any) of Examples 5, 11, and 12, labeling each step "stated premise," "tacit premise," or "intermediate step."

5. Do you think Example 4 is *deductive?* Explain.

For each of the following arguments, identify the conclusion, the stated premises, and the tacit premises (if any). Remember: Often you have some latitude in formulating premises and conclusions, stated and tacit. Do not worry about formulations. Just make sure in each case that you have distinguished the conclusion from the other steps and that you have distinguished each premise from the other steps.

6. All Podunk students are smart. But some people are not smart. So some people are not Podunk students.

* 7. I'm opposed to deregulating natural-gas prices, because deregulating the price of any good imposes an unfair burden on the poor.

8. SLA members often sincerely desire to better mankind. But terrorists are never thus sincere. So no terrorists are SLA members.

* 9. Dracula must be a jet setter because he enjoys a great night life.

10. I think Snow White is entitled to maternity insurance. After all, she must be a polyandrist, living as she does with a bunch of dwarfs.

* 11. If we adopt the bill, we're in for trouble. But if we reject it, we're in for trouble as well. *We're in for trouble!*

12. If we decontrol natural-gas prices, we place an unfair burden on the poor. But if we continue to regulate the price of natural gas, we impose unjust costs on future generations. Therefore, either we place an unfair burden on the poor, or we impose unjust costs on future generations.

* 13. If personality traits were hereditary, he-men would have he-children.

14. Why outlaw pornography? We know now that it does no psychological harm. And surely naked bodies per se are not evil.

* 15. You think God can do *anything?* Can He make a rock so big He cannot lift it?

16. Compared with smoking cigarettes, failing to have an annual dental examination does trivial harm to one's health. Consequently, it's unlikely that a person who troubles to have an annual dental examination would ever smoke cigarettes.

* 17. We all regard ourselves as having free will, because we all deliberate about alternative courses of action.

* 18. Societies are subject to the same ethical standards as individuals. But individuals may not kill others except in self-defense. Specifically, individuals

may not kill others just for the sake of retribution or deterrence. So society may not use capital punishment.

19. Owing to the danger of executing innocent people, capital punishment ought to be abolished.

20. Because almost everyone executed is poor, capital punishment is discriminatory.

21. Look and listen for arguments in books, magazines, newspapers, television shows, lectures, discussions, barroom disputes, lovers' quarrels, etc. Write down four. Identify stated premises, tacit premises (if any), intermediate steps (if any), and conclusions.

2

Deductive Validity

2.1. KANGAROOS AND VALID ARGUMENTS

The only animals in this house are cats.

Every animal is suitable for a pet that loves to gaze at the moon.

When I detest an animal, I avoid it.

No animals are carnivorous unless they prowl at night.

No cats fail to kill mice.

No animals ever take to me except what are in this house.

Kangaroos are not suitable for pets.

None but *Carnivora* kill mice.

I detest animals that do not take to me.

Animals that prowl at night always love to gaze at the moon.

Conclusion: I always avoid a kangaroo.

What you have just seen is a deductive argument—a *deductively valid* one, as it happens. It is *deductive* because its *conclusion purportedly follows* from its premises: its author, Lewis Carroll, held that truth of the premises would not only support but necessitate truth of the conclusion—that the conclusion must be true if the premises be true. It is *deductively valid* because (roughly speaking) Lewis Carroll was right: the *conclusion does follow* from the premises; the conclusion must indeed be true if the premises be true.

Note the difference between calling an argument *deductive* and calling it deductively *valid*. In a deductive argument, the conclusion *purpor-*

tedly follows from the premises—whether or not it actually follows. In a deductively valid argument, the conclusion does follow from the premises—whether or not it purports to follow. In the case of a deductive argument, the author *holds*, rightly or wrongly, that truth of the premises would necessitate truth of the conclusion. In the case of a deductively valid argument, truth of the premises *would* necessitate truth of the conclusion, whether or not the author thinks so or says so.

Here are three more deductively valid arguments:

Whoever is reading is literate.	true
You are reading.	true
Therefore, you are literate.	true
Whoever is reading is dead.	false
You are reading.	true
Therefore, you are dead.	false
Whoever is dead is reading.	false
You are dead.	false
Therefore, you are reading.	true

Observe that a deductively valid argument can have one or more false premises. While some have false conclusions as well, others have true conclusions.

The first argument has true premises. Its conclusion also is true. I gave no example of a deductively valid argument with true premises and a false conclusion. There is none. Why? (Do not proceed till you have answered this question!)

What makes an argument deductively valid—*valid*, for short—is not true premises or a true conclusion or both, but a certain *connection* between premises and conclusion: roughly speaking, the conclusion has to be true if the premises be true—which is not to say it is or they are.

A *sound* argument is *both valid and has true premises.* Of the three examples above, only the first is sound. Besides true premises, a sound argument (as just defined) always has a true conclusion. Why? (Do not proceed till you have answered this question!)

Examples of *invalid* (hence unsound) arguments:

If you are reading, you are literate.	true
You are literate.	true
Therefore, you are reading.	true

Whoever is reading is dead.	false
You are dead.	false
Therefore, you are reading.	true
If you are taking an exam, you are literate.	true
You are literate.	true
Therefore, you are taking an exam.	false
Whoever is literate is taking an exam.	false
Either you are taking an exam, or you are not reading.	false
Therefore, if you are literate, you are not reading.	false

In the first of these four examples, the premises and conclusion are true. Yet the argument is not valid. Although the conclusion is true, this fact is not guaranteed by the true premises. The conclusion did not have to be true, even given the truth of the premises. It just happens to be true, independently of the premises. In an invalid argument, the premises may or may not be true, and in either case the conclusion may or may not be true.

The premises and conclusion of an *in*valid argument can possess any combination of truth and falsity. That an argument is invalid tells us nothing about the truth or falsity of premises or conclusion. The premises and conclusion of a *valid* argument can possess any combination of truth and falsity save one: true premises plus false conclusion. That an argument is valid tells us just that it does not have *both* true premises *and* a false conclusion—though it may have either.

Here are several common ways to say the same thing about a given argument:

It is valid (deductively valid, logically valid).

The conclusion follows (follows logically) from the premises.

The conclusion is a valid consequence (logical consequence) of the premises.

The premises logically imply (validly imply, entail) the conclusion.

The conclusion must be true if the premises be true.

Truth of the premises would not merely support but necessitate truth of the conclusion.

It is impossible for the premises to be true without the conclusion being true as well.

You deny this when you say:

> The conclusion is independent (logically independent) of the premises.

2.2. VALIDITY AND OTHER VIRTUES

Validity is just one virtue a deductive argument can have, invalidity just one defect. Deductive arguments can be good or bad in many ways. They can be or fail to be clear, concise, polite, interesting, correctly spelled, important, nonequivocal, reverent, persuasive, elegant, inoffensive, clever, patriotic, pleasant, grammatical, funny, fair, and so on and on.

Here are three particularly important virtues even a valid argument might lack:

(i) *Truth of premises* True premises plus validity make an argument sound. False premises make even a valid argument unsound.

Once you have shown that an argument has at least one false premise, you have decisively refuted it, even if it is valid and its conclusion is true. For anyone aware of what you have shown can no longer accept one of the ultimate reasons (premises) offered in defense of the conclusion. The conclusion might still be true, but not for the reasons given.

(ii) *Sufficient plausibility of premises* For an argument to provide any support for its conclusion, its premises must be plausible—plausible enough, anyway, to enhance the conclusion's credibility to some degree.

False premises often are not sufficiently plausible. But even true premises can fail to be sufficiently plausible. Of the following two arguments, each is valid, each has a true conclusion, and one (we do not know which) has only true premises, hence is sound:

> There have been living things on Mars.
>
> Anything on Mars is in the solar system.
>
> Therefore, there have been living things in the solar system.

> There have never been living things on Mars.
>
> Anything born on Mars is a living thing on Mars.
>
> Therefore, you were not born on Mars.

Yet each of these arguments has a first premise that is not plausible enough to support its conclusion. So a *sound* argument need not be a *good* argument: it can fail to provide any support whatever for its conclusion. Soundness is not the inclusive virtue it is sometimes touted to be.

A particularly glaring case of a premise that is not sufficiently plausible is a *question-begging* premise—one that is identical or close to the conclusion it is used to support. Example:

> Only a Communist would support busing.
>
> Therefore, any supporter of busing must be a Communist.

Just as a true premise can fail to be sufficiently plausible, so a sufficiently plausible premise can turn out to be false. You probably find these statements eminently plausible: "The author of this book never was a professional barber." "The author of this book never had a job playing the role of a ventriloquist's dummy." Both are false.

If your premises are plausible enough and your argument otherwise virtuous, you have argued well—you have given what we should normally consider a pretty good argument—even if one of your premises turns out to be false. It is reasonable to demand that people make the best use of the information available to them. It is not reasonable to demand omniscience.

Plausibility can vary with audience and time. One man's axiom (God exists) is another's absurdity. New truths are discovered (Germs cause disease), erstwhile truisms discarded (Noxious effluvia cause disease). Lesson: When giving or evaluating an argument, define and keep in mind the intended audience—and date of performance.

(iii) *Evidence of validity*   The validity of a valid argument is not always evident. Although (roughly speaking) the conclusion must be true if the premises be true, this connection between premises and conclusion may not be obvious.

The two arguments about dead readers obviously are valid. Although valid, Lewis Carroll's argument about kangaroo-avoidance is not *obviously* valid. To make its validity evident, we must add suitable *intermediate steps*. If we succeed, we shall have *deduced* or *derived* the conclusion *from* the premises, and our words will constitute a *deduction* or *derivation* or *proof* of the conclusion from the premises. Example:

Premises
1. The only animals in this house are cats.

2. Every animal is suitable for a pet that loves to gaze at the moon.

3. When I detest an animal, I avoid it.

4. No animals are carnivorous unless they prowl at night.

5. No cats fail to kill mice.

6. No animals ever take to me except what are in this house.

7. Kangaroos are not suitable for pets.

8. None but *Carnivora* kill mice.

9. I detest animals that do not take to me.

10. Animals that prowl at night always love to gaze at the moon.

11. Kangaroos do not love to gaze at the moon.   from 2 and 7

12. Kangaroos do not prowl at night.   from 10 and 11

13. Kangaroos are not carnivorous.   from 4 and 12

14. Kangaroos do not kill mice.   from 8 and 13

15. Kangaroos are not cats.   from 5 and 14

16. Kangaroos are not animals in this house.   from 1 and 15

17. Kangaroos never take to me.   from 6 and 16

18. I detest kangaroos.   from 9 and 17

19. I always avoid a kangaroo.   from 3 and 18

Such a derivation normally would be set out more colloquially, like this:

Kangaroos are not suitable for pets (premise). But every animal is suitable for a pet that loves to gaze at the moon (premise). Therefore, kangaroos do not love to gaze at the moon (intermediate step), and thus, since animals that prowl at night always love to gaze at the moon (prem.), kangaroos do not prowl at night (i.s.). But no animals are carnivorous unless they prowl at night (prem.). Consequently, kangaroos are not carnivorous (i.s.), and hence, since none but *Carnivora* kill mice (prem.), kangaroos do not kill mice (i.s.), so that kangaroos are not cats (i.s.), inasmuch as no cats fail to kill mice (prem.). But the only animals in this house are cats (prem.), hence not kangaroos (i.s.), and no animals ever take to me except what are in this house (prem.). Therefore, kangaroos do not take to me (i.s.). As a result, I detest kangaroos (i.s.), since I detest animals that do not take to me (prem.). But when I detest an animal, I avoid it (prem.). Hence, I always avoid a kangaroo (conclusion).

Or consider the second argument about life on Mars. In case it is not completely obvious that the conclusion follows from the premises, we can make it obvious by adding an intermediate step:

There have never been living things on Mars. (premise)

But anything born on Mars is a living thing on Mars. (premise)

So nothing was born on Mars. (intermediate step)

In particular, then, you were not born on Mars. (conclusion)

The proofs you constructed in high-school geometry were attempted derivations of theorems from axioms. Each was a valid argument whose premises were the axioms of Euclidean geometry, whose conclusion was the theorem proved, and whose intermediate steps were the various steps you concocted to prove the theorem. Considerable time and ingenuity sometimes were required. There is no practicable, foolproof, generally applicable recipe for the construction of a correct derivation. Sometimes the deductive genius of a great mathematician is needed. Sometimes that is not enough.

2.3. A MATTER OF FORM

Roughly speaking, a deductively valid argument is one whose conclusion must be true if its premises be true. But only roughly speaking. It is time for some refinement.

What makes an argument valid is its *form*, its *shape*, its *structure*. Take:

Every alien is a potential spy.

François Abdul Benito Wahrhaftig is an alien.

Therefore, François Abdul Benito Wahrhaftig is a potential spy.

It is valid. It has this form:

Every A is a S.

w is a A.

∴ w is a S.

In any argument of this form, if the premises are true, so is the conclusion. The form guarantees that the conclusion is true if the premises are. Some arguments of this form have false premises. But those with true premises have true conclusions as well. *That* is what makes the "spy" argument valid.

A (deductively) *valid argument* is one with this virtue:

EVERY ARGUMENT OF THE SAME FORM WITH TRUE
PREMISES ALSO HAS A TRUE CONCLUSION

that is:

NO ARGUMENT OF THE SAME FORM HAS BOTH TRUE
PREMISES AND A FALSE CONCLUSION.

A *valid argument-form* is an argument-form of which each argument
with true premises has a true conclusion—an argument-form of which
no argument has both true premises and a false conclusion. So a valid
argument-form is the form of some valid argument, and a valid argument is one whose form is valid.

An *invalid argument* is one that is not valid, hence one for which some
argument of the same form has both true premises and a false conclusion. Example:

Every spy is an alien.

François Abdul Benito Wahrhaftig is an alien.

Therefore, François Abdul Benito Wahrhaftig is a spy.

This argument has the form:

Every S is a A.

w is a A.

∴ w is a S.

It is invalid because some arguments of this form have true premises
along with false conclusions. Example:

Every fraction is a number.	true
3 is a number.	true
Therefore, 3 is a fraction.	false

An argument automatically is invalid if it has true premises and a
false conclusion. Some invalid arguments are not like this. They have
false premises, or true premises plus true conclusions. They cannot be
proved invalid by the simple route of pointing to true premises and a
false conclusion. To prove them invalid on the basis of my definition,
one must produce *another* argument of the *same form* with true premises and a false conclusion.

Sometimes an argument has true premises and a false conclusion, hence is invalid, yet its invalidity also must be established indirectly, because truth of the premises or falsity of the conclusion is not obvious and not easily established. Example: the second "spy" argument just above. In such a case, one must cite another argument of the same form with true premises and a false conclusion, but one whose premises *obviously* are true and whose conclusion *obviously* is false.

An *invalid argument-form* is an argument-form of which at least one argument has true premises along with a false conclusion. So an invalid argument-form is the form of some invalid argument.

An argument of a given form sometimes is called an *example* of that form. If its premises are true and its conclusion false, thereby establishing its own invalidity and that of the given form, then it is a *counter-example* to that form. (You will learn a different use of the term "counter-example" in Chapter 9.)

Although a valid argument-form can have only valid instances (examples), there is a sense in which an invalid argument-form can have valid as well as invalid instances. Consider:

> It is not snowing.
>
> It is raining or cloudy.
>
> Therefore, it is cloudy.

It is invalid. It has this form:

> not-A.
>
> B or C.
>
> ∴ C.

Some arguments of this form have true premises along with false conclusions. (Find one!) Yet there is a sense in which other arguments of this form are quite valid, witness:

> It is not raining.
>
> It is raining or cloudy.
>
> Therefore, it is cloudy.

This valid argument has the invalid form lately cited, but only in the sense that it has the *more specific, valid* form:

> not-A.
>
> A or C.
>
> ∴ C.

Do you see why the second form is a more specific version of the first? Look at it this way: Arguments of the first form come in two varieties: those in which the A clause and B clause are the same, and those in which the A clause and B clause are different. The arguments of the former variety are precisely those of the second, more specific form. So every argument of the second form also is of the first, less specific form, but not vice versa.

Many invalid argument-forms become valid when made more specific. For example, the argument-form:

A.

∴ B.

is invalid. (Prove this with a counter-example!) But the following, more specific form is valid:

B and C.

∴ C.

Lesson: Although one argument can have various forms, some more specific than others, THE form of an argument—that form which alone can bestow invalidity on the argument—is the *most specific* form it has.

2.4. ARGUMENTS AND ARGUMENT-FORMS: EXAMPLES AND COUNTER-EXAMPLES

Example 1   All huskies are dogs.
                Every dog is a mammal.
                So all huskies are mammals.

                All H are D.
                Every D is a M.
                ∴ All H are M.

VALID.

Example 2   No Republican is a Democrat.
                Some Republican is a cucumber.
                Therefore, some cucumber is not a Democrat.

                No R is a D.
                Some R is a C.
                ∴ Some C is not a D.

VALID. Remember: Validity is just one virtue of arguments. A valid argument need not be a good argument. A bad argument can nevertheless be valid.

Example 3   All huskies are mammals.
Every husky is a dog.
So all dogs are mammals.

All Hs are Ms.
Every H is a D.
∴ All Ds are Ms.

INVALID. Counter-example:

All huskies are dogs.	true
Every husky is a mammal.	true
∴ All mammals are dogs.	false

An invalid argument can nevertheless have true premises and a true conclusion. Note that a counter-example can sometimes be couched in the terms of the very argument whose invalidity it demonstrates. That is useful to keep in mind when looking for counter-examples.

Example 4   No conservative is a liberal.
But some Republicans are liberals.
So some Republicans are not conservatives.

No C is a L.
Some Rs are Ls.
∴ Some Rs are not Cs.

VALID.

Example 5   No liberal is a Republican.
But some Republicans are conservatives.
So some liberals are not conservatives.

No L is a R.
Some Rs are Cs.
∴ Some Ls are not Cs.

INVALID. Counter-example:

No positive number is a negative number.
Some negative numbers are numbers.
∴ Some positive numbers are not numbers.

This counter-example illustrates two important points:

First, an example of an argument-form, hence a counter-example to an argument-form, can contain a multiword phrase ("positive number") where the form contains a single letter ("L"). In constructing a counter-example to an argument-form, one replaces each place-holder letter with an English expression. That expression need not be a single word.

Second, elementary arithmetic is a good source of counter-examples. The premises of a good counter-example are *obviously* true and the conclusion *obviously* false. Because elementary arithmetic is familiar to everyone, simple arithmetic statements tend to be obviously true if true, obviously false if false.

Example 6   Some Presidents have been wealthy.
                John Kennedy was a President.
                Therefore, John Kennedy was wealthy.

                Some Ps have been W.
                k was a P.
            ∴ k was W.

INVALID. Counter-example:

    Some Presidents have been wealthy.
    Abraham Lincoln was a President.
  ∴ Abraham Lincoln was wealthy.

Anticipating a convention introduced in Chapter 4, I am using lower-case letters ("k") as place holders for proper names ("John Kennedy") and other expressions labeling single objects ("the world's ugliest logician"). But you may use any letters you like for now.

Example 7   All Presidents have been wealthy.
                Abraham Lincoln was a President.
                So Abraham Lincoln was wealthy.

                All Ps have been W.
                l was a P.
            ∴ l was W.

VALID.

Example 8   If Professor Q. E. Demonstratum succeeds in proving the theorem before class begins, he will not kill himself.

                But he does kill himself.

So he does not succeed in proving the theorem before class begins.

If S, not-K.
K.
∴ not-S.

VALID.

In Examples 1–6, the significant structure consists in the way words form clauses, so place-holder letters stand for words. In Example 8, the significant structure consists in the way clauses form complete sentences, so place-holder letters stand for clauses.

Notice how I displayed the logical form of Example 8. Having represented the clause "he will kill himself" as "K," I then represented the clause "he will *not* kill himself" simply by prefixing "not" to "K," although the original clause does not begin with "not." Such simplifications are permissible, even desirable, when exact fidelity would be pointlessly cumbersome.

Example 9   The La Tour is preferable to the Château Margaux, which in turn is preferable to the Haut Brion.

Thus, the La Tour is preferable to the Haut Brion.

t is P to m.
m is P to b.
∴ t is P to b.

INVALID. Counter-example:

1 is next to 2.
2 is next to 3.
∴ 1 is next to 3.

If you thought Example 9 was valid, perhaps you were tacitly assuming the additional premise:

If one thing is preferable to a second and the second is preferable to a third, then the first is preferable to the third.

The best counter-examples—those that most clearly demonstrate invalidity—often seem silly and contrived. That is no objection to them. When one constructs a counter-example, it is good strategy to use statements whose truth or falsity is so childishly obvious as to make the example seem silly.

A counter-example proves invalidity. But failure to find a counter-example does not prove validity: it does not prove there is none to be found. How to decide, in general, whether an argument is valid?

For some important classes of arguments, there are easily mastered methods of ascertaining validity. One such method is given in Part Two. For now, I leave you to your logical intuitions and your imagination. Faced with an argument whose validity you wish to ascertain, read it carefully, display its form, make an intuitive judgment of validity, and seek a counter-example to its form if validity is not evident. If the argument seems valid and you have found no counter-example, there is a good chance it is indeed valid—though it still may not be. If it seems *in*valid but you have found no counter-example, keep looking until you find one or feel satisfied there is none to be found. In seeking a counter-example, start with statements that are simple, trivial, even silly—ones whose truth (in the case of premises) or falsity (in the case of conclusions) is absurdly obvious.

In a genuine counter-example, it is obvious that the premises are true and the conclusion false. In a *near* counter-example, it obviously is *possible*, although not obviously the case, that the premises are true and the conclusion false. If you cannot find a genuine counter-example, seek a near counter-example. Here is a near counter-example to the form of Example 6:

> Some men have been fat.
> Ignatz was a man.
> ∴ Ignatz was fat.

Although it is not obvious that the premises are *in fact* both true and the conclusion false, it obviously is *possible* (depending on who Ignatz is) for the premises to be true and the conclusion false.

EXERCISES

For each of the following arguments, display its *form* and say whether it is *valid*. If it is *not valid*, prove this by giving a *counter-example* to its form—a genuine counter-example if you can, a near counter-example if that is the best you can do.

*   1. Socrates is a man.
     All men are mortal.
     So Socrates is mortal.

*   2. Communists admire Marx.
     Some faculty members admire Marx.
     Therefore, some faculty members are Communists.

*   3. Whoever is reading is literate.
You are reading.
Therefore, you are literate.

*   4. Whoever is reading is literate.
You are literate.
Therefore, you are reading.

    5. All conservatives are Republicans.
But no Democrat is conservative.
Thus, no Democrat is a Republican.

    6. All conservatives are rich.
Every Republican is rich.
So all Republicans are conservatives.

*   7. No worker is rich.
Some Democrats are workers.
So some Democrats are not rich.

*   8. No worker is rich.
Some Republicans are not rich.
So some Republicans are not workers.

    9. Some Communists are atheists.
Therefore, some atheists are Communists.

  10. All Communists are atheists.
Therefore, all atheists are Communists.

* 11. If Senator McGraft is honest, I'm a monkey's uncle.
Senator McGraft is honest.
So I'm a monkey's uncle.

  12. No one can die who is made of dead men.
Frankenstein is made of dead men.
Consequently, Frankenstein cannot die.

  13. Someone is a politician.
Someone is greedy.
Thus, someone is a greedy politician.

* 14. Whoever is prudent shuns hyenas.
No banker is imprudent.
So no banker fails to shun hyenas. (Lewis Carroll)

* 15. Some pillows are soft.
No pokers are soft.
Therefore, some pokers are not pillows. (Lewis Carroll)

  16. Taxes are theft.
Licensing fees are theft.
Thus, licensing fees are taxes.

  17. No capitalist belongs to a union.
Some professors are capitalists.
So some professors do not belong to unions.

3

Logical Form

3.1. FORM AND MATTER

There are many ways to impute form, shape, or structure to a bicycle, to a university, to a cantaloupe, or to a deductive argument. Every argument has a specific syntactic structure; it consists of a specific string of syllables; it is spelled a specific way. That form, shape, or structure which determines whether an argument is *valid* is called its *logical form*.

In depicting an argument's logical form, we delete certain expressions, replacing them with place-holder letters, but leave in certain others. Take:

> Bertha is a wolf.
>
> Every wolf is a mammal.
>
> So Bertha is a mammal.

Its logical form is:

> b is a W.
>
> Every W is a M.
>
> ∴ b is a M.

I depicted it by deleting these expressions, treating them as nonstructural—as part of the *content* or *matter* of the argument:

> Bertha   wolf   mammal.

I left these expressions, treating them as part of the argument's *form*, or *structure:*

> *is a*   *every*

Because the latter constitute the logical form of the argument, they are called *logical expressions*. The others—those deleted—are *nonlogical expressions*.

How, in general, do we decide which expressions are logical and which nonlogical? Why, from a logical point of view, do we regard expressions like "every" as bones of an argument and "wolf" as flesh? Consider:

> Jacob is a descendant of Isaac.
>
> Isaac is a descendant of Abraham.
>
> Therefore, Jacob is a descendant of Abraham.

Were "descendant" a logical expression, the argument would be valid, since it would then have the form:

> a is a descendant of b.
>
> b is a descendant of c.
>
> ∴ a is a descendant of c.

and every argument of this form with true premises has a true conclusion. But classifying "descendant" as flesh rather than bone makes the argument *in*valid, because it imputes to it the form:

> a is a D of b.
>
> b is a D of c.
>
> ∴ a is a D of c.

and *some* arguments of this form have true premises along with false conclusions, witness:

> Jacob is a son of Isaac.
>
> Isaac is a son of Abraham.
>
> Therefore, Jacob is a son of Abraham.

As a matter of fact, logicians do *not* regard "descendant" as a logical expression. So they do not regard the "descendant" argument as valid.

But why? What makes "every" and "is a" logical expressions but "descendant" not a logical expression?

Maybe this: Genuine logical expressions occur in virtually all sciences and all general fields of discourse, regardless of subject matter. Nonlogical expressions do not. *Logical* expressions are *subject-independent*. *Non*logical expressions are *subject-specific*.

This criterion justifies the accepted view that the following are logical expressions:

and	or	not
every	some	is

while these are nonlogical:

descendant	Bertha	wolf
mammal	kangaroo	animals I detest

But the subject-independence criterion does not always yield a clear classification. For example, it is not completely clear whether these expressions pass the test of subject-independence:

because	possible	true	in order to
everywhere	more———than	while	

Subject-independence may be a *correct* criterion for distinguishing logical from nonlogical expressions. But it is an *imprecise* one: it admits of borderline cases.

Logicians often single out certain logical expressions for separate study, ignoring others—or rather, treating all others on a par with nonlogical expressions. In so-called propositional logic, for example, one studies separately the logic of "and," "or," "not," "if———then," and cognate expressions. That is, one develops a theory of validity that treats these expressions alone as logical. While studying this branch of logic, one deliberately—but temporarily—acts as though such logical expressions as "every" and "some" were nonlogical. Logicians have even investigated the "logic" of expressions not customarily regarded as logical, treating them as though they were logical. Examples:

———prefers . . . to - - -
It is possible that———
———asserts that . . .   ——— believes that . . .
It will happen in the future that ———.

One might take the view that nothing is a logical expression intrinsically, absolutely, or of itself, but only *relative to* a particular logical investigation or branch of logic—one that *treats it as* a logical expression—and that any expression can, in principle, be a logical expression relative to some logical investigation or branch of logic. Our tendency to regard just the subject-independent expressions as really logical would then be explained by the fact that it is especially useful to study the logic of expressions that are especially prevalent.

By counting "descendant" as a logical expression, we make our little "descendant" argument valid, but at the cost of an enlarged logic—a criterion of validity complicated by the inclusion of "descendant," along with "and," "not," "every," and the like, among the logical expressions. By counting "descendant" as nonlogical, we save on logic at the cost of validity: our criterion of validity is then simpler, but our "descendant" argument no longer is valid. We can restore validity with no increase in logic by adding this premise, or construing it as an unstated premise of the original "descendant" argument:

> Whenever one thing is a descendant of another and the second is a descendant of a third, the first is a descendant of the third. (In short, descendants of descendants are descendants.)

In general, by counting an expression as logical, we save on premises and preserve the validity of some appealing arguments, but at the cost of added logic (of a more complicated criterion of validity); by counting it as nonlogical, we save on logic at the cost of added premises or the invalidity of some appealing arguments.

Strictly speaking, when depicting the logical form of an argument, it is not enough to delete the nonlogical expressions, marking their positions with letters. We must also specify, implicitly or explicitly, the *category* of expressions meant to fill each position. Here is a valid argument and its logical form:

> Bertha kissed Ignatz.
>
> Therefore, Bertha kissed something.
>
> b K i.
>
> ∴ b K something.

But the following *in*valid argument seems to share this form:

> Bertha kissed nothing.
>
> Therefore, Bertha kissed something.

The trouble is that the "i" position is meant to be filled only by a proper name ("Ignatz") or other expression used to label a single object ("the tallest boy in the class"). But "nothing" is not of this sort. There is no such thing as nothing, let alone a single such thing. So "nothing" is not among the expressions meant to fill the "i" position. Therefore, the second argument does not really have the same form as the first.

Confused by all this? So am I. How exactly to distinguish logical from nonlogical expressions and categories is an unresolved issue in the philosophy of logic.

3.2. HOW TO DEVELOP GOOD FORM

So much for theory. Here are four rules of thumb to help you depict the logical forms of arguments:

1. When distinguishing logical from nonlogical expressions, follow these guidelines:

> By and large, *logical* expressions are those that seem intuitively to constitute the overall *form* or *shape* or *structure* of arguments; *nonlogical* expressions seem intuitively to constitute the *content* or *matter* of arguments.

> *Logical* expressions are *subject-independent*. Unlike nonlogical expressions, they do not express the specific topic or content or subject matter of arguments.

> Be *generous* to an argument's author: treat borderline cases as logical expressions if that is needed to make the argument valid.

> *Nonlogical* expressions include words, phrases, and clauses that stand for specific things ("Ignatz," "the tallest boy in the class"), for specific types or kinds of things ("dog," "beer," "assassinated archdukes"), for specific properties or traits or features of things ("canine," "heliotrope," "artfully naïve"), for specific sorts of action or event ("rains," "chews Bazooka"), for specific relations among things ("chews," "lies between"), and for specific putative facts ("she left him," "the moon is one-quarter the size of the earth").

> Although most verbs are nonlogical, "to be" is logical.

> Although most adjectives are nonlogical, certain adjectives of *quantity*, notably "all," "every," "some," and "most," are logical.

> Although most adverbs are nonlogical, "not" is logical, as are all expressions of *negation*—"it is not the case that," "un" (as in "ungrammatical"), "fail" (as in "he failed to come"), and so on.

2. Because *the* form of an argument is the *most specific* form it has, do not convict an argument of invalidity until you have uncovered *all* of its relevant structure. Even if it has an invalid form, the argument also

could have a more specific, valid form. In a sense, this *valid* argument:

> Bertha is a wolf.
>
> Every wolf is a mammal.
>
> Therefore, Bertha is a mammal.

has the *in*valid form:

> A.
>
> B.
>
> ∴ C.

What makes it valid is that it also has the more specific, valid form:

> b is a W.
>
> Every W is a M.
>
> ∴ b is a M.

3. Once you have imputed a valid form to an argument, you may stop. There is no need to seek more structure. An argument with a valid form automatically is valid, even if that form is not THE form of the argument—not the most specific form it has. Reason: If an argument-form is valid, so is any more specific form. Example:

> If all humans are mortal, then Socrates is mortal.
>
> All humans are mortal.
>
> Therefore, Socrates is mortal.

This has the valid form:

> If P, then Q.
>
> P.
>
> ∴ Q.

That is enough to establish the argument's validity. It does not matter that the argument also has the more specific (no less valid) form:

> If all F are G, then a is G.
>
> All F are G.
>
> ∴ a is G.

4. When depicting the forms of arguments, feel free to *ignore features that play no logical role in the argument*. Besides making the work easier, this often enhances clarity and uncovers important structural similarities.

How to tell whether a structural feature plays a role in the argument? Sometimes it is intuitively obvious that a structural feature is merely grammatical or stylistic, not logical. And sometimes an expression's significant structural components do not occur elsewhere in the argument, in which case the expression's internal structure is not related to the rest of the argument and may be ignored.

Here are two valid arguments:

> Unless something is an animal, it is not a wart hog.
>
> Therefore, whatever kisses a wart hog kisses an animal.

> Unless something has legs, it does not dance.
>
> Therefore, whatever is a nose of a dancer is a nose of something that has legs.

It is perfectly proper to depict their respective forms as follows:

> Unless something is an F, it is not a G.
>
> ∴ Whatever Hs a G, Hs an F.

> Unless something F, it does not G.
>
> ∴ Whatever is an H of a G-er is an H of something that F.

But one can also simultaneously depict the form of both arguments this way:

> Unless something F, it not-G.
>
> ∴ Whatever Hs G, Hs F.

Because this form represents just those features common to the first two forms, it is simpler than they are. It is pretty obvious, I think, that those features represented in either of the first two forms but not in the third are merely grammatical and stylistic—not relevant to questions of validity.

Or consider this argument:

> There will be a run on the Pound if the Government lose their majority.
>
> There is indeed a run on the Pound.
>
> Therefore, the Government will lose their majority.

I should depict its form as follows:

P if Q.

P.

∴ Q.

This form obviously is invalid. (Stop and find a counter-example to it!)
Yet one need not seek more structure. One need not depict the internal
structure of the clauses "there will be a run on the Pound" and "the
Government lose their majority." Such additional structure plays no
role in the argument. For the clause "there will be a run on the Pound"
shares no significant structural component with any other clause in the
argument, so its internal structure is unrelated to the rest of the argument. Similarly for "the Government lose their majority."

3.3. MORE ARGUMENTS, ARGUMENT-FORMS, AND COUNTER-EXAMPLES

Example 1   Only Communists are atheists. But some atheists are
congressmen. Hence, some congressmen are Com-
munists.

Only Cs are As.

Some As are Ms.

∴ Some Ms are Cs.

VALID.

Example 2   None but atheists are Communists. But Madalyn is an
atheist. Hence, Madalyn must be a Communist.

None but As are Cs.

m is an A.

∴ m is a C.

INVALID. Counter-example:

None but human beings are U.S. senators.

The Ayatollah Khomeini is a human being.

∴ The Ayatollah Khomeini is a U.S. senator.

Example 3   Whoever wears a heavy fur coat must be warm. Thus, whoever is not warm cannot be wearing a heavy fur coat.

Whoever C W.

∴ Whoever not-W not-C.

VALID. Because no significant structural component of "wears a heavy fur coat" occurs elsewhere in the argument, the internal structure of this phrase is not related to the rest of the argument, so it may be ignored.

Example 4   Those who drink heavily do not drive safely. But Tom drinks heavily. So Tom does not drive safely.

Those who H not-S.

t Hs.

∴ t not-S.

VALID. Because this form is valid as is, there is no need to make it more specific by displaying the internal structure of "drinks heavily" and "drive safely."

Example 5   Heavy drinkers do not drive safely. But Mormons do not drink at all. Consequently, Mormons drive safely.

H K-ers don't V S-ly.

Ms don't K at all.

∴ Ms V S-ly.

INVALID. Counter-example:

Heavy eaters don't eat moderately.

Rocks don't eat at all.

∴ Rocks eat moderately.

It was not necessary to display the internal structure of the phrase "drives safely." It *was* necessary to display the internal structure of "heavy drinkers," though, because one of its structural components, "drink," occurs by itself in the second premise. When showing an argument to be invalid, it is safer to display too much structure than too little.

Example 6   Every philosopher in Pittsburgh is a Fanatical Jogger or a Violent Vegetarian. But Preston is neither a Fanatical Jogger nor a Violent Vegetarian. Yet Preston is in Pittsburgh. Hence, Preston is not a philosopher.

Every S A is a P or a V.

n is neither a P nor a V.

n is A.

∴ n is not an S.

VALID.

Example 7   If Bertha is the culprit, Ignatz is not. In fact, Bertha is not the culprit. It follows that Ignatz must be the culprit.

If b is the C, i is not (the C).

b is not the C.

∴ i is the C.

INVALID. Counter-example:

If 3 is the number 4, 3 + 2 is not (the number 4).

3 is not the number 4.

∴ 3 + 2 is the number 4.

Example 8   All socialists are for Medicare. But some liberals are for Medicare. Hence, some liberals are socialists.

All Ss are M.

Some Ls are M.

∴ Some Ls are Ss.

INVALID. Counter-example:

All bananas are fruit.

Some strawberries are fruit.

∴ Some strawberries are bananas.

3.4. LOGICAL TRUTH AND CONSISTENCY

Validity is a formal property of arguments. But it is the business of logic to study certain kindred formal properties of statements and sets of statements as well. Two such properties are worth calling to your attention:

(i) *Logical truth*   A statement is *logically true* if, and only if, *every statement of the same logical form is true.* In other words, a logical truth is a statement for which no statement of the same logical form is false.
Compare:

> Every dog is a cat.
>
> Every dog is an animal.
>
> Every dog is a dog.

Because it is false, the first statement automatically fails to be logically true. Although true, the second statement is not *logically* true. For it has the form:

> Every A is a B,

and *some* statements of this form, for example:

> Every number is a rock,

are false. But the third statement is logically true. It has the form:

> Every A is a A,

and *every* statement of this form is true: no false statement has this form.
Three more examples of logical truths and their forms:

> If it is raining, it is raining.
>
> If P, P.

> Either it is raining or not.
>
> Either P or not-(P).

> Either someone is non-Albanian, or else everyone is Albanian or Liechtensteinian.
>
> Either someone is non-A, or else everyone is A or B.

Logical truth and validity are different concepts. One applies to statements; the other, to arguments. One is a species of truth; the other is not: a valid argument can consist partly or wholly of falsehoods, so long as no argument of the same form consists of true premises plus a false conclusion. Despite their differences, logical truth and validity are both defined in terms of truth and logical form. And they are further connected this way:

Corresponding to every argument is the statement "If _____ then . . .," in which the "if" part is filled by the premises of the argument and the "then" part by the conclusion. An argument is valid if, and only if, its corresponding "If–then" statement is logically true. Examples:

ARGUMENT	CORRESPONDING "IF–THEN" STATEMENT
Every alien is a potential spy. But François Abdul Benito Wahrhaftig is an alien. There-fore, François Abdul Benito Wahrhaftig is a potential spy. (valid)	If every alien is a potential spy and François Abdul Benito Wahrhaftig is an alien, then François Abdul Benito Wahrhaftig is a potential spy. (logi-cally true)
Every spy is an alien. But François Abdul Benito Wah-rhaftig is an alien. Therefore, François Abdul Benito Wah-rhaftig is a spy. (invalid)	If every spy is an alien and François Abdul Benito Wah-rhaftig is an alien, then Fran-çois Abdul Benito Wahrhaftig is a spy. (not logically true)

Note, by the way, that the "If–then" statement corresponding to an argument is not itself an argument. When you give an argument, you affirm, in effect, that the premises and conclusion are true. When you make the corresponding "If–then" statement, you do not thereby affirm that the "If" part (corresponding to the premises) or the "then" part (corresponding to the conclusion) is true. All you affirm is that the "then" part is true *if* the "If" part is true.

(ii) *Consistency* A *consistent* statement is one for which *some state-ment of the same logical form is true*. So truth is a species of consistency: every true statement is consistent, though not vice versa.

Compare:

Every adult man was born with a heart.

Every man is feathered.

Some men are not men.

Because the first statement is true, it is perforce consistent. Although false, the second statement still is consistent, because it has the logical form:

Every A is B,

and some statements of this form are true. (Find one!) But the third statement is not even consistent. Besides being false, it has the logical form:

Some As are not As,

and every statement of this form is false; no true statement has this form.

Statements that are *not* consistent are called *inconsistent*. The clearest cases are statements of this form:

A and not-A.

Such statements are called *explicit contradictions*. Often the label "contradiction," or "contradictory statement," is applied to inconsistent statements generally.

The negation of a logical truth is inconsistent; that of an inconsistent statement, logically true. Thus, "Every philosophy professor is or is not smart" is logically true, while its negation, "It is not the case that every philosophy professor is or is not smart," is inconsistent; and "Some philosophy professor is *and* is not smart" is inconsistent, while its negation, "It is not the case that some philosophy professor is and is not smart," is logically true.

The concepts of consistency and inconsistency apply to *sets* of statements as well as single statements. Each of these statements is consistent:

Ignatz kissed Bertha.

Ignatz did not kiss Bertha.

But they are *jointly in*consistent—inconsistent with each other. They constitute an inconsistent set. They have the forms:

A

Not-A,

and no two statements of these forms are *both* true.

The following statements, too, are each consistent but jointly inconsistent:

It is raining.

It is not both raining and snowing.

If it is not snowing, I'll be home by five.

Either I won't be home by five, or it is not raining.

They constitute an inconsistent set: no four statements of the same forms as these are all true. If that is not obvious, I can make it so by deducing an explicit contradiction from the four statements:

Assume they are all true. Then it is not both raining and snowing. But it is raining. Hence, it is not snowing. But then, by virtue of the third statement, I'll be home by five, and thus, by virtue of the fourth statement, it is not raining. So it is both raining and not raining.

Because the explicit contradiction, "It is both raining and not raining," follows from the four statements above, if any four statements of the forms:

A.

Not both A and B.

If not-B, C.

Either not-C, or not-A.

were all true, so would be the corresponding statement of the form:

A and not-A.

But no statement of the latter form is true. Hence, no four statements of the forms just displayed are all true.

In general, if an explicit contradiction follows from a set of statements, those statements must be jointly inconsistent. So one way to show that a set of statements is inconsistent is to deduce from it an explicit contradiction.

People are said to be inconsistent when they hold positions that are singly or jointly inconsistent. And we call someone's words or thoughts inconsistent when his utterances or beliefs constitute an inconsistent set.

Logical truth and consistency are related to validity in a way you may find surprising and disturbing: An argument with *inconsistent premises* or a *logically true conclusion* is perforce *valid*, however unrelated its premises be to its conclusion. Reason: No argument of the same form can have both true premises and a false conclusion: there are no counter-examples to its form. (Think about it!) Examples:

This book is easy to read. E

This book is not easy to read. Not-E $\Big\}$ (inconsistent)

Therefore, Queen Elizabeth II is a vampiress. Q

It is raining champagne. R

Therefore, this book is easy to read, or this book is not easy to read. E or not-E (logically true)

Because no argument of the former form can have true premises, while none of the latter form can have a false conclusion, there is no counter-example to either form, which is to say both arguments are valid.

You will not get too upset by this if you recall that validity is just one virtue of arguments. A perfectly valid argument can be very bad in other ways; a very bad argument can still be perfectly valid. Major evils often entail minor goods: accidents encourage safety, war engenders heroism, ignorance occasions inquiry, and inconsistent premises ensure validity.

3.5. BEYOND LOGICAL FORM (optional)

Validity, logical truth, consistency, and inconsistency are *formal* properties: whether an argument is valid depends solely on its logical form; similarly for the logical truth of statements and the consistency and inconsistency of statements and sets of statements.

Validity, logical truth, and inconsistency are the strictly formal versions of certain more inclusive, nonformal properties. The latter are worth calling to your attention if only to avoid confusion with their narrower, strictly formal kin.

Some truths are *necessarily* true: they could not possibly be false. (Those truths that are not necessarily true are called *contingent* truths.)

Logical truths are necessarily true. Besides being true, they could not possibly be false. But the logical truths do not exhaust the necessary truths. Some necessarily true statements are not logically true.

Here are four truths:

(1) All women are under twenty feet tall.

(2) There is no greatest integer.

(3) Every bachelor is male.

(4) Every bachelor is a bachelor.

Although true, (1) is *not necessarily* true. It is possible (even if extremely unlikely) that there is a woman twenty feet tall or more. (2)–(4) are necessarily true. But only (4) is logically true. It has the form:

Every A is an A,

and every statement of this form is true. (2) and (3) have the respective forms:

There is no A-est B,

Every A is B,

and *some* statements of these forms are false. (Find one each! Do not proceed till you have done so!) So necessary truths are not always logically true.

Besides logical truths—statements true by virtue of their logical forms alone—the necessary truths include *mathematical truths*. They also include *verbal truths*—statements true by virtue of the meanings of their component words. (2) is a mathematical truth, (3) a verbal truth.

Are there other necessary truths? Are there necessary truths that are neither logically nor mathematically nor verbally true? That is a deep, debatable philosophical issue. Perhaps certain moral, metaphysical, or methodological principles ("One is obligated to do what one has promised," "Every event has a cause," "No hypothesis can be verified on the basis of a biased sample") count as necessary truths. I am not sure.

Sometimes the logical and verbal truths are lumped together under such rubrics as "analytic statements," "tautologies," and even "logical truths" (though not, of course, in my strictly formal sense).

Some falsehoods nevertheless are *possibly* true. A possible truth must, at the very least, be *consistent*. But some consistent statements fail to be possible truths in other ways.
Compare:

(5) There are nine planets.

(6) There are twelve planets.

(7) There are twelve apostles and nine planets and exactly as many planets as apostles.

(8) There are nonmale bachelors.

(9) There are nonmale males.

Being true, (5) automatically is *possibly* true. Although false, (6) is possibly true as well: there could have been twelve planets. (7)–(9) are not even possible truths. But of these, only (9) is inconsistent in the sense defined earlier. Only (9) is false by virtue of its logical form alone. It has the form:

There are non-M Ms,

and every statement of this form is false. But (7) and (8) have the respective forms:

There are t As and n Ps and exactly
as many As as Ps,

There are non-M Bs,

and some statements of these forms are true. (Find one each!)

Although consistent, (7) fails to be a possible truth because it is false on mathematical grounds, and (8) because it is verbally false—false by virtue of the meanings of its component words. Besides being consistent, a possible truth must not be mathematically or verbally false (although it can be false on other grounds, such as astronomical observation).

Necessity and possibility are interdefinable: A necessary truth is one that not only is true but cannot *possibly* be false. A possible truth is a statement which, even if false, is not *necessarily* false.

Very often, possible truths are called consistent (though in a narrower sense than mine), and statements that are not possibly true are called inconsistent (though in a broader sense than mine).

The categories I have been discussing are related to each other as follows:

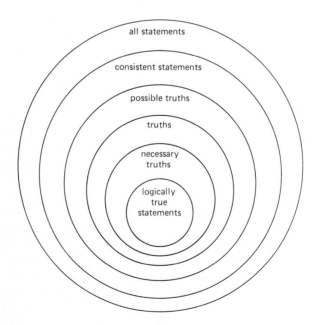

Sometimes arguments are called valid, or their conclusions are said to follow from their premises, even though they are not valid in the narrow, strictly formal sense I have tried to explain. An argument is valid in the broader, nonformal sense so long as its premises would, if true, necessitate the truth of its conclusion—so long as it would be impossible for the premises to be true without the conclusion being true as well. This is the rough notion of validity introduced in §2.1 and polished to formal luster in §2.3.

Compare these four arguments:

(1) Ron is a Republican. Therefore, Ron is a cucumber.

(2) There are twelve apostles. And there are nine planets. Therefore, there are more apostles than planets.

(3) Ignatz is someone's brother. Therefore, Ignatz is male.

(4) Bertha is a Democrat. But all Democrats are cucumbers. Therefore, Bertha is a cucumber.

(1) is not valid in any sense: it is quite possible for its premises to be true without its conclusion being true. (2)–(4) are valid in the broad sense: in each case, it would be impossible for the premises to be true without the conclusion being true as well. But only (4) is valid in the narrow, formal sense. It has the form:

b is a D.

All Ds are Cs.

∴ b is a C.

and no argument of this form has both true premises and a false conclusion. By contrast, (2) and (3) have the respective forms:

There are t As.

There are n Ps.

∴ There are more As than Ps.

i is someone's B.

∴ i is M.

and some arguments of each of these forms have true premises plus false conclusions. That is, there are counter-examples to each form. (Stop and find a counter-example to each form!)

Adding the necessary truth "Twelve soandsos are always more than nine suchandsuches" to the premises of (2) makes (2) formally valid.

And adding the necessary truth "Every brother is male" to the premises of (3) makes (3) formally valid. In general, an argument that is valid in the broad sense (truth of premises would necessitate truth of conclusion) but not the narrow, formal sense (every argument of same form with true premises has true conclusion) can be made formally valid by adding one or more necessary truths to the premises. In real-life cases, such necessary truths can reasonably be regarded as tacit premises of the arguments in question, so those arguments can be regarded as formally valid.

EXERCISES

Depict the *logical forms* of the following arguments. In each case, if the argument is (formally) valid, write "VALID" (what else?). Do not bother to give a derivation. If the argument is not (formally) valid, write "INVALID," and prove invalidity by giving a counter-example to the invalid form—a genuine counter-example if possible, a near counter-example if that is the best you can do.

* 1. Any punishment that deters crime is justified. And capital punishment deters crime. So capital punishment is justified.

* 2. If capital punishment deterred crime, it would be justified. But it does not deter crime. So it is not justified.

3. No Albanian speaks with a proper Irish brogue. Consequently, whoever speaks with a proper Irish brogue is no Albanian.

4. Whoever has a great night life is a jet setter. But Count Dracula has a great night life. So Count Dracula is a jet setter.

* 5. If Count Dracula is a jet setter, then he has a great night life. Indeed, Count Dracula has a great night life. Thus, Count Dracula is a jet setter.

6. All Republicans are rich. But some politicians are not Republicans. So some politicians are not rich.

* 7. All policies recommended by the White House have some merit. But some energy policies do not have any merit. So some energy policies have not been recommended by the White House.

8. Either professors justify the way they spend their time, or the legislature has the right to impose work loads. But professors do not justify the way they spend their time. It follows that the legislature has the right to impose work loads.

* 9. Either we decontrol oil prices, or we deprive our posterity of energy sources, or both. But we indeed decontrol oil prices. Consequently, we do not deprive our posterity of energy sources.

10. If we have desires, we suffer from frustration. If we do not have desires, we suffer from boredom. Therefore, either we suffer from frustration, or we suffer from boredom. (Schopenhauer)

* 11. If we ratify the treaty, there will be resentment. But if we reject the treaty, there will be resentment. Therefore, there will be resentment.

12. If we ratify the treaty, there will be resentment. But if we reject the treaty, there will be resentment. And either we ratify the treaty or we reject it. Therefore, there will be resentment.

* 13. All Podunk students are smart. But some people are not smart. Therefore, some people are not Podunk students.

14. If we ratify the treaty, there will be resentment. But if we do not ratify the treaty, there will be resentment. Therefore, there will be resentment.

* 15. Homosexual acts involving only consenting adults have no victims. But every crime has a victim. Consequently, a homosexual act involving only consenting adults is no crime.

16. "Every person residing in Maine who earns less than $4,000 annually shall be furnished a hearing aid free of charge by the Department of Health and Welfare" (bill proposed in Maine Legislature, 1969, by Representative Robert Soulas of Bangor, cited in Pospesel, *Arguments*). Therefore, every person residing in Maine who has excellent hearing but earns less than $4,000 annually shall be furnished a hearing aid free of charge by the Department of Health and Welfare.

It is somewhat more difficult to display the logical forms of the following arguments, almost all of which are valid:

* 17. Standard IQ tests are culturally biased. But whatever is biased is discriminatory. And whatever is discriminatory is unconstitutional to use in public schools. So it is unconstitutional to use standard IQ tests in public schools.

18. Any woman who lives with a bunch of dwarfs must be a polyandrist. But polyandrists are married. And a married woman is entitled to maternity insurance. What's more, Snow White is a woman who lives with a bunch of dwarfs. Thus, Snow White is entitled to maternity insurance.

* 19. Everybody doesn't like somebody. Therefore, there is somebody everybody doesn't like.

20. No political partisan is unbiased about politics. But politics is what political-science professors teach. And most political-science professors are political partisans. Therefore, most political-science professors are biased about what they teach.

* 21. If something is outlawed, whoever does it is a criminal. So if owning guns is outlawed, only criminals own guns.

22. It is wrong to break the law. But to do what the law forbids is to break the law. And a law is just if it forbids only what is wrong. Consequently, every law is just.

23. All countries that automatically behead convicted murderers have fewer assassinations in a century than the U.S. has in one year. But any country that has fewer assassinations in a century than the U.S. has in one year has a positive contribution to make to the U.S. criminal-justice system. And no country that has such a contribution to make should be judged offhandedly to be barbarous. So no country that automatically beheads convicted murderers should be judged offhandedly to be barbarous.

* 24. Believing in God amounts to high potential gain and no chance of loss. And not believing in God amounts to high potential loss and no chance of gain. But high potential gain and no chance of loss is safer than high potential loss and no chance of gain. So believing in God is safer than not believing in God. (Pascal's "Wager")

* 25. If there is no morally relevant difference between two things and if one is wrong, so is the other. But there is no morally relevant difference between banning *Hustler* and banning *T.V. Guide*. Therefore, because it would be wrong to ban *T.V. Guide*, it would be wrong to ban *Hustler*.

* 26. If a thing does not exist in reality, then something greater than it can be conceived. But nothing greater than any god can be conceived. So some god exists in reality.

27. If we decontrol natural-gas prices, we place an unfair burden on the poor. But if we do not decontrol natural-gas prices, we impose unjust costs on future generations. Therefore, either we place an unfair burden on the poor, or we impose unjust costs on future generations.

* 28. If we fail to control population growth, the world will become over-crowded. But if we control population growth, we interfere with individual liberty. So if we do not interfere with individual liberty, the world will become over-crowded.

29. Either we decrease government spending, or we increase inflation. But if we decrease government spending, we increase unemployment. And if we increase inflation, we hurt those with fixed incomes. So we must increase unemployment or hurt those with fixed incomes.

* 30. Either God does not want to prevent evil, or God cannot prevent evil. But if God does not want to prevent evil, then God is not benevolent. And if God cannot prevent evil, then God is not omnipotent. Therefore, God is not both benevolent and omnipotent.

* 31. You cannot fool all the people all the time. Therefore, there is a person whom you can never fool.

* 32. God exists in the imagination. If a thing exists in the imagination but not in reality, something greater than it can be conceived. But nothing greater than God can be conceived. Therefore, God exists in reality.

33. Millard Fillmore is dead. So either the Captains Regent of San Marino will decide to devastate Liechtenstein with a neutron bomb delivered by the Goodyear Blimp, or they will not.

34. It is both raining and not raining. So 2 + 2 = 3.

For each of the following *statements*, say whether it is LOGICALLY TRUE and whether it is CONSISTENT. Also say whether it is NECESSARILY TRUE and whether it is POSSIBLY TRUE. If it is consistent, prove it so by citing a true statement of the same logical form. If it is not logically true, prove this by citing a false statement of the same logical form.

* 35. It is raining champagne.

* 36. It is or is not raining champagne.

* 37. It never rains champagne.

* 38. It is and is not raining champagne.

* 39. Whenever it rains champagne, it rains wine.

  40. Every square has four sides.

  41. 7 + 5 = 13.

  42. Every sister is a sibling.

* 43. Red is a color.

  44. Some sister is a sibling.

* 45. Everyone is such that, if he is a sibling, then someone is a sibling.

  46. Some sister is not a sibling.

  47. It is not raining champagne or not raining Pabst Blue Ribbon if, and only if, it is not the case that it is both raining champagne and raining Pabst Blue Ribbon.

  48. If Abyssinia started and lost World War II, then Abyssinia lost World War II and started World War II.

  49. Some square has just three corners.

* 50. The man who shaves all and only those men who do not shave themselves shaves himself if, and only if, he does not shave himself.

* 51. There is a man who shaves all and only those men who do not shave themselves.

PART · 2

PICTURES

Classes and Venn Diagrams

4.1. CLASSY LANGUAGE

I shall show you a diagrammatic technique for depicting the contents of statements that express simple class relationships. You can ascertain the validity of any argument composed of such statements by checking whether the diagram of the premises also depicts the contents of the conclusion.

By a *class* I mean any batch, bunch, collection, or totality of things—a *set*, in the language of mathematics—not just a social stratum, course meeting, or group of fellow graduates. There is a class of dogs, a class of drops of sealing wax, and a class of two-eyed furry things without spots; a class of dumb professors, a class of smart things that are either midget university students or assassinated archdukes, and a class consisting of my bicycle, your first love, and the left nostril of Prince Franz Josef of Liechtenstein. Exotic technical exceptions aside, there is a class comprising those things that fit any given description, simple or complex, natural or ad hoc, humdrum or bizarre.

Dogs and they alone *belong to*—are *members of*—the class of dogs. Smart things that are either midget university students or assassinated archdukes and they alone belong to the class of smart things that are either midget university students or assassinated archdukes. In general, soandsos and they alone belong to—are members of—the class of soandsos.

When some member of one class belongs to another class, those classes *overlap*. The class of dogs overlaps the class of Schwartz-family pets: Bertha belongs to both. The class of armadillos and the class of Schwartz-family pets do not overlap.

When every member of a class X belongs to a class Y, X is *included in*, or is a *subclass of*, Y. The class of poodles is included in the class of dogs. Every class is included in itself.

Classes are the *same* when they have the *same members*, that is, when each is included in the other. Thus, the class of anti-Socialist postwar British prime ministers is the same as the class of post-1950 Tory leaders.

If there are no soandsos, the class of soandsos has *no members*; it is *empty*. But like an empty barrel, the class itself still exists. The class of unicorns is empty. So is the class of centaurs. Because these classes have *no* members, they do not differ in membership: they have exactly the same members—none. So they are the same class. In general, empty classes are all the same. That is, there is *just one empty class*, variously describable as the class of unicorns, the class of centaurs, and the class of round squares.

Some English statements involve express reference to classes. I have just written a few. Others can be regarded as assertions about classes, although they involve no express reference to classes. Examples:

STATEMENT	CLASS-INTERPRETATION
3 is an odd number.	3 belongs to the class of odd numbers.
Harold Stassen is an American politician and not an odd number.	Harold Stassen belongs to the class of Americans and to the class of politicians but not to the class of odd numbers.
There are no unicorns.	The class of unicorns is empty.
Every politician is greedy.	The class of politicians is included in the class of greedy things (in other words, the class of non-greedy politicians is empty).
Some women ran for the U.S. Senate in 1980.	The class of women overlaps the class of those who ran for the U.S. Senate in 1980.
Whoever is dishonest but does not have dandruff must be a lion-tamer or a clergyman.	The class of dishonest persons who have no dandruff is included in the class of those who are either lion-tamers or clergymen.

A *singular term* is any proper name, definite description, demonstrative pronoun, or other expression used to designate, to label, to refer to a unique object in order to say something about that object. As ordinarily used, "Bertha McGillicuddy" is a singular term. So is "3." So are "that," "this book," "the Queen Mother's left ear lobe," "the dumbest student in the class," and "the present president of the United States." Many people may be named "Bertha McGillicuddy." But when this name is used ordinarily, the user means to refer to *exactly one* of those people. That is what makes this name a singular term. Although there could be several maximally dumb students in the class, whoever calls someone the dumbest student in the class means to refer to just one person, implying (falsely, perhaps) that that person is dumber than everyone else in the class.

When I call something a singular term, I do not mean it is singular rather than plural. I mean it purports to refer to a *single object*.

A *general term* is a word or phrase that expresses some property, feature, or trait of things. General terms include verbs and verb phrases, nouns and noun phrases, and adjectives and adjectival phrases. "Ate," "dog," and "red" are general terms. So is "general term." So are "loves Bertha," "two-eyed furry thing without spots," and "smart things that are either midget university students or assassinated archdukes."

The sentences listed above contain these fifteen general terms:

odd number	women	dishonest but
American	ran for the U.S.	does not
politician	Senate in	have
American	1980	dandruff
politician	dishonest	lion tamers
and not an	has dandruff	clergyman
odd number	does not have	lion tamer or
unicorns	dandruff	clergyman
greedy		

Observe that a general term can contain other, simpler general terms.

Exotic technical exceptions aside, there is a class corresponding to every general term.* It is the class of those things to which the term truly applies. Corresponding to "red" is the class of red things; to "ate," the class of creatures who have eaten; to "lion tamer or clergyman," the class of people who are lion tamers or clergymen; to "unicorn," the class of unicorns, that is, the empty class.

Henceforth, singular and general terms will be treated as nonlogical expressions; "every," "all," "some," "is," "are," and similar expressions used to build statements out of singular and general terms will be treated as logical expressions; "and," "or," "not," and similar expres-

---

*For the record, one famous such exception is the general term "does not belong to itself." Were there a corresponding class, it would comprise all and only those things that did not belong to themselves. But then, if it belonged to itself, it would not belong to itself, and if it did not belong to itself, it would belong to itself.

sions used to build complex general terms from simple ones will be treated as logical expressions also.

When depicting the logical forms of statements, let us use lower-case Roman letters for singular terms, and upper-case Roman letters for general terms. Thus, the six statements listed above have these forms:

t is an O.

h is an AP and not an O.

There are no U.

Every P is G.

Some W R.

Whoever is dis-H but not-D must be a L or a C.

4.2. DIAGRAMING STATEMENTS WITH ONE GENERAL TERM

To *diagram* a statement containing a single general term, A, begin with a circle:

The page near the circle, including the circle itself, is the *universe region*. It represents the class of everything. The circle is the *A region*. It represents the *A class*, the class of things to which A truly applies. The part of the universe region outside the circle is the *non-A region*. It represents the *non-A class*, the class of things to which A does not truly apply. So if A = "dog," the circle represents the class of dogs; the rest of the universe region, the class of nondogs. The label "A" is part of the diagram; it indicates which term (and, therefore, which class) corresponds to the circle.

Some statements, their logical forms, their class-interpretations, and their diagrams:

— Stalin is a Georgian.

s is a G.

s (Stalin) belongs to the class of Gs (Georgians).

These statements can be diagramed the same way:

Harold ran for president.   h R.   h belongs to the class of
                                        those who R.

Jimmy is chilly.   j is C.   j belongs to the class of
                            C things.

- Zog no longer rules Albania.

  z no longer R.

  z does *not belong* to the class of those who R.

- Something itches.

  Something I.

  Something or other belongs to the class of
  things that I, that is, the I
  class is *not empty*.

The fat dot represents nonemptiness. Read "●" as "something." Write
"●" in the region representing a class to say that *something*—meaning *at
least one thing*—belongs to that class. These statements also are depicted by the last diagram:

Someone is happy.	Someone is H.
There are unicorns.	There are U.
Unicorns exist.	U exist.

- Something is not cheap.

  Something is not C.

  Something does not belong to the C class.

- There are no unicorns.

  There are no U.

  Nothing belongs to the U class, that is, the U class is *empty*.

Shading represents *emptiness*. Shade the region corresponding to a class
to show that nothing belongs to that class. These statements are depicted the same way as the last:

Nothing is supernatural.	Nothing is S.
Ghosts don't exist.	G don't exist.
No one loves me.	No one L.

- Everything is material.

  Everything is M.

  The M class exhausts the universe:
  everything belongs to it; there
  is nothing outside it.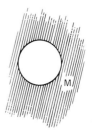

4.3. STATEMENTS WITH TWO GENERAL TERMS

To diagram a statement containing *two* general terms, A and B, begin with two overlapping circles, representing the A class and the B class:

The entire double circle—the A circle plus the B circle—is the *A-or-B region*. It represents the A-or-B class, the class of things that belong to the A class or the B class or both (called the *union* of the A class and the B class). The football-shaped overlap area is the *AB region*. It represents the AB class, the class of those things that belong *both* to the A class *and* to the B class (called the *intersection* of the A class and the B class). The A circle minus the football is the *A−B* (A minus B) *region*. It represents the A−B class, the class of things that belong to the A class but not to the B class (called the *complement* of the B class with respect to the A class). The B circle minus the football represents the B−A class. The outer region, the *neither-A-nor-B region*, represents the class of things that are neither A nor B.

Some more statements, class-interpretations, forms, and diagrams:

- Bertha is a vicious dog.

  b is a VD.

  b belongs to the V class and to the
  D class—or simply to the VD class.

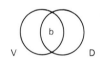

- Bertha is vicious but not hungry.

  b is V but not H.

  b belongs to the V class but not to the
  H class, that is, b belongs to
  the V−H class.

"Klaghorn lost the election without losing his cool" is depicted the same way.

- Bertha is vicious or hungry.

  b is V or H.

  b belongs to the V class or to
  the H class (or possibly to both).

The connecting line tells us that b belongs to *one* of the classes represented by a region in which the letter "b" occurs, without telling us *which* one. In other words, it tells us that b belongs to the V−H class *or* to the VH class *or* to the H−V class. Read a connecting line as "or."

- Bertha is neither vicious nor hungry.

  b is neither V nor H.

  b does not belong to the V class or to the H class.

- Some dogs are vicious.

  Some D are V.

  The D and V classes overlap: something belongs to both.

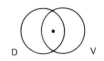

This statement is depicted the same way:

> There are friendly ghosts.   There are FG.

- Some dogs are not vicious.

  Some D are not V.

  Something belongs to the D class without belonging to the V class, that is, something belongs to the D−V class.

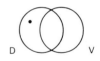

- Someone is rich or a liar.

  Someone is R or a L.

  The R-or-L class is not empty: something belongs to it, that is, to the R class or to the L class (or possibly to both).

As before, the connecting line means "or." It tells us that something belongs to *at least one* of the classes corresponding to a region occupied by "•," without telling us *which* class.

Of the last two diagrams, the former is stronger even though simpler: it says more. The latter says that something belongs to at least one of the two classes at issue. It does not say which one. The former diagram says which one.

Every politician is greedy.

Every P is G.

The P class is included in
the G class, that is, nothing belongs to the P class
without belonging to the
G class as well.

Shading the P—G region is like erasing it, thereby pushing the whole P
region into the G region. *Study this example very carefully. Think about it.
Remember it.* The following statements are depicted the same way:

Whatever is a poodle is a dog.	Whatever is a P is a D.
All poodles are dogs.	All P are D.
None but dogs are poodles.	None but D are P.
Only dogs are poodles.	Only D are P.
Whoever itches enjoys scratching.	Whoever I E.

Note the equivalences of these four forms:

All As are Bs.	Only Bs are As.
Every A is a B.	None but Bs are As.

Changing "all" or "every" to "only" or "none but" is equivalent to
reversing the order of general terms. *All* U.S. senators are American
citizens. *Only* American citizens (*none but* American citizens) are U.S.
senators.

No politician is honest.

No P is H.

The P class does not overlap the H class, that is,
the PH class is empty.

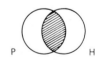

These statements can be represented the same way:

There are no honest politicians.	There are no HP.
Honest politicians don't exist.	HP don't exist.
Politicians are never honest.	P are never H.
No cyclist jumps hurdles.	No C J.

4.4. STATEMENTS WITH THREE GENERAL TERMS

To depict a statement with three general terms, A, B, and C, begin with a pretzel:

The interpretation should by now be obvious.
   Some statements with three general terms:

- Bertha is mean or vicious
   but not hungry.

   b is M or V but not H.

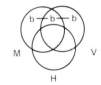

- All politicians are greedy scoundrels.

   All P are GS.

- All greedy politicians are honest.

   All GP are H.

- Some politicians are greedy but honest.

   Some P are G but H.

- Politicians are always
   greedy or honest but
   never both.

   P are always G or H but never both.

• Politicians and clergy-men are sometimes greedy.

P and G are sometimes C.

4.5. THE GENERAL PROCEDURE

The diagraming technique I have just presented was invented by the nineteenth-century English logician John Venn. The diagrams are called *Venn diagrams.*

Obviously, a statement with two general terms cannot be represented in a one-circle diagram, and a statement with three general terms cannot be represented in a two-circle diagram. But a statement with one or two general terms *can* be represented in a two- or three-circle diagram (which will prove convenient when we have occasion later to represent two or more statements in one diagram). Thus, "Some politicians are liars" can be depicted this way:

Summary of rules for representing a statement by means of a Venn diagram:

1. For a statement containing one general term, A, divide a "universe region" into at least two parts, representing the A class and the non-A class. For two general terms, A and B, divide the region into at least four parts, representing the AB class, the A−B class, the B−A class, and the neither-A-nor-B class. For three general terms, A, B, and C, divide the region into at least eight parts, representing the ABC class, the AB−C class, and so forth.

2. Divide a universe region into two parts by drawing a circle, into four parts by drawing two overlapping circles, and into eight parts by drawing three overlapping circles. In each case, a circle corresponds to a simple (rather than a complex) general term, representing the class of things to which the term truly applies.

3. To show that an object designated by a given singular term belongs to a given class, mark the singular term (or letter symbol) in the region representing that class. If this region is di-

vided, write the singular term in each subregion and connect its several inscriptions with lines.

4. To show that *something or other* belongs to a given class, mark "•" in the region representing that class. If this region is divided, mark "•" in each subregion and connect these "•"s with lines.

5. To show that a class is *empty*, shade the corresponding region.

Some useful corollaries:

1. To show that the X class is *included in* the Y class, shade the X−Y region—the part of the X region that lies outside the Y region.

2. To show that the X class *overlaps* the Y class, put a fat dot (or chain of linked dots) in the XY region.

3. To show that the X class does *not overlap* the Y class, shade the XY region.

When diagraming sentences, I first displayed their logical forms. This is useful because a sentence's logical form comprises just those features of the sentence that are relevant to diagraming and because it provides letter-symbols for singular and general terms. But displaying logical form is not essential to the task of diagram construction.

4.6. ARGUMENTS

Test an argument for validity by representing all the argument's premises in a single Venn diagram, then checking whether the diagram verifies the conclusion—whether the information expressed by the conclusion is represented in the diagram of the premises.

Example 1   Only crooks are politicians.   Only C are P.
               Some politicians are Democrats.   Some P are D.
               So some Democrats are crooks.   Some D are C.

Because there are three general terms, we need a three-circle diagram. The first premise is represented thus:

If we were diagraming the second premise by itself, we should inscribe two connected "●"s in the PD region, as follows:

Since what we want to do is represent the *two* premises in a *single* diagram, we might simply combine the two diagrams (represent the first premise and then the second in one diagram):

Having shaded the P–C region to represent the first premise, however, we need not put a "●" in the shaded area when representing the second premise. We need not say that something belongs to at least one of two classes (to the PD–C class or to the PDC class) when we have already said that nothing belongs to the first of the two classes (the PD–C class). Especially since we *began* by shading the PD–C region (to represent the first premise) it is simpler to represent the second premise this way:

In this diagram, there no longer is a left-hand "●." In the previous diagram, the shading effectively erases the left-hand "●." The information represented is exactly the same in either case. *Either diagram is correct.*

In general, *shading* a region containing a "●" or singular term effectively *erases* the "●" or term.

Because the diagram of the premises shows that something belongs to the DC class, it verifies the conclusion, proving the argument valid.

Note that the conclusion *by itself* would be represented as follows:

This tells us that something belongs to the DC class. The diagram of the premises tells us more: that something belongs to the PDC class. An argument is valid so long as the premise-diagram *verifies* the conclusion—so long as it represents all the information expressed by the conclusion. It is permissible for the premise-diagram to *go beyond* the conclusion, representing more information than is expressed by the conclusion.

Example 2   Only crooks are politicians.   Only C are P.
                   Some Texans are crooks.   Some T are C.
                   Therefore, some Texans are politicians.   Some T are P.

Premise-diagram:

The conclusion says that something belongs to the TP class. The diagram does not verify this. It tells us that something belongs *either* to the TP class *or* to the TC class. But it does not tell us which. So the argument is *not valid.*

4.7. EXAMPLES

Here are some arguments, their logical forms, and their premise-diagrams. There is a diagram next to each premise, representing that premise plus all preceding premises (if any). So only the last diagram with each argument represents all the premises of that argument. I set it up this way to display the successive steps involved in diagraming an argument's premises. *You* need not do this. You may successively depict all the premises of an argument in one diagram.

Example 3   Socrates is a man.

              s is a H.

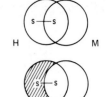

              All men are mortal.

              All H are M.

Therefore, Socrates is   **VALID**   According to the diagram, s
mortal.   belongs to the M class.

s is M.

Example 4   Madalyn is an atheist.

              m is an A.

              All Communists are atheists.

              All C are A.

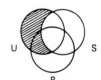

Therefore, Madalyn is a   **INVALID**   According to the diagram,
Communist.   m does not necessarily
                                            belong to the C class;
m is a C.   m might belong to
                                            the A−C class.

Example 5   All Podunk students are smart.

              All U are S.

              But some people are not smart.

              Some P are not S.

Therefore, some people   **VALID**   According to the diagram,
are not Podunk students.   something belongs to the
                                         P−U class.

Some P are not U.

Example 6   Whoever is prudent shuns hyenas

Whoever is P Ss.

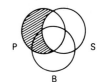

No banker is imprudent.

No B is im-P.

[The B class does not intersect the non-P class.]

Therefore, no banker fails   VALID
to shun hyenas.

No B fails to S.

According to the diagram, the B class does not intersect the non-S class.

Example 7   Some pillows are soft.

Some W are S.

No pokers are soft.

No K are S.

Therefore, some pokers   INVALID
are not pillows.
Some K are not W.

The diagram does not show that something belongs to the K−W class.

Example 8   Every politician is greedy or fanatical.

Every P is G or F.

Not every politician is fanatical.

Not every P is F.

["Every P is F" means the P−F class is empty. So "*Not* every P is F" means the P−F class is *not* empty.]

Therefore, some greedy   VALID
things are not fanatical.

Some G are not F.

The diagram shows the G−F class to be nonempty.

Example 9   All politicians are greedy.

All P are G.

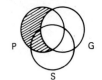

Some statesmen are not politicians.

Some S are not P.

So some statesmen are   INVALID The diagram does not
not greedy.   require that anything
                                   belong to the S−G class.
Some S are not G.

Example 10   Centaurs do not exist.

C do not exist.

Therefore, all centaurs are VALID Yes, the diagram does
ugly.   show the C class to be
                                    included in the U class.
All C are U.   Look at it this way: For
                                    the conclusion to be
                                    false, there would have to
                                    be at least one good-looking
                                    centaur. (The class-
                                    inclusion interpretation
                                    of "all-are" sentences
                                    simplifies ordinary English,
                                    perhaps, but I see
                                    no harm.)

Example 11   SLA members often sincerely desire
             to better mankind.

Ss often D.

But terrorists are never thus sincere.

Ts never D.

Therefore, no terrorists   INVALID The diagram allows
are SLA members.   (although it does not
                                    require) the T class to
No Ts are Ss.   intersect the S class.

When two premises of an argument called for shading, I used a different style of shading for each premise. I shall continue to do this as an aid to exposition, but it is not essential to the Venn-diagram method.

EXERCISES

1. Draw a single circle twice, using a fifty-cent piece as template. Draw two overlapping circles several times. Make sure the second circle comes to about the center of the first. Labeling the circles A and B, specify the A-or-B, neither-A-nor-B, AB, A−B, and B−A regions. Draw three overlapping circles ten times. Make sure the third circle comes to the center of the football formed by the first two. With the circles labeled A, B, and C, specify the interpretation of each of the eight undivided parts constituting the universe region.

For each of the following arguments, display its *logical form*, draw a *single Venn diagram* of *all* its premises (not one diagram per premise), and state whether the argument is *valid*.

* 2. Every husky is a dog. But all dogs are mammals. So each husky is a mammal.

* 3. Every husky is a mammal. And every husky is a dog. So all dogs are mammals.

* 4. No Republican is a Democrat. But some Republican is a cucumber. So some cucumber is not a Democrat.

* 5. All Communists are atheists. Therefore, all atheists are Communists.

6. Some Communists are atheists. Therefore, some atheists are Communists.

* 7. Someone is a politician. Someone is greedy. So someone is a greedy politician.

8. All men are mortal. Therefore, all purple men are mortal.

9. No conservative is a liberal. But some Republicans are liberals. So some Republicans are not conservatives.

* 10. No liberal is a Republican. But some Republicans are conservatives. So some liberals are not conservatives.

11. No capitalists are artists. But all businessmen are capitalists. So no businessmen are artists.

* 12. Some U.S. presidents have been wealthy. John F. Kennedy was a U.S. president. So John F. Kennedy was wealthy.

* 13. All U.S. presidents have been wealthy. And Lincoln was a U.S. president. So Lincoln was wealthy.

14. All conservatives are Republicans. But no one is both a Democrat and a Republican. So no Democrat is conservative.

* 15. All conservatives are rich. And every Republican is rich. So every Republican is a conservative.

16. There are no rich workers. But some Democrats are workers. So there are Democrats who are not rich.

* 17. No workers are rich. And some Republicans are not rich either. So some Republicans are not workers.

18. Some capitalists are not artists. But all businessmen are capitalists. So no businessmen are artists.

* 19. Some restrictions create new opportunities. Whatever creates new opportunities is liberating. Thus, some restrictions are liberating.

20. Whoever is an alien is a potential spy. François Abdul Benito Wahrhaftig is an alien. Therefore, François Abdul Benito Wahrhaftig is a potential spy.

* 21. Communists admire Marx. So do some faculty members. Therefore, some faculty members are Communists.

22. Dracula enjoys a great night life. But whoever enjoys a great night life is a jet setter. Consequently, Dracula is a jet setter.

* 23. Dracula enjoys a great night life. But every jet setter enjoys a great night life. Therefore, Dracula is a jet setter.

24. No one can die who is made of dead men. But Frankenstein is made of dead men. So Frankenstein cannot die.

* 25. Whoever is reading is literate. And you are reading. Therefore, you are literate.

26. Whoever is taking an exam is literate. And you are literate. Therefore, you are taking an exam.

* 27. A homosexual act involving only consenting adults has no victim. But every crime has a victim. So a homosexual act involving only consenting adults is no crime.

28. There have been living things on Mars. But anything on Mars is in the solar system. Therefore, there have been living things in the solar system.

* 29. All socialists are for Medicare. But some liberals are for Medicare. Hence, some liberals are socialists.

30. All policies are harmful or expensive. But no policies are expensive. Therefore, no policies are harmful.

* 31. Only a Communist would support busing. Therefore, any supporter of busing must be a Communist.

32. No platypus flies. All platypuses lay eggs. Therefore, some egg layers do not fly.

* 33. No platypus flies. All platypuses lay eggs. There are platypuses. Therefore, some egg layers do not fly.

34. Everyone who has met both Henry and Cy loves Cy. But some who've met Cy do not love him. Thus, some who've met Cy have not met Henry.

* 35. Some atheists are Communists. And some professors are atheists. So some professors are Communists.

36. Whoever drinks heavily does not drive safely. But Matilda drives safely. So Matilda does not drink heavily.

* 37. I eat everything. Therefore, I eat everything I do not eat.

5

Diagrams:
Refinements and
Ramifications

5.1. IMPLICIT GENERAL TERMS

Sometimes a sentence expresses a diagrammatically representable class relationship but does not contain general terms corresponding to all the relevant classes. Example:

They only do it at night.

Class-interpretation:

The class of times at which they do it is included in the class of night times.

Diagram:

Although this sentence is about the class of times at which they do it, the sentence does not contain the general term "times at which they do it" or its ilk. This term, let us say, is an *implicit general term*: it is a complex general term foreign to the sentence in question but needed to label one of the circles in the sentence's Venn diagram.

Some more examples:

► Everywhere that Mary went the lamb was sure to go.

The class of places to which Mary went is included in the class of places to which the lamb was sure to go.

places to which Mary went

places to which the lamb was sure to go

- She sometimes wears pants on Sunday.

The class of days on which she wears pants overlaps the class of Sundays.

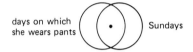

days on which she wears pants

Sundays

- Decontrolling gas prices would not seriously hurt the poor.

The class of acts of decontrolling gas prices does not overlap the class of acts that would seriously hurt the poor.

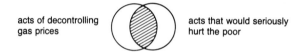

acts of decontrolling gas prices

acts that would seriously hurt the poor

- Believing in God involves potential gain and no possible loss.

The class of (possible) cases of believing in God is included in the class of cases of potential gain minus the class of cases of possible loss.

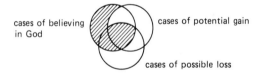

cases of believing in God

cases of potential gain

cases of possible loss

When a sentence concerns a class whose corresponding general term is implicit, that class often is a class of *times* (or other temporal denominations), of *places* (or other spatial denominations), of *actions*, or of *cases*. So implict general terms often have the forms "times at which . . .," "places at which . . .," and the like.

When *all* the circles in a diagram are labeled "*times* at which . . .," it is convenient to interpret the universe region as representing the class of *all times* rather than the class of all entities whatever. This way we can interpret the region outside a circle labeled "times at which it rains" as representing the class of times at which it does not rain rather than the class of *nontimes plus* those times at which it does not rain.

Now some arguments:

Example 1   She only wears pants on Sunday.

Today is Sunday.

So she is wearing pants today.

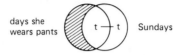

The shading represents the first premise; the two-"t" chain ("t" for "today"), the second. The argument is INVALID. The premise-diagram does not require today (t) to belong to the class of days she wears pants.

Example 2   When something is outlawed, whoever does it is a criminal.

Owning guns is outlawed.

So only criminals own guns.

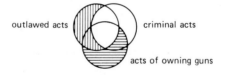

Alternatively:

VALID.

   In testing Examples 2 and 3 for validity, I did not bother to display the logical forms of these arguments. Although often helpful, displaying logical form is not essential to the diagram test. And in cases involving implicit general terms, it is not all that helpful.

5.2. WHEN A SINGULAR TERM OCCURS IN MORE THAN ONE PREMISE

Here is a valid argument, its logical form, and its diagram:

Example 3   Bertha is a Vegetarian or a Prohibitionist. b is a V or a P.

But she is not a Prohibitionist.   b is not a P.

Therefore, Bertha is a Vegetarian.   b is a V.

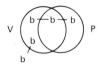

The chain of three "b"s represents the first premise; that of two "b"s, the second. Because the two chains coincide only in the V−P region, the premise-diagram tells us that b belongs to the V−P class, hence to the V class, thereby verifying the conclusion. In other words, the three-"b" chain tells us that b belongs to one of the three classes in this list:

the V−P class,   the VP class,   the P−V class;

and the two-"b" chain tells us that b belongs to one of the two classes in this list:

the V−P class,   the neither-V-nor-P class;

whence it follows that b belongs to the V−P class, the one class common to the two lists. In general, a diagram with two or more distinct chains of the same singular term locates the term in that region in which the chains coincide.

Having inscribed the three-"b" chain to represent the first premise and the two-"b" chain to represent the second, we can make our diagram more vivid by *crossing out* those "b"s that lie outside the V−P region, the region in which the two chains coincide, thus:

This device of crossing out singular terms enables us to construct diagrams that are not only more vivid but simpler. Having represented the first premise of Example 3 by the three-"b" chain, we need not then represent the second premise by the two-"b" chain. We can represent it more simply by crossing out the two "b"s incompatible with the second premise, thus:

The second premise says b does not belong to the P class. So instead of writing "b" in the non-P region as before, I crossed "b" out of the P region.

Henceforth, follow this rule: *When a premise-diagram already contains a chain of some singular term, depict any new premise involving that term by crossing out links of the existing chain instead of inscribing a new chain.* For the sake of uniformity, always cross out a singular term this way: ⧸ .

Given this rule, no premise-diagram will ever contain more than one chain of the same singular term. As a result, we need no longer inscribe connecting lines; they were needed only to make clear to which chain each occurrence of a term belonged. Henceforth, *you may omit connecting lines between occurrences of singular terms.* So the first premise of Example 3 may now be depicted this way:

We must still *read* the diagram as though the connecting lines were present. That is, the diagram says that b belongs *either* to the V−P class *or* to the VP class *or* to the P−V class. It does not say that b belongs to all three classes—an inconsistent thing to say. In this chapter and the next, you will find diagrams that would be illegibile but for the omission of connecting lines.

Note that the policy of omitting connecting lines applies only to chains of *singular terms*, not to chains of "●"s, clsc we could not distinguish these two cases:

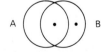

There exist at least two Bs, one of which is an A and one of which is not an A.

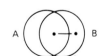

There exists at least one B.

When one premise of an argument calls for a chain of some singular term and subsequent premises require that *all* links in that chain be crossed out, stop immediately and conclude that the argument is valid. Reason: Taken together, the premises say of a certain object both that it does and that it does not belong to a certain class. So the premises are jointly inconsistent. But an argument with inconsistent premises is automatically valid (see §3.4 above).

Besides crossing out singular terms already present in a diagram, we can represent premises by *adding crossed-out singular terms*—terms added only to be crossed out immediately. Let us reverse the premises of Example 3:

Bertha is not a Prohibitionist.	b is not a P.
But she is a Vegetarian or a Prohibitionist.	b is a V or a P.
Therefore, Bertha is a Vegetarian.	b is a V.

We can depict the first premise either of two ways:

That is, we can inscribe a two-"b" *chain* in the non-P region as before, symbolizing b's *presence* in the non-P class; or we can inscribe *crossed-out* "b"s in each subdivision of the P region, symbolizing b's *absence* from the P class. The information conveyed is the same in either case. The second diagram is a more direct, more obvious representation of the first premise. But either alternative is correct.

On the second alternative, the simplest way to add the information contained in the second premise is the following:

I added "b" to the V-or-P region because the second premise says b belongs to the V-or-P class. I added "b" only to the left-most part, instead of marking "b" in all parts, because "b" already is marked absent from the middle and right parts. *Never mark a singular term in a region from which it has already been excluded by crossing out or shading.*

A crossed-out singular term (or letter symbol) represents absence of the corresponding object. Crossing out is a little like shading. But whereas shading bars everything from the shaded region, crossing out bars a single object. It is a selective embargo rather than a general one.

Example 4   Ignatz is greedy or dishonest.   i is G or dis-H.

                      Ignatz is honest but not well regarded.   i is H but not W.

                      Therefore, Ignatz is greedy but honest.   i is G but H.

I represented the first premise by inscribing an "i"-chain throughout the G-or-dis-H region, that is, the G region plus the non-H region. I represented the second premise by crossing out those "i"s already present that do not occur in the H−W region. As a result, "i" remains only in the GH−W region, verifying the conclusion.

    To sum up:

> If a singular term, σ, occurs in an argument, represent the first premise that contains σ either by a chain of σ's (omitting connecting lines, if you wish) or by one or more crossed-out σ's. Once your diagram contains a crossed-out σ in a given region, do not mark σ in that region (it has already been barred). Once your diagram contains a σ-chain, represent every subsequent premise containing σ by crossing out links (occurrences of σ) in that chain; do not add any new chains or new crossed-out σ's.

When crossed-out occurences of a singular term, σ, occur throughout a given region of a diagram, take care to *read* the diagram as though a σ-chain occupied the *remaining* region. Reason: Absence from one part of the universe is equivalent to presence somewhere or other in the remaining part.

Example 5   Everything is material or spiritual.   Everything is M or S.

                      But God is not material.   g is not M.

                      So God is spiritual.   g is S.

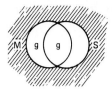

The shading represents the first premise; the crossed-out "g"s, the second. The argument is VALID. Because the neither-M-nor-S region is shaded and "g" has been crossed out of the M region, we must read the diagram as though "g" (a one-link "g"-chain) occupied the remaining region—the S−M region.*

Arguments containing more than one singular term raise special difficulties that make them unprofitable to treat at this point. They are best left to the more general method of Chapter 6.

5.3.   ARGUMENTS WITH FOUR GENERAL TERMS

As presented so far, the diagram technique enables us to decide the validity of arguments with one, two, or three general terms. For arguments with *four* general terms, say A, B, C, and D, we need a diagram that divides a universe region into sixteen parts—an ABCD part, an ABC−D part, an ABD−C part, and so on. But four overlapping circles will not divide a region into sixteen parts (try it). What to do?

For arguments with four general terms, I offer three approaches. The first two usually are the simplest when applicable. Only the third is always applicable.

First approach   If one premise says the A class is *included* in the B class, draw a three-circle diagram containing a B circle but not an A circle; then draw an A circle *inside* the B circle, to represent class-inclusion, this way:

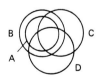

---

*I assume, of course, that any sentence under consideration containing a singular term implies or presupposes the existence of a corresponding object. The contrary case is easily enough handled with Venn diagrams. But it would not be profitable to take up such a fussy complication at this point.

Example 6	Every politician is greedy.	Every P is G.
	But no greedy Republicans ever get elected.	No GR ever E.
	Yet some Republicans get elected.	Some R E.
	So some Republicans are not politicians.	Some R are not P.

Thanks to the first premise, we can draw the P circle inside the G circle. The resulting premise-diagram verifies the conclusion, proving the argument valid:

Second approach If a premise says (in effect) the A class does *not* overlap the B class, draw a four-circle diagram with the A and B circles *separated*, thus:

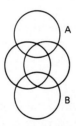

Make sure the A and B circles both pass through the vertical football but do not overlap or even touch each other.

Example 7	No politician is honest.	No P is H.
	Jimmy is either an honest Crest-user or a Crest-using politician.	j is either an H U-er or a U-ing P.
	Whoever uses Crest is toothy.	Whoever Us is T.
	Consequently, someone who is toothy is a dishonest politician or an honest nonpolitician.	Someone who is T is a dis-H P or an H non-P.

The first premise allows us to draw the P and H circles separated. This diagram shows the argument to be valid:

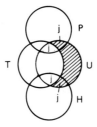

Third approach　To a pretzel, add a *squash*:

A pretzel (three overlapping circles) divides the universe region into eight parts. The squash divides these parts into two parts each, yielding sixteen parts altogether.

These squash diagrams represent Examples 6 and 7:

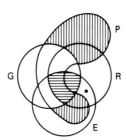

The vertical shading represents the first premise; the horizontal shading, the second; the "●," the third.

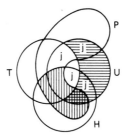

The vertical shading represents the first premise; the "j"-chain, the second; the horizontal shading, the third.

Example 8   No Democrat is honest.   No D is H.

             No Democrat believes in fiscal   No D Bs.
             responsibility.

             Some Republicans believe in fiscal   Some R B.
             responsibility.

             So some Republicans are honest.   Some R are H.

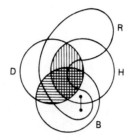

The vertical shading represents the first premise; the horizontal shading, the second; the connected "●"s, the third. The conclusion is not verified. It says something belongs to the H class. All the diagram tells us is that something belongs *either* to the H class *or* to the B class; it does not tell us which. So the argument is INVALID.

Example 9   All Potentates and Grand Viziers who've met Cy have met Henry.

             Some Potentates have met Henry or Cy.

             Thus, some Potentates or Grand Viziers have met Henry.

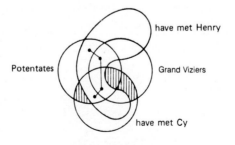

The shading represents the first premise; the "●"-chain, the second. The argument is VALID.

5.4. IDENTIFYING APPROPRIATE REGIONS

When you have to mark a region with shading or other matter, you usually can spot the region at a glance. But not always: sometimes it is hard to tell exactly where to mark just by looking. Example:

Some politicians are neither greedy nor dishonest.
Some P are neither G nor dis-H.

To diagram this sentence, begin with a pretzel:

You need to inscribe a "●" (or "●"-chain) in the P region minus the G-or-dis-H region, that is, in the part of the P region that lies outside the G-or-dis-H region. If it is not apparent which region this is, you can locate it in steps. First, mark the dis-H region with the numeral "1," as follows:

Next, continue to mark "1" throughout the G region (part of which already is marked "1"):

Because the G-or-dis-H region is the G region plus the dis-H region, it is the region marked "1." To inscribe a "●" in the P region minus the G-or-dis-H region, that is, in the P region minus the "1" region, merely inscribe "●" in the part of the P circle devoid of "1":

Here is a more complex example:

> Paupers who work hard are neither lazy nor unintelligent.
> P who W are neither L nor un-I.

This says the PW class is included in the neither-L-nor-un-I class. To identify the neither-L-nor-un-I region, I first mark "1" throughout the L-or-un-I region, that is, the L region plus the un-I region:

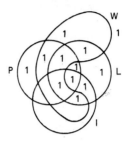

The remaining region—the area so far unmarked—is then the neither-L-nor-un-I region. This I mark with "2," after which I mark the PW region with "3":

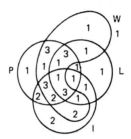

To show that the PW class is included in the neither-L-nor-I class, I shade the PW region minus the neither-L-nor-un-I region. That is, I shade the "3" region minus the "2" region:

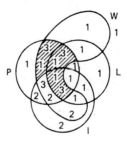

Now three arguments:

Example 10   Whoever is not hot is not wearing a coat.   Whoever is not H is not W.

Therefore, whoever is wearing a coat is hot.   Whoever is W is H.

I marked the not-H region with "1" and the not-W region with "2," then shaded the area marked "1" but not "2," that is, the not-H region minus the not-W region. The conclusion is verified.

Example 11   Whoever is wearing a coat   Whoever is W is H.
              is hot.

              Therefore, whoever is not hot   Whoever is not H
              is not wearing a coat.   is not W.

To represent the premise, I shaded the W-H region; numerical markers were not needed. The conclusion requires shading of the not-H region minus the not-W region. Because it is not immediately apparent which this region is, I marked the not-H region with "1" and the not-W region with "2." The not-H region minus the not-W region is then the "1" region minus the "2" region, which indeed is shaded. So the argument is VALID.

By the way, the last two diagrams show that the two sentence-forms:

All X are Y   All non-Y are non-X

are logically equivalent: each is deducible from the other. That is a useful fact to remember.

Example 12   Whenever tariffs are high and imports drop, labor is
              happy but Japan is unhappy.

              But Japan is now happy.

              So labor is now happy or tariffs are not now high.

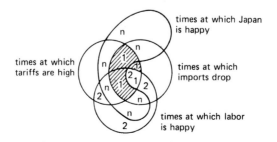

I marked "1" in the region corresponding to times at which tariffs are high and imports drop, and "2" in the region corresponding to times at which labor is happy but Japan is unhappy. I then represented the first premise by shading the area containing "1" but not "2," thereby showing that the class of times at which tariffs are high and imports drop is included in the class of times at which labor is happy but Japan is unhappy. The "n"-chain ("n" for "now") represents the second premise. The conclusion is not verified, because not every link of the "n"-chain falls within the happy-labor or no-high-tariffs region.

5.5. ARGUMENTS WITH MORE THAN FOUR GENERAL TERMS (optional)

How to assess the validity of arguments with *more than four* general terms? Sometimes a judicious combination of nested circles and nonoverlapping circles does the trick, as in this argument with six general terms:

Example 13

All Republicans are conservatives.	All R are C.
But no conservative supports socialized medicine or deficit spending.	No C Ms or Ds.
Yet some supporters of socialized medicine or deficit spending are for free trade.	Some M-ers or D-ers are F.
Whoever is for free trade opposes tariff increases.	Whoever is F Ts.
So not only Republicans oppose tariff increases.	Not only R T.

The first premise allows us to nest the R circle in the C circle; the second, to separate the M and D circles from the C circle. So far we have:

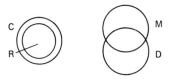

The fourth premise allows us to nest the F circle in the T circle. We must ensure, of course, that the F and T circles intersect the C, R, M, and D circles. Our developing diagram looks like this:

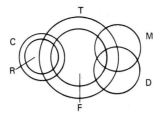

I have already depicted the second and fourth premises. The third calls for a "●"-chain in the part of the M-or-D-region that overlaps the F circle. We get the premise-diagram:

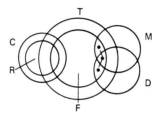

which verifies the conclusion.

A method that always works, regardless of the number of general terms and regardless of whether the premises license nesting or separation of circles, is to construct a *matrix,* or *table.* Here is a matrix suitable for Example 13:

	TMD	TM$\overline{\text{D}}$	T$\overline{\text{M}}$D	T$\overline{\text{MD}}$	$\overline{\text{T}}$MD	$\overline{\text{T}}$M$\overline{\text{D}}$	$\overline{\text{TM}}$D	$\overline{\text{TMD}}$
RCF								
RC$\overline{\text{F}}$								
R$\overline{\text{C}}$F								
R$\overline{\text{CF}}$								
$\overline{\text{R}}$CF								
$\overline{\text{R}}$C$\overline{\text{F}}$								
$\overline{\text{RC}}$F								
$\overline{\text{RCF}}$								

This divides the universe region into the appropriate sixty-four minimum subregions, which are the cells of the matrix. The cell determined by the third column (the T$\overline{\text{M}}$D column) and the second row (the RC$\overline{\text{F}}$ row), for example, is the TDRC-but-neither-M-nor-F-region.

One can formulate the column labels for this matrix by constructing the following tree:

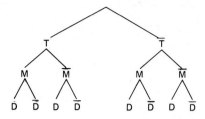

The first column label is "TMD," the second "TMD̄," and so forth. Similarly for the row labels. The decision as to which general terms to use for column labels and which for row labels was quite arbitrary. I could, for example, have labeled the columns "CTR," "CTR̄," "CT̄R," and so on, and the rows "DMF," "DMF̄," and the like.

The first premise of Example 13 calls for shading (I shall use vertical) of the R−C region. The second calls for shading of the overlap of the C region with the M-or-D region. I have marked "1" in the M-or-D region, then horizontally shaded the overlap of this region with the C region. The third premise calls for a "●"-chain in the part of the M-or-D region (marked "1") that overlaps the F region. And the final premise calls for shading (acute) of the F−T region. We get the validating premise-diagram:

	TMD	TMD̄	T̄MD	T̄MD̄	T̄̄MD	T̄̄MD̄	T̄̄̄MD	T̄̄̄MD̄
RCF	1	1	1		1	1	1	
RCF̄	1	1	1		1	1	1	
RC̄F	1	1	1		1	1	1	
RC̄F̄	1	1	1		1	1	1	
R̄CF	1	1	1		1	1	1	
R̄CF̄	1	1	1		1	1	1	
R̄C̄F	1●—1●—1●—				1●	1●	1●	
R̄C̄F̄	1	1	1		1	1	1	

For an argument with N general terms, we need a 2^N-cell matrix.

Example 14   Believing in God amounts to potential gain and no potential loss.

Not believing in God amounts to potential loss and no potential gain.

But potential gain without potential loss is safe.

On the other hand, potential loss without potential gain is unsafe.

And what is safe is reasonable.

But what is unsafe is unreasonable.

So believing in God is reasonable; and not believing, unreasonable.

The general terms needed to label the rows and columns of the matrix are implicit. Let:

B = cases of believing in God,

G = cases of potential gain,

L = cases of potential loss,

S = cases of doing what is safe, and

R = cases of doing what is reasonable.

Let the *universe* consist just of *cases*. To test the argument for validity, I begin with the bare matrix:

	BGL	BGL̄	BḠL	BḠL̄	B̄GL	B̄ḠL̄	B̄ḠL	B̄LḠ
SR								
SR̄								
S̄R								
S̄R̄								

According to the first premise, the B class is included in the G−L class. I shall represent this by vertically shading the B region minus the G−L region, having marked the latter with "1." According to the second premise, the non-B class is included in the L−G class. This I shall represent by horizontally shading the non-B region minus the L−G region, having marked the latter with "2." The third premise says the G−L class is included in the S class. This calls for shading (acute) of the G−L region (marked "1") minus the S region. Similarly, the fourth premise calls for shading (acute again) of the L−G region (marked "2") minus the non-S region. The fifth premise just calls for shading (oblique) of the S−R region, and the sixth for shading (oblique) of the non-S region minus the non-R region. The result:

	BGL	BGL̄	BḠL	BḠL̄	B̄GL	B̄GL̄	B̄ḠL	B̄ḠL̄
SR		1	2			1	2	
SR̄		1	2			1	2	
S̄R		1	2			1	2	
S̄R̄		1	2			1	2	

The premise-diagram verifies the conclusion, since it requires the B class to be included in the R class (the B−R region is shaded) and the non-B class to be included in the non-R class (the non-B region minus the non-R region is shaded).

5.6. MODIFIERS AND RELATIONAL EXPRESSIONS (optional)

Compare:

Example 15	Bimbo is a gray elephant.	b is a G E.
	Every elephant is an animal.	Every E is an A.
	Therefore, Bimbo is a gray animal.	b is a G A.
Example 16	Bimbo is a small elephant.	b is a S E.
	Every elephant is an animal.	Every E is an A.
	Therefore, Bimbo is a small animal.	b is a S A.

The first of these arguments is valid, as shown by the diagram:

The second surely is invalid. Yet it seems to have the same logical form as the first.

The apparent anomaly is due to the fact that "gray" is a general term but "small" is not. "Gray elephant" means "both gray and an elephant." "Small elephant" does not mean "both small and an elephant." "Small" modifies the simple general term "elephant," yielding the complex general term "small elephant." But "small" by itself is not a general term. It stands for no class. There is a class of gray things but no class of small things, else a small elephant that was nevertheless large for an animal would both belong and fail to belong.

Other modifiers that are not general terms are "good" and "with remarkable agility" as in:

Hitler was a good orator.

Every orator is a person.

Therefore, Hitler was a good person.

Mohammad Ali boxes with remarkable agility.

Mohammad Ali composes verse.

Therefore, Mohammad Ali composes verse with remarkable agility.

An expression functions as a *pure modifier* when it modifies a general term but does not function as a general term itself. In the examples above, "small," "good," and "with remarkable agility" are pure modifiers; "gray" is not.

When constructing a premise-diagram for an argument containing a pure modifier, M, represent M by a circle *inside* each circle that represents a general term modified by M. This requires more than one M circle when M modifies more than one general term. Here is the proper premise-diagram for Example 16:

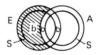

Because "small" modifies both "elephant" and "animal," there are separate "small" circles inside the "elephant" and "animal" circles. The S circle inside the E circle represents *small elephants*, not *small things*, and the S circle inside the A circle represents small animals. Fortunately, the premise-diagram does not verify the conclusion.

Venn diagrams do not apply to all arguments. They are inapplicable, in particular, to many arguments containing *relational expressions*—words and phrases, like "loves," "next to," "picture of," and "greater than," that stand for relations among things rather than classes of things. Thus, the evident validity of this argument cannot be demonstrated diagrammatically:

There is a boy whom all the girls in the class love.	There is a B whom all the Gs L.
Bertha is a girl in the class.	b is a G.
So Bertha loves some boy.	b Ls some B.

Still, we can apply diagrams to many arguments involving relational expressions, to wit, those whose relational expressions can be paraphrased as general terms with modifiers attached.

Example 17   All horses are animals.   All Es are As.

Therefore, all heads of horses   All Hs of Es are Hs
are heads of animals.   of As.

We can paraphrase the conclusion, which contains the relational expression "heads of," as follows:

All horse heads are animal heads.   All EHs are AHs.

Now "horse" and "animal" serve as *general terms* in the premise, but as *pure modifiers* in the conclusion. Because they are related to each other as general terms, their circles must overlap. But because they are related to "heads" only as pure modifiers, we can draw their circles wholly inside the "heads" circle. Here is the argument's premise-diagram:

Regarding E and A as general terms, the premise requires shading of the E−A region. This must be preserved when we draw E and A circles inside the H circle. Because the E circle inside the H circle represents horse *heads* and the A circle inside the H circle represents animal *heads*, the diagram tells us that every horse head is an animal head, verifying the conclusion.

In general, *diagrammatic representations of class relationships among general terms are preserved when these terms recur as pure modifiers.* So when an expression is used in one argument both as a general term and as a pure modifier, include all information from its general-term representation in its modifier representation.

In Example 17 I paraphrased the original conclusion to make it clear that I interpret it as containing pure modifiers. But the paraphrase was not essential. We could simply have regarded "of horses" and "of animals" as pure modifiers of "heads," represented by overlapping circles inside the "head" circle.

Example 18	Everyone who buys a ticket receives a prize.	Everyone who Bs a T Rs a P.
	There are no prizes.	There are no Ps.
	So nobody buys a ticket. (from Quine, *Methods of Logic*)	Nobody Bs a T.

"Ticket" and "prize" serve as pure modifiers in the first premise and conclusion. "Prize" serves as a general term in the second premise. Inside the B and R circles, the T and P circles represent ticket *buyers* and prize-*receivers*. The vertical shading represents the first premise; the horizontal shading, the second. The diagram obviously verifies the conclusion.

My treatment of Example 18 might be clarified by the following paraphrase:

Every ticket buyer is a prize-receiver.

There are no prizes.

So nobody is a ticket buyer.

Problem: This argument obviously is invalid:

No Chevrolet is a Buick.	No C is a B.
So no Chevrolet manufacturer is a Buick manufacturer.	No CM is a BM.

Yet the following diagram seems to prove it valid:

Not really, though. Outside the M circle, the C and B circles represent Chevrolets and Buicks. Inside the M circle, they represent Chevrolet *manufacturers* and Buick *manufacturers*. The same is true of the CB region. Outside the M circle, the CB region represents *hybrid* cars—cars that are each both a Chevrolet and a Buick—and of these there is none, as the premise says. Inside the **M** circle, then, the **CB** region represents *manufacturers of Chevrolet-Buick hybrids*, not manufacturers of both cars. So the premise-diagram just shows that no one makes hybrid cars, not that no one makes both cars.

EXERCISES

1. Draw ten *pretzels*. Add a *squash* to each. Make sure the squash divides the eight minimum subregions of the pretzel diagram (including the outer region) into two parts each, yielding sixteen parts altogether. Construct a *matrix* for *six* general terms.

Diagrammatically test each of these arguments for validity:

* 2. It is now raining. But when it rains, the streets are wet. Therefore, the streets are now wet.

* 3. Frankenstein cannot both die and be made of dead men. But he is made of dead men. So he cannot die.

* 4. All babies are illogical. Nobody is despised who can manage a crocodile. Whoever is illogical is despised. Therefore, no babies can manage a crocodile. (Lewis Carroll)

5. No politicians are unsociable. But some who are unsociable are zealots. So some zealots are not politicians.

6. Drinkers do not drive safely. But Baptists do not drink. So Baptists drive safely.

* 7. Any woman who lives with a bunch of dwarfs must be a polyandrist. But only married women are polyandrists. And every married woman is entitled to maternity insurance. What's more, Snow White is a woman who lives with a bunch of dwarfs. Consequently, Snow White is entitled to maternity insurance.

8. Every political scientist in Alaska is a pinko or a Violent Vegetarian. Irving is neither a pinko nor a Violent Vegetarian. Irving is in Alaska. Hence, Irving is not a political scientist.

* 9. Either Dracula did not have a great night life, or he was a jet setter. But he did. So he was.

10. Whoever has an Albanian accents fails to have a proper Irish brogue. But only Albanians have Albanian accents. Therefore, Albanians do not have proper Irish brogues.

* 11. Bertha never wears pants on Sunday. But today is not Sunday. So Bertha wears pants today.

12. No kitten that loves fish is unteachable. No kitten without a tail will play with a gorilla. Kittens with whiskers always love fish. No teachable kitten

has green eyes. No kittens have tails unless they have whiskers. Therefore, no kitten with green eyes will play with a gorilla. (Lewis Carroll)

* 13. Either Bertha is both vicious and hungry, or else she is senile. But she is not vicious. So she is senile.

14. Every Egyptologist in Gross Tête, Louisiana, is a secret agent of the Hanseatic League. Bertha is not an Egyptologist. But she is in Gross Tête, Louisiana. Hence, Bertha is not a secret agent of the Hanseatic League.

* 15. Whenever imports are high, tariffs rise. But labor is happy only when imports are not high. And Japan is happy only when tariffs do not rise but imports are high. Consequently, labor is happy only when Japan is unhappy.

16. Whoever has an Albanian accent fails to have a proper Irish brogue. But all Albanians have Albanian accents. Therefore, Albanians do not have proper Irish brogues.

* 17. Whatever is not inflammable does not burn. But matches are inflammable. Hence, matches burn.

18. Those who are poor but work hard are neither lazy nor unintelligent. But Ignatz is neither poor nor unintelligent. Consequently, Ignatz is not both lazy and hard-working.

* 19. Some who are rational smoke cigarettes. But no one who is rational and who cares enough about his health to get his teeth examined would smoke cigarettes. Consequently, not all who are rational care enough about their health to get their teeth examined.

20. Heavy drinking interferes with safe driving. But Tom has done nothing to interfere with safe driving. Consequently, Tom has not drunk heavily.

* 21. Any punishment that involves the danger of killing innocent people ought to be abolished. Capital punishment is a punishment. And it involves the danger of killing innocent people. So capital punishment ought to be abolished.

22. Some politicians are neither greedy nor dishonest. Klaghorn is greedy. But he is not a politician. So Klaghorn is honest.

* 23. Whenever imports are high, tariffs rise. But labor is happy only when imports are not high. And Japan is happy only when tariffs do not rise but imports are high. Consequently, whenever Japan is unhappy, imports are not high.

24. The President believes Russia outguns us. But either she will not sign the agreement, or she does not believe Russia outguns us, or she does not seek the country's best interests. Indeed, she does not sign the agreement. Therefore, she seeks the country's best interests.

* 25. An unjustified punishment would not deter crime. But capital punishment is a punishment that does not deter crime. Consequently, capital punishment is justified.

26. Ignatz is innocent or cautious. But he is not cautious. And whoever is not innocent is cautious. So Ignatz is not innocent.

* 27. Ignatz is a great lover. Ignatz is a logician. Therefore, there is a great logician.

* 28. She is a tall woman. So she is tall.

* 29. He's an invertebrate zoologist. So he's an invertebrate.

30. Raising taxes would make someone unhappy. But not raising taxes also would make someone unhappy. So someone will be unhappy.

* 31. All countries that automatically behead convicted murderers have fewer assassinations in a century than the United States has in one year. But any country that has fewer assassinations in a century than the United States has in one year has a positive contribution to make to the United States criminal-justice system. And no country that has such a contribution to make should be judged offhandedly to be barbarous. So no country that automatically beheads convicted murderers should be judged offhandedly to be barbarous.

32. You are illiterate, or you are taking an exam. But you are not taking an exam. So you are illiterate.

* 33. To decontrol natural-gas prices is to impose unfair costs on the poor. But to continue to regulate the price of natural gas is to impose unjust burdens on future generations. Consequently, unfair costs on the poor or unjust burdens on future generations are imposed.

34. She will kiss only a unicorn. But there are no unicorns. So she will kiss nothing.

* 35. Everyone on the committee is a Democrat or a Republican. Democrats are boorish. Jones is not boorish. Neither is he a Republican. So Jones is not on the committee.

36. Without hunger, we wouldn't enjoy eating. But we do, on occasion, enjoy eating. Hunger is evil, though. And enjoyment of eating is good. Thus, good can involve evil.

* 37. To decontrol natural-gas prices is to impose unfair costs on the poor. But not to decontrol natural-gas prices is to impose unjust burdens on future generations. Consequently, unfair costs on the poor or unjust burdens on future generations are imposed.

38. Standard IQ tests are culturally biased. And nothing that is culturally biased can fail to be discriminatory. But whatever is constitutional to use in public schools is nondiscriminatory. And nothing that is unconstitutional to use in public schools is permissible. So standard IQ tests are permissible.

* 39. Whoever loves a Frenchman loves a lover, since all Frenchmen are lovers.

40. Either God does not want to prevent evil, or God cannot prevent evil. But whoever does not want to prevent evil is not benevolent. And whoever cannot prevent evil is not omnipotent. Therefore, God is not benevolent.

* 41. What is right for society is right for the individual. But it is not right for the individual to kill for retribution or deterrence. And capital punishment is killing by society for retribution or deterrence. So capital punishment is not right.

42. All the girls in the class love some boy. Bertha is a girl. And Bertha is in the class. So Bertha loves some boy.

* 43. You can fool all the people some of the time. And you can fool some of the people all the time. But you cannot fool all the people all the time. Hence, there is some person such that some of the time you can fool him and some of the time you cannot fool him.

6

More Structure, More Diagrams (optional)

6.1. COMPOUND STATEMENTS. CONNECTIVES

Some statements contain others. Examples:

The King lost his throne *and* the Grand Vizier lost his head.

The King lost his throne *or* the Grand Vizier lost his head.

If the King lost his throne *then* the Grand Vizier lost his head.

The Grand Vizier lost his head *because* the King lost his throne.

The Grand Vizier lost his head *while* the King lost his throne.

The King is *not* dead.

Maybe the King is dead.

Bertha believes the King is dead.

The first five statements contain the shorter statements "the King lost his throne" and "the Grand Vizier lost his head." The rest contain the single shorter statement "the King is dead."

A statement containing no others is *simple*, or *atomic*. A statement containing others is *compound*, or *molecular*. Note that the last three examples are compound, even though each contains just one other statement. (Yes, the logical meanings of "statement" and "compound" are broader than their grammatical meanings.)

Connectives are expressions used to form molecular statements from atomic ones. The examples above contain the connectives "and," "or," "if-then," "because," "while," "not," "maybe," and "Bertha believes." Note that the last three are connectives, even though they do not do any connecting.

Corresponding to every statement, simple or compound, is a class: the class of possible cases in which the statement is true. A *possible case* can also be called a possible world, situation, or state of affairs. It is a complete specification of one way the world might be. Let t be the *true* case—the actual state of affairs, the real world. In effect, every statement says of t that it belongs to the corresponding class. Thus, "It is raining" amounts to: "t belongs to the class of possible cases in which it is raining." This way of interpreting statements enables us to give a diagrammatic representation of many compound statements and a diagrammatic test of the validity of many arguments involving compound statements.

Let the universe region represent the class of all possible cases (states of affairs, worlds) rather than the class of all entities whatever.

Where X is any statement, the class of possible cases in which X is true is the *X class*.

To represent an atomic statement diagrammatically, locate "t" in the corresponding circle or squash, that is, mark "t" throughout that figure, or mark "$\cancel{t}$" throughout the remaining region, or cross out preexisting "t"s foreign to that figure. Example:

Franklin beat Alf. (B)

Class interpretation:

> t belongs to the B class (the class of possible cases in which Franklin beat Alf).

Diagram:

A compound statement of the form:

X and Y

corresponds to the class of possible cases in which X and Y are both true. It amounts to:

> t belongs to the X class and to the Y class.

And we can depict this by locating "t" in the overlap of the X and Y regions, that is, by marking "t" throughout the XY region or by marking "$\cancel{t}$" throughout the remaining region or by crossing out preexisting "t"s foreign to the XY region. Example:

Franklin won and Alf lost. (F and A.)

We can represent statements of the forms:

X but Y   X although Y   X yet Y

the same way as "and" statements. Each affirms the joint truth of its two component statements.
Let us interpret:

X or Y

as: X or Y or both   (inclusive "or")

rather than: X or Y but not both   (exclusive "or")

in the absence of any strong contrary indication. Then such a statement corresponds to the class of possible cases in which X or Y or both are true, that is, to the X class plus the Y class. It amounts to:

t belongs to the X class or to the Y class (or to both).

We can depict it by locating "t" in the X-or-Y region, that is, by marking "t" throughout the X-or-Y region or by marking "$\not{t}$" throughout the neither-X-nor-Y region or by crossing out preexisting "t"'s foreign to the X-or-Y region. Example:

Franklin won or Alf lost. (F or A.)

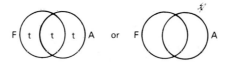

These diagrams are equivalent. Each locates "t" in the F-or-A region. Each excludes "t" from the neither-F-nor-A region. Remember: Presence in one part of the universe is the same as absence from the remaining part.
Statements of the forms:

Either X or Y   X or else Y
Either X or else Y   X unless Y

can be represented the same way as "or" statements. Each affirms, in effect, that at least one of its two component statements is true. Yes, "unless" amounts to "or." So "He'll come home unless he meets Bertha" amounts to "Either he'll come home or he'll meet Bertha." Think about that. Remember it.

Occasionally we gainsay a statement X by prefixing "not" to X, as in "Not everyone in this room relishes armadillo quiche." More often we add "not" or "does not" or some such thing to the main verb of X, as in "She has not come home," "She does not love him." Either way, let us refer to the result as:

Not X

This corresponds to the class of possible cases in which X is false. It amounts to:

t does not belong to the X class.

We can depict it by excluding "t" from the X region, that is, by marking "t̸" throughout the X region or by marking "t" throughout the non-X region or by crossing out preexisting "t"s in the X region. Example:

Alf did not win. (Not W.)

Statements of the forms:

It is not the case that X
It is false that X

obviously admit of the same class interpretation and diagrammatic representation as "not" statements.

Controversy surrounds the interpretation of:

If X then Y.

According to the so-called *material* interpretation, this statement-form amounts to:

Either not X or Y

or equivalently: Not both X and not Y.

So the corresponding class is the non-X class plus the Y class. And the class interpretation is the following:

t belongs to the non-X class or to the Y class

or equivalently:

t does not belong to the X−Y class.

We can depict it by excluding "t" from the X−Y region, that is, by marking "t̸" throughout the X−Y region or by marking "t" throughout the remaining non-X-or-Y region or by crossing out preexisting "t"s in the X−Y region. Example:

If Franklin won then Alf lost. (If F then A.)

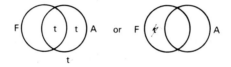

These two diagrams represent the same information. Excluding "t" from the F−A region is the same as locating "t" in the remaining region—the non-F-or-A region.

These statement-forms are equivalent; they can be depicted the same way:

If X then Y.	If X, Y.
X only if Y.	Y if X.
Only if Y, X.	Assuming X, Y.
Y, provided that X.	Suppose X. Then Y.

Notice the way "only" reverses the order of component statements. Notice that moving "if" from in front to between component statements also reverses order. Study these forms. Remember their equivalence.

Under the material interpretation, a statement of the form:

If X then Y

is rather weak. Because all it says is that t does not belong to the X−Y class, the only possibility it rules out is that in which X is true and Y false. As a result, it automatically is true so long as X is false or Y is true or both, however unrelated X and Y may be. Thus, "If 2 + 2 = 5 then I'm a monkey's uncle" and "If a cure for cancer is discovered tomorrow then 2 + 2 = 4" are automatically true.

I discuss a stronger interpretation of "if-then" in §6.4. Until then, let us give this connective the material interpretation—admitting that many colloquial uses of "if-then" might call for stronger interpretations.

The examples I have cited contain one connective each. Here are four statements containing two or more connectives each:

- Unless the legislature does not impose   Unless not W, L.
  work loads, the university will lose prestige.

Because "unless" means "or," this statement calls for a "t"-chain in the non-W-or-L region, that is, in the non-W region plus the L region.

- If tariffs are high, labor is happy but   If T, L but not J.
  Japan is unhappy.

This calls for "*t*"s in the T region minus the L−J region. After marking the L−J region with "1," I fill the T region minus the "1" region with "*t*."

- It would be false to hold that either   It would be false to
  the King will not die or the Grand   hold that either
  Vizier will not resign.   not K or not V.

This denies the assertion: not K or not V. So it calls for "*t*"s in the non-K-or-non-V region, that is, in the non-K region plus the non-V region.

- If the King dies but the Crown Prince does not succeed him, then the Grand Vizier will have been assassinated and the Magnates of the Realm will not have supported the monarchy.

If K but not P, then V and not M.

This calls for "ƚ"s in the K−P region minus the V−M region. After marking "1" in the K−P region and "2" in the V−M region, I fill the "1" region minus the "2" region with "ƚ."

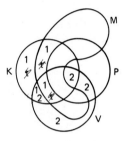

Many English connectives I have not mentioned can be paraphrased in terms of those I have discussed and represented by the same diagrammatic technique. Thus:

X instead of Y

amounts to: X and not Y.

So we can represent it by locating "t" in the X−Y region. Example:

We ate at home instead of dining out.　　H instead of D.

A statement of the form:

X if, and only if, Y

amounts to: If X then Y, and if Y then X.

So we can represent it by excluding "t" from the X−Y region and from the Y−X region. Example:

Franklin won if, and only if, Alf lost.　　F if, and only if, A.

And a statement of the form:

$$\text{X or Y but not both} \qquad \text{(exclusive "or")}$$

calls for locating "t" in the X−Y plus Y−X region (omitting the XY region). Example:

Franklin won or Alf won but not both.   F or A but not both.

6.2. ARGUMENTS CONTAINING COMPOUND STATEMENTS

In discussing the following arguments, I treat only *connectives* as logical expressions. That is, I assess the validity of the *connective structure* of each argument, ignoring all other logical structure—ignoring, in other words, the internal structure of atomic statements. In §6.3 I show how to combine connective structure with the internal subject-predicate structure of atomic statements when assessing validity.

Example 1   Either professors justify   Either J or W.
the way they spend their
time, or the legislature
has the right to impose
work loads.

Professors do not justify   Not J.
the way they spend their
time.

So the legislature has   W.
the right to impose work
loads.

The three-"t" chain represents the first premise, and the crossing out of the first two links in that chain represents the second. Remember: Once a premise-diagram contains a "t"-chain, represent subsequent premises by crossing out links in that chain, not by adding new "t"s or "ŧ"s. Because the diagram at hand forces "t" into the W region, it verifies the conclusion. So the argument is VALID.

Example 2	Either we decontrol natural-gas prices, or there will be shortage of natural gas.	Either D or S.
	But we shall indeed decontrol natural-gas prices.	D.
	So there will not be a shortage of natural gas.	Not S.

The three-"t" chain represents the first premise, and the crossing out of the third "t"—the one foreign to the D circle—represents the second. Because the premise-diagram does not wholly exclude "t" from the S circle, it does not verify the conclusion. So the argument is INVALID.

Example 3	If there is a coup, the Grand Vizier will lose his head.	If C, H.
	But there is a coup.	C.
	Therefore, the Grand Vizier loses his head.	H.

The "*t*" represents the first premise; the plain "t," the second. In depicting the second premise, I marked "t" just in the CH region instead of marking a two-"t" chain in the whole C region. That is because "t" was already excluded from the left part of the C region. As a result, "t" occurs just in the H region, verifying the conclusion.

| Example 4 | If exile is urged for the Crown Prince, then defenestration will be recommended for the Grand Vizier. | If E, then F. |

| If defenestration is rec-ommended for the Grand Vizier, then decapitation will be prescribed for the King. | If F, then C. |

| Therefore, if exile is urged for the Crown Prince, then decapitation will be prescribed for the King. | If E, then C. |

The two "*ʒ*"s in the E−F region represent the first premise; those in the F−C region, the second. The diagram excludes "t" from the E−C region, verifying the conclusion.

Example 5

If there is a coup, the King loses his head.	If C, K.
The King does lose his head.	K.
Thus, there is a coup.	C.

Because the premise-diagram does not force t into the C class (all it shows is that t belongs *either* to the CK class *or* to the K−C class), it does not verify the conclusion.

Example 6

If imports drop, tariffs are high.	If I, T.
If tariffs are high, labor is happy but Japan is unhappy.	If T, L but not J.
As it happens, Japan is happy.	J.
So labor must not be happy.	Not L.

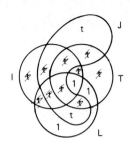

The "⚡"s in the I–T region (the four left-most "⚡"s) represent the first premise; those in the T region minus the L–J region (marked "1") represent the second; and the two plain "t"s represent the third. Because the diagram does not exclude "t" from the L region, it does not verify the conclusion.

Example 7	If the Republicans win or unemployment rises, there will be a recession or inflation.	If W or U, R or I.
	If unemployment rises or there is a recession, the stock market will hit a slump.	If U or R, S.
	But the stock market will not hit a slump.	Not S.
	And the Republicans will win.	W.
	Hence, there will be inflation.	I.

	WUR	WUR̄	WŪR	WŪR̄	W̄UR	W̄UR̄	W̄ŪR	W̄ŪR̄
IS	1⚡ 2 3	1⚡ 2 3	1⚡ 2 3	1⚡ 2	1⚡ 2 3	1⚡ 2 3	2⚡ 3	2⚡
ĪS	1⚡ 2 3	1⚡ 2 3	1⚡ 2 3	1 t 2	1⚡ 2 3	1·r' 2 3	2⚡ 3	2
IS̄	1⚡ 2 3	1⚡ 3	1⚡ 2 3	1⚡	1⚡ 2 3	1⚡ 3	2⚡ 3	⚡
ĪS̄	1⚡ 2 3	1⚡ 3	1⚡ 2 3	1⚡	1·r' 2 3	1⚡ 2 3	2⚡ 3	

I represented the first premise by "⚡"s in the W-or-U region (marked "1") minus the R-or-I region (marked "2"), the second premise by "⚡"s in the U-or-R region (marked "3") minus the S region, the third premise by "*"'s in the S region, and the fourth by a "t" in the one cell of the W region from which "t" has not been excluded. Because the lone "t" lies in the I region, the premise-diagram verifies the conclusion.

6.3. MIXING CONNECTIVE STRUCTURE WITH SUBJECT-PREDICATE STRUCTURE

Sometimes a valid argument containing connectives has an invalid connective structure: Its valid logical form is more specific than its invalid connective structure. Its validity depends on a combination of its connective structure and the internal subject-predicate structure of its component atomic statements.

Example 8   Every Republican is a conservative.

So if no conservative can win, no Republican can win.

Although valid, this has the invalid connective structure:

A.
∴ If B, C.

The validity of Example 8 depends in part on the internal structures of the atomic statements "Every Republican is a conservative," "no conservative can win," and "no Republican can win."

A technique for ascertaining the validity of such arguments is virtually at hand. I illustrate it with Example 8.

The first step (helpful though not essential) is to *display the argument's entire logical structure,* including the internal structure of every atomic component. The second is to *label all atomic components,* preferably with upper-case Roman letters not already used for general terms, or with numerals or Greek letters if that is easier. The result:

$$\overset{\displaystyle P}{\overbrace{\text{Every R is a C.}}}$$

$$\overset{\displaystyle Q \qquad\; S}{\therefore \text{If } \overbrace{\text{no C W}}, \overbrace{\text{no R W.}}}$$

The next step is to *test the argument's connective structure for validity,* as in §6.2. Here is the premise-diagram:

The "t"-chain in the P region represents the single premise. The conclusion requires t's absence from the Q–S class. But the diagram does not ensure this. Because the "t"-chain overlaps part of the Q–S region—the heavily outlined area—the diagram does not exclude "t" from that part.

Had the connective structure been valid, the argument would have been valid, and the procedure would have stopped here.

The fourth step is to *identify the area from which "t" would have to be excluded to verify the conclusion*. It is the heavily outlined area.

The fifth step is to *list those atomic statements or negations of such whose combination is represented by this area*. Since the heavily outlined area is the PQ–S region, it represents the following combination of atomic statements or negations of such:

(P)	Every R is a C.
(Q)	No C W.
(not S)	It is not the case that no R W.

To complete the test of validity, *check whether this combination of statements is consistent*. If it is—if P, Q, and not-S are jointly consistent—then the logical form of these statements does not justify excluding "t" from the PQ–S region, so the argument is invalid. If, on the other hand, P, Q, and not-S are not jointly consistent, then the logical forms of these statements ensures that no possible state of affairs can belong to the PQ–S class, so we may scratch "t" from the PQ–S region, verifying the conclusion. In short, *the argument is valid if, and only if, the region from which "t" would have to be excluded to verify the conclusion represents an inconsistent combination of statements*.

To test P, Q, and not-S for joint consistency, we try to represent all these statements in one diagram. If we succeed, they are jointly *consistent*, so the argument is *invalid*. If we fail, they are jointly *inconsistent*, so the argument is *valid*. I use vertical shading for P, horizontal for Q:

The third statement, not-S, denies that nothing belongs to the RW class. It affirms, therefore, that something belongs to this class. So it calls for a "•" in the RW region. But there is no way to mark a "•" in the RW region: it is entirely shaded. Thus, the three statements cannot all be represented in one diagram. This shows them to be inconsistent, hence the argument to be valid.

When testing for joint consistency, it is easiest to begin with those statements that require shading.

Seven more examples:

Example 9   Every husky is a dog.

So if any dog can pull a sled, some husky can.

Logical form, with atomic components labeled:

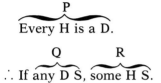

$$\overbrace{\text{Every H is a D.}}^{\text{P}}$$

$$\therefore \text{If } \overbrace{\text{any D S,}}^{\text{Q}} \overbrace{\text{some H S.}}^{\text{R}}$$

Premise-diagram of connective structure:

Connective structure INVALID.

Region from which "t" would have to be excluded to verify conclusion: the PQ−R region (heavily outlined).

The combination of statements represented by this region:

    (P)   Every H is a D.
    (Q)   Some D S.
  (not R)   No H S.

Note that I have written Q as:

Some D S

rather than: *Any* D S.

Reason: Standing alone, "any" means "every." But when preceded by "if," it means "some." Watch out for that. Note also that I wrote not-R as:

No H S

rather than: It is not the case that some H S.

Either is correct. The former is simpler.

Diagram of P, Q, and not-R to test their joint consistency:

I depicted P with the vertical shading, then not-R with the horizontal shading, and finally Q with the "•". (Remember: When testing statements for joint consistency, it is easiest to begin with those statements that call for shading.) Since the three statements can indeed be represented in a single diagram, they are jointly consistent.

Verdict: The argument is INVALID.

Example 10   If everyone pollutes, everyone will breathe dirty air.

                So everyone will breathe dirty air if he pollutes.

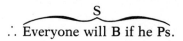

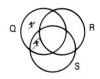

Connective structure INVALID.

Region from which "t" would have to be excluded to verify conclusion: the R−S region plus the outer region. There does not seem to be any one combination of atomic statements or negations of such represented by the combined region. Rather, the R−S region represents:

        (R) Everyone will B,

and (not S) Not everyone will B if he Ps,

while the outer region represents:

(not Q) Not everyone Ps,

(not R) Not everyone will B,

and (not S) Not everyone will B if he Ps.

So there are two combinations to test for consistency. If both are *incon-sistent*, then the argument is valid, since we may then mark "⊄" throughout the R−S and outer regions, verifying the conclusion. But if even *one* of the combinations is *consistent*, then the argument is *not* valid, since we cannot then wholly exclude "t" from the region whence it would have to be excluded to verify the conclusion. So if the first combination we test proves *in*consistent, we must go on to test the second, judging the argument valid if the second proves inconsistent as well, invalid otherwise. But if the first combination we test proves con-sistent, that would show the argument to be invalid, and there would be no need to test the second.

Consider the second combination: not-Q, not-R, and not-S. Each of these statements calls for a "•"-chain. But two or more "•"-chains can-not conflict with each other. A "•"-chain can only conflict with shading. So it is automatically possible to represent the second combination of statements in a single diagram. We do not even have to try it. Therefore, the second combination is consistent, and we may conclude, without bothering with the first combination, that the argument is INVALID.

An argument with an invalid connective structure still is valid if all those regions of its premise-diagram from which "t" would have to be excluded to verify the conclusion represent inconsistent combinations of statements. Usually there is just one such region, hence one combina-tion of statements to test for consistency. But when there is more than one such region, *each* must represent an inconsistent combination for the argument to be valid. If even one region represents a consistent combination, then we are not entitled (by the logical forms of the pre-mises) to exclude "t" from that region, so the argument is not valid.

Example 11   All members of the committee are Republicans.

But if no Republicans are for socialized medicine, then no liberals are Republicans.

Consequently, if any liberals are members of the committee, then some Republicans are for socialized medicine.

$$\overset{A}{\overbrace{\text{All the Ms are Rs.}}}$$

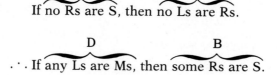

$$\overbrace{\text{not B}}\qquad\overbrace{\text{not C}}$$
If no Rs are S, then no Ls are Rs.

$$\overbrace{\text{D}}\qquad\qquad\overbrace{\text{B}}$$
∴ If any Ls are Ms, then some Rs are S.

Notice that I have treated "no Republicans are for socialized medicine" (not B) as the negation of "some Republicans are for socialized medicine" (B) and "no liberals are Republicans" (not C) as the negation of "some liberals are Republicans" (C). Although not essential, this makes the work a bit easier. It increases the amount of structure counted as connective structure, improving the chance that the connective structure will be valid. It also decreases the number of atomic statements, enhancing diagrammatic tractability.

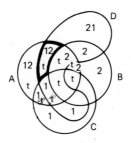

The eight-"t" chain in the A region represents the first premise. The crossing out of those "t"s (those links) that occur in the non-B region (marked "1") minus the non-C region (marked "2") represents the second premise.
Connective structure INVALID.

Region whence "t" must be excluded to insure validity: the AD$\overline{BC}$ (AD-but-neither-B-nor-C) region (heavily outlined).

Statements to test for joint consistency:

(A) All the Ms are Rs.

(D) Some Ls are Ms.

(not B) No Rs are S.

(not C) No Ls are Rs.

Note how I changed "any" to "some" when displaying D by itself (outside the "if"-context).

Diagram of A (vertical shading), not-B (horizontal), and not-C (acute):

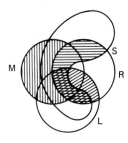

D requires "•" in the LM region, which is wholly shaded. So the four statements cannot be represented in one diagram: they are jointly inconsistent.

Verdict: The Argument is VALID.

Example 12   All policies recommended by the President have some merit.

Some energy policies do not have any merit.

Therefore, some energy policies have not been recommended by the President.

This argument contains no connectives. So it requires just a one-diagram test of the sort treated in previous chapters. I leave details for an exercise.

Example 13   If the King dies but the Crown Prince does not ascend the throne, either the Grand Vizier will be assassinated or the Magnates of the Realm will not continue to support the monarchy.

Consequently, supposing the Magnates of the Realm continue to support the monarchy and the Crown Prince does not ascend the throne, if the King dies then the Grand Vizier will be assassinated.

       P   not Q   R
If K Ds but p not-T, either v will be A or
        not W
the Ms will not S.

          W   not Q   P
∴ Supposing the Ms S and p not-T, if k Ds
          R
then v will be A.

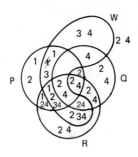

The premise is represented by a "*t*" in the P–Q region (marked "1") minus the R-or-not-W region ("2"). The conclusion requires "t" 's exclusion from the W–Q region ("3") minus the region corresponding to:

If P then R.

That is the non-P-or-R region ("4"). To verify the conclusion, then, the premise-diagram must exclude "t" from the "3" region minus the "4" region, which it does. So the connective structure alone is valid, and we may conclude, without a second diagram test, that the argument is VALID.

Example 14   The dollar is strengthened or tariffs rise only if the labor lobby is effective or the Japanese delegation fails.

Therefore, if the Japanese delegation does not fail or tariffs rise, then it is not the case that both the dollar is strengthened and tariffs fail to rise.

This argument has an *in*valid connective structure (I leave details for an exercise). But its atomic components obviously bear no internal structural relationships to one another: no two of them share a significant structural component. So we may conclude that the argument is INVALID, without looking beyond its connective structure, hence without a second diagram test.

Example 15   If everything is spiritual, than nothing is material.

But God is spiritual.

So God is not material.

$$\overbrace{\text{If everything is S,}}^{P} \text{ then } \overbrace{\text{nothing is M.}}^{Q}$$

$$\overbrace{\text{g is S.}}^{R}$$

$$\text{not V}$$
$$\therefore \overbrace{\text{g is not M.}}$$

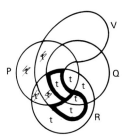

Two combinations of statements to test for consistency:

$\left\{\begin{array}{l} \text{(P) Everything is S.} \\ \text{(Q) Nothing is M.} \\ \text{(R) g is S.} \\ \text{(V) g is M.} \end{array}\right.$

$\left\{\begin{array}{l} \text{(R) g is S.} \\ \text{(V) g is M.} \\ \text{(not P) Not everything is S.} \end{array}\right.$

Diagram of R, V, and not-P:

Because the second combination of statements is consistent, we can ignore the first and conclude that the argument is INVALID.

6.4. TRUTH-FUNCTIONAL CONNECTIVES AND OTHERS

Every statement has one of two *truth values*. The truth value of a true statement is TRUTH; that of a false statement, FALSITY.

A *truth-functional connective* is one with this feature: The truth value of a compound statement formed by applying the connective to shorter statements is completely determined by (is a function of) the truth values of the shorter statements. As interpreted in §6.1, the connectives "not," "and," "or," and "if-then" are truth-functional. A "not"-statement is true if its component statement is false, false if its component statement is true. An "and"-statement is true if both its component statements are true, false otherwise. An "or"-statement is true if at least one of its component statements is true, false otherwise. An "if-then"-statement is true if the "if" part is false or the "then" part is true, false if the "if" part is true and the "then" part is false. In short:

X	Y	not X	X and Y	X or Y	if X then Y
true	true	false	true	true	true
true	false	false	false	true	false
false	true	true	false	true	true
false	false	true	false	false	true

Not all connectives are truth-functional. Because I believe some but not all truths and some but not all falsehoods, the truth value of:

I believe that X

is not determined solely by the truth value of X. So the connective "I believe that" is not truth-functional. Neither are "she knows that," "it is possible that," "it is necessary that," "because," and many other connectives.

Truth-functional connectives can be represented simply by locating "t" appropriately in a Venn diagram. Non-truth-functional connectives cannot. But they often can be represented by means of shading or "•" or a combination of these and "t." Several illustrations:

Statement: I believe that it is snowing but warm.
Class interpretation: The class of possible cases compatible with what I
                      believe is included in the class of possible cases in
                      which it is snowing but warm.

Diagram:

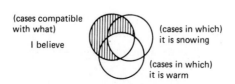

(cases compatible with what) I believe
(cases in which) it is snowing
(cases in which) it is warm

Statement: I want you to be home by five or leave a message.
Class interpretation: The class of possible cases compatible with what I want (cases in which my wants are all fulfilled) is included in the class of possible cases in which either you are at home by five or you leave a message.

Diagram:

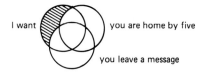

Statement: I'm not certain that it is raining.
Class interpretation: The class of possible cases compatible with what I'm certain of is not included in the class of possible cases in which it is raining.

Diagram:

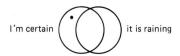

Statement: I don't believe he'll win.
Class interpretation: The class of possible cases compatible with what I believe does not overlap the class of possible cases in which he'll win.

Diagram:

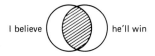

Note this quirk of language: "I don't believe" does not merely *deny* belief; it *affirms disbelief*. "I don't believe he'll win" means "I believe he won't win," not "It is false that I believe he'll win." The latter is depicted thus:

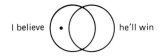

Statement: It is possible that it is both snowing and warm.
Class interpretation: The class of possible cases in which it is both snowing and warm is nonempty.

Diagram:

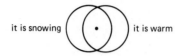

it is snowing (•) it is warm

Statement: Necessarily, the bill will pass or it will be defeated.
Class interpretation: Every possible case is one in which the bill is passed or defeated.

Diagram:

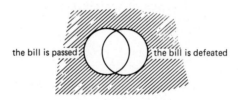

the bill is passed / the bill is defeated

Statement: The match failed to ignite because it was wet.
Class interpretation: t belongs to the class of possible cases in which the match was wet, and that class is included in the class of possible cases in which the match failed to ignite.

Diagram:

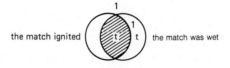

the match ignited (t) t the match was wet

After marking "t" in the wet-match region, I marked the failure-to-ignite region with "1," then shaded the wet-match region minus the "1" region.

Under the *material* interpretation, presented in §6.1, a statement of the form:

If X then Y

is true so long as t does not belong to the X−Y class, hence so long as X is false or Y is true or both. This interpretation makes "if-then" truth-functional.

Under a stronger interpretation, called the *strict* interpretation, such a statement does not merely exclude t from the X−Y class; it excludes *all* possible cases from the X−Y class. It amounts to:

Every possible case in which X is a case in which Y.

So it can be represented by shading the X−Y region. Example:

If Billy is a brother, he is a sibling.

Material (truth-functional) Strict interpretation:
     interpretation:

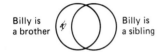

When a statement contains a non-truth-functional connective, whether it is true can depend on how broadly or narrowly we construe the class of possible cases in which each component statement is true. I am about to strike a match. Someone says, "If you strike the match, it will light." Interpreted strictly, is this statement likely to be true? Is it likely that every possible case of my striking is a case of the match lighting? Not if the *possible* cases of striking include *all imaginable* cases of striking, certainly. But the statement could well be true if the possible cases of striking are construed, more narrowly, to consist of just normal cases of striking consistent with what is generally known about my current circumstances.

How should *you* interpret "if-then," materially or strictly? That depends on context. There is no general rule. Rarely is the question important, though. If the conclusion of an argument contains a non-truth-functional connective, then the validity of the argument could depend on how we interpret "if-then" in the premises. Otherwise, the argument's validity can*not* depend on which way we interpret "if-then." Reason: If the conclusion contains only truth-functional connectives, then it only says something about the location of t, and the strict and material interpretations of:

If X then Y

have exactly the same effect on the location of t: each interpretation just ensures t's absence from the X−Y class.

Now an argument:

Example 16   If unemployment gets worse, the King will abdicate.

The King believes unemployment will get worse.

Whatever the King believes is true.

Therefore, the King will abdicate because unemployment gets worse.

Premise-diagram, with "if-then" interpreted materially:

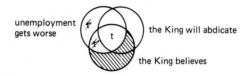

The "⫫"'s represent the first premise; the shading, the second; the "t," the third. The diagram does not verify the conclusion, because it does not show the unemployment-gets-worse class to be included in the King-abdicates class.

Premise-diagram, with "if-then" interpreted strictly:

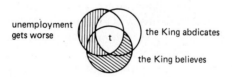

This does verify the conclusion.

EXERCISES

For each of the following arguments, display just its *connective structure* (ignoring the internal structure of atomic components), and test its connective structure for validity by diagram. Interpret all connectives truth-functionally.

*   1. Frankenstein cannot both die and be made of dead men. But he is made of dead men. So he cannot die.

* 2. Either Ignatz is innocent, or Bertha is. But Ignatz is innocent. And if he is innocent, he is not guilty. So Bertha is guilty.

3. If Dracula had a great night life, he was a jet setter. He did. So he was.

* 4. Either God does not want to prevent evil, or God cannot prevent evil. If God does not want to prevent evil, He is not benevolent. And if God cannot prevent evil, He is not omnipotent. Therefore, God is not both benevolent and omnipotent.

5. Either Ignatz is innocent, or Bertha is. But Ignatz is not innocent. So Bertha is innocent.

6. If we have desires, we suffer from frustration. If we do not, we suffer from boredom. Therefore, either we suffer from frustration or we suffer from boredom. (Schopenhauer)

* 7. If we fail to control population growth, the world will become over-crowded. But if we control population growth, we interfere with individual liberty. So if we do not interfere with individual liberty, the world will become over-crowded.

8. Either we decrease government spending, or we increase inflation. If we decrease government spending, we increase unemployment. But if we increase inflation, we hurt those with fixed incomes. So we must increase unemployment or hurt those with fixed incomes.

* 9. If capital punishment deterred crime, it would be justified. It doesn't. So it isn't.

10. If we decontrol natural-gas prices, we place an unfair burden on the poor. But if we do not decontrol natural-gas prices, we impose unjust costs on future generations. Therefore, either we place an unfair burden on the poor, or we impose unjust costs on future generations.

* 11. If it would not be wrong to ban *Hustler*, then it would not be wrong to ban *T.V. Guide* unless there is a morally relevant difference between these two acts of banning. But there is no morally relevant difference between these acts. And it would indeed be wrong to ban *T.V. Guide*. So it would be wrong to ban *Hustler*.

12. Supposing gas prices rise hugely if interstate gas is decontrolled, interstate gas should not be decontrolled. In fact, interstate gas should not be decontrolled. Therefore, either gas prices rise hugely or interstate gas should be decontrolled.

* 13. Unemployment cannot be cured unless the federal government spends beyond its income. So if the federal government spends beyond its income, unemployment will be cured.

14. If mind and body are the same, then since body is divisible, so is mind. But mind is indivisible. Hence, mind and body are not the same.

15. If Cain married his sister, their marriage was incestuous. If he did not marry his sister, then Adam and Eve were not the progenitors of the entire human race. It follows that Adam and Eve were the progenitors of the entire human race only if Cain's marriage was incestuous. (from Pospesel, *Arguments*)

* 16. It is raining and not raining. So 2 + 2 = 4.

* 17. Millard Fillmore is dead. So it is raining or not raining.

* 18. Bertha is a Vegetarian or a Prohibitionist. But she is not a Prohibitionist. So she is a Vegetarian.

19. If the King abdicates or dies, the Grand Vizier will resign and there will be no coup. But the Grand Vizier won't resign if the King abdicates. And there will be a coup if the King does not abdicate. Consequently, the King won't die.

* 20. Ignatz is greedy or dishonest. And he is honest but not well-regarded. So he is greedy and honest.

21. If imports are high, tariffs rise. But labor is happy only if imports are not high. And Japan is happy only if tariffs do not rise but imports are high. Consequently, labor is happy only if Japan is unhappy.

* 22. Either Bertha is both vicious and hungry, or else she is senile. But she is not vicious. So she is senile.

23. If we adopt the treaty, we will cause resentment. But if we reject the treaty, we will cause resentment. Therefore, we will cause resentment.

* 24. If the government falls, there will be no economic recovery. And if there is no economic recovery, unemployment will rise. So if unemployment does not rise, the government will not fall.

25. If the King dies, it is not the case that both the Crown Price abdicates and the Grand Vizier resigns. But it is false that either the Crown Prince does not abdicate or the Grand Vizier does not resign. Hence, the King dies.

* 26. If we adopt the treaty, we will cause resentment. But if we do not adopt the treaty, we will cause resentment. Therefore, we will cause resentment.

27. If the pince-nez belongs to the parlor maid, then the Dowager Marchioness did not stab Lord Cucumber. But if she did not stab Lord Cucumber, then the footman has lied to the police. Therefore, if the footman has not lied to the police, then the pince-nez does not belong to the parlor maid.

* 28. If we adopt the treaty, we will cause resentment. But if we reject the treaty, we will cause resentment. And either we adopt the treaty or we reject it. Therefore, we will cause resentment.

For each of the following arguments, display its full logical form (not just its connective structure) and test it for validity, interpreting all connectives truth-functionally. In many cases, a multiple-diagram test is necessary. But not in all cases.

* 29. Some professors are Republicans. And no Republican belongs to a union. So if some professors belong to a union, then some others do not belong.

* 30. Someone is a Democrat or someone is a Republican. But every Republican is repulsive. So someone is repulsive.

* 31. The Grand Vizier is shrewd and honest. But whoever is shrewd is either intellectual or dishonest. Consequently, there exists at least one intellectual.

* 32. If anything is spiritual, then whatever is not material is spiritual. And if anything thinks, then whatever is spiritual thinks. But something spiritual does indeed think. Thus, whatever is not material thinks.

33. The Grand Vizier is shrewd. But whoever is shrewd is either intellectual or dishonest. And whoever is dishonest is shrewd. So the Grand Vizier is dishonest.

34. Someone is a liberal Republican. But every Texan is illiberal. And there are Texans. Therefore, there are liberals and there are nonliberals.

35. Taxes are theft. And licensing fees are taxes. So licensing fees are theft.

36. The dollar is strengthened or tariffs rise only if the labor lobby is effective or the Japanese delegation fails. Therefore, if the Japanese delegation does not fail or tariffs rise, then it is not the case that both the dollar is strengthened and tariffs fail to rise.

37. Either God is good or Satan is evil. But if anything is good or anything is evil, then everything is either good or evil. Something, however, is not evil. Hence, something is good.

38. She'll take either Business Administration or Economics. But both are taught by pinkos. So she'll take something taught by a pinko.

* 39. All policies recommended by the President have some merit. But some energy policies do not have any merit. Therefore, some energy policies were not recommended by the President.

* 40. Supposing there will be a coup if the Crown Prince does not renounce his claim, then the Regent will have lost the confidence of the army and of the Magnates of the Realm. But the Regent does indeed lose the confidence of the Magnates of the Realm. Consequently, the Crown Prince does not renounce his claim.

41. If any ministers know of the Lord High Chancellor's indiscretion, they all know. So if some ministers do not know of the Lord High Chancellor's indiscretion, then some also know.

* 42. If any ministers know of the Lord High Chancellor's indiscretion, they all know. So if some do not know, then none knows.

43. Every husky is a dog. So if no dog can pull a sled, no husky can.

* 44. If every minister is a liberal or a socialist, then none is a nationalist. But some are liberal nationalists. Therefore, some are neither liberals nor socialists.

45. If God has foreknowledge, then nothing is free. Therefore, God cannot both have foreknowledge and be free.

* 46. Madalyn is an atheist. And she will not become a candidate for Pope. So some atheist becomes Pope if Madalyn becomes a candidate for Pope.

47. If either everything is material or everything is abstract, then nothing is spiritual. But some things are both spiritual and intelligible. So something is neither material nor abstract.

* 48. Either every member of the committee is Republican, or none is. But some members are liberals. And no Republicans are liberals. So no member of the committee is Republican.

49. All the ministers knew, or none of them knew. But some ministers are lovers of the Queen. And none who knew is a lover of the Queen. So no ministers knew.

* 50. Either something is spiritual, or everything is material. But God is not material. So God is spiritual.

51. Either everything is spiritual, or God is material. But God is not material. So God is spiritual.

Test the following arguments for validity by diagram. They involve relational expressions and non-truth-functional connectives.

52. I love everyone who loves me. So if no one loves me, I love no one.

53. If anyone can beat Muhammad Ali, Schwartz can. Muhammad Ali can beat himself. Therefore, Schwartz can beat Muhammad Ali.

* 54. I do not want to go to bed. Whatever I want comes true. If I do not go to bed, I'll be grouchy tomorrow. It is not possible for me both to be grouchy tomorrow and to keep my job. Therefore, I will not keep my job.

55. Japan attacked the United States because the United States cut off trade with Japan. But the United States did this because Japan was ruthlessly ravaging China. Consequently, Japan attacked the United States because Japan was ruthlessly ravaging China.

* 56. Only those who love the Queen are rewarded by the King. But the Queen is a bitch. And no one who loves a bitch is rewarded by anyone. So no one loves the Queen.

57. The Queen believes the King will find out about her indiscretion or be assassinated. But she does not believe he will find out about her indiscretion. And whatever she wants to happen, she believes will happen. So she wants the King to be assassinated.

PART·3
EVALUATIONS

7

Reconstructing Arguments

7.1. HOW TO EVALUATE AN ARGUMENT: PREVIEW

In this chapter and the next two, I present a general method for evaluating any deductive argument. It consists of three main steps:

Step one

Reconstruct the argument:

Standardize the argument, listing its express premises followed by its conclusion, each formulated as a fully explicit declarative sentence with a clear logical form and no extraneous matter.

Test the argument as it stands for *validity*.

If it is not valid, supply *validating premises* if possible.

Step two

Check whether the argument *depends on any ambiguity*—whether the argument owes its appeal (the appearance of plausible premises plus interesting conclusion plus valid form) to some expression's having different meanings at different points in the argument, yet owes its validity to the expression's having the same meaning throughout.

Step three

Evaluate the premises, looking for premises that are false or not sufficiently plausible to support the conclusion drawn from them. More specifically:

Read the premises carefully and critically.

Check whether the premises are *self-defeating* and whether any is *question-begging*.

133

Look for *counter-examples* to general premises.

Test each premise for *sufficient generality*, asking whether it can reasonably be made more general.

Criticisms found at Steps Two and Three can lead to revisions—to modifications of the original argument—and therewith to reapplications of the first three steps.

I explain and illustrate Step One in this chapter, Step Two in Chapter 8, Step Three in Chapter 9. Although I discuss only *deductive* arguments in these three chapters, any argument can be construed as deductive without impairment (see §1.4), and the general method also applies, by and large, to whatever species of nondeductive argument there may be.

Although testing for validity is just one part of Step One, the concept of validity and the ability to distinguish valid from invalid arguments obviously play starring roles throughout Steps One and Two. The third part of Step One, for example, consists not in assessing validity, but in turning an admittedly invalid argument into a valid one (if possible); validity is less a trait to be found in arguments than a constraint to be fulfilled by reconstructions. That is why I have laid such stress on the concept and the ability to apply it.

You can use my three-step procedure to evaluate, criticize, and improve *your own* arguments as well as those of others. And you can use it to help *discover* good arguments for a given position and to help *decide* whether a given position is true: As crudely and concisely as you like, list all the reasons (arguments) you can think of for the position you wish to defend, or for and against the position whose truth you wish to decide. Then reconstruct and evaluate each reason according to Steps One, Two, and Three, rejecting some reasons, accepting the rest, and improving some of those you accept.

I think you will find that virtually every argument with an interesting conclusion is open to some criticism. This does not mean that virtually every such argument is poor. It means that hardly any such argument is perfectly conclusive. To give a good criticism is not necessarily to give a decisive refutation. It is to remark a debatable or questionable feature. And only perfectly conclusive arguments lack these.

7.2. STANDARDIZING

As the first part of Step One, list the candidate argument's *express premises* followed by its *conclusion*, even if the conclusion was unstated. Formulate each step as a separate, fully explicit declarative sentence, even if this requires some rewriting. If you can make the argument's logical form more transparent or more nearly valid by some strictly stylistic modification, do so. Omit all repetition and extraneous matter. At this stage in the reconstruction process, omit tacit premises and intermediate steps; we shall get to them later.

This task is not a matter of testing typical textbook specimens for validity or other virtues, but of turning colloquial arguments into typical textbook specimens.

Eleven things to keep in mind:

Thing 1. Arguments rarely occur in isolation. Normally an argument is part of a larger discourse, whence it must be extracted.

Thing 2. *Premises* often are introduced by such premise-indicators as "because," "since," "for," "for the reason that." But not always. An express premise of an argument is any statement that meets these four conditions:

(i)   It is expressly formulated in the argument (though perhaps in an abbreviated form).

(ii) Its truth is affirmed (in effect) in the argument.

(iii) It is offered as a reason for believing the conclusion.

(iv) It is not itself defended in the argument—no further reason is offered in the argument for believing it—although it might be the conclusion of another argument.

What makes something an express premise of an argument is not the words it contains or its position in the argument, but the role it plays. It plays the role of express premise if, and only if, it fulfills (i)–(iv).

Thing 3. *Conclusions* often are introduced by such conclusion-indicators as "therefore," "it follows that," "so," "thus," "consequently," "we may conclude that." But not always. Often a conclusion comes first, presented as the thesis, proposal, or idea to be defended. What makes something the conclusion of an argument is not the words it contains or its position in the argument, but the role it plays. The conclusion is the position the argument is designed to defend, to give reasons for believing.

Thing 4. Sometimes the conclusion of an argument is unstated, as in this example, cited earlier: "I oppose capital punishment because it has not been shown to be an effective deterrent." The conclusion is not: "*I oppose* capital punishment." It is something like: "Capital punishment is wrong." Whether or not the conclusion was stated, list it along with the express premises.

Thing 5. Premises and conclusions often contain *extraneous expressions*—merely decorative and other words and phrases that do not contribute to an argument's validity. Common examples: "as a matter of fact," "on the other hand," "to be perfectly frank," "I say that." Delete these.

Thing 6. Arguments often are laced with *extraneous statements*—statements that are neither premises nor conclusions nor intermediate steps. These include repetitions, variations, elucidations, and illustrations of premises and conclusions, as well as personal, historical, and other asides. Remember to omit all such statements.

Thing 7. Eliminate *repetition*.

Thing 8. A premise or conclusion might occur otherwise than as a *declarative sentence*. Reformulate it as such in that case.

Thing 9. List distinct statements as separate premises, even if they were originally conjoined.

Thing 10. Expand all ellipses and other abbreviating devices. If a premise as originally formulated contains a relative pronoun or other abbreviation of an expression occurring outside the premise, replace the abbreviation with the full expression it abbreviates.

Thing 11. Do not hesitate to make minor modifications of a strictly stylistic (not substantive) character in the original formulation of an argument if that makes the argument's logical form more nearly valid, or at least simpler or more transparent and, therefore, easier to test for validity.

Example 1   Socrates is a man, and all men are mortal, so Socrates is mortal.

Express premises and conclusion:

Socrates is a man.

All men are mortal.

∴ Socrates is mortal.

I listed the two premises separately, even though they were conjoined in the original version. Always separate clearly distinct premises.

Very well, I promise not to use that example again. Here is a meatier argument:

Example 2   The bigger the burger, the better the burger, and the burgers are bigger at Burger King.

Express premises and conclusion:

The bigger the burger, the better the burger.

The burgers are bigger at Burger King.

∴ The burgers are better at Burger King.

I made the tacit conclusion explicit.

Example 3   How do I know he's guilty, you ask? Well, wasn't he found dressed in black, on the balcony of the ransacked room, panting and giggling, a sack of the dowager marchioness's jewelry slung over his shoulder?

Express premise and conclusion:

He was found dressed in black, on the balcony of the ransacked room, panting and giggling, a sack of the dowager marchioness's jewelry slung over his shoulder.

∴ He's guilty.

I changed the express premise from interrogative to declarative form.

Example 4   This is what I think of the Electoral College: Its members are either useless or dangerous—useless if they do their job, dangerous if they don't.

Express premises and conclusion:

The members of the Electoral College are useless if they do their job.

The members of the Electoral College are dangerous if they don't do their job.

∴ The members of the Electoral College are either useless or dangerous.

I expanded the highly elliptical original premises, turning them into complete declarative sentences and replacing the relative pronoun "they" by its antecedent, "the members of the Electoral College."

Example 5   Since, admittedly, he is *responsible* for what he did, he could not have been *caused* (by his genes, his upbringing, his environment, or whatnot) to act as he did, else he would not have acted *freely*.

Express premises and conclusion:

He is responsible for what he did.

Either he was not caused to act as he did, or else he did not act freely. (Equivalently: If he was caused to act as he did, he did not act freely.)

∴ He was not caused to act as he did.

The clause "else he did not act freely" was elliptical for the second premise.

Example 6   We should go to war no more, whatever the provocation, since the costs always outweigh the benefits.

Express premise and conclusion:

The costs of going to war always outweigh the benefits (of going to war).

∴ We should go to war no more.

For the first premise, I could not simply have copied: "the costs always outweigh the benefits." The costs and benefits of *what*? In the original context, "costs" and "benefits" are plainly abbreviations for "costs of war" and "benefits of war." I omitted "whatever the provocation," because this phrase does not seem to be an essential part of the conclusion. Its role is to lend emphasis to the conclusion and to tell us to read the conclusion quite literally.

Example 7   I grant for the sake of argument that fetuses are living human persons. Still, I'm in favor of allowing voluntary abortions. For no creature—hence no living human person—has the right to use another's body to support its life.

Express premise and conclusion:

No creature has the right to use another's body to support its life.

∴ Voluntary abortions should be allowed.

The conclusion is unstated. It is not: "I'm in favor of allowing voluntary abortions." There seem to be unstated premises. But the sentence:

I grant for the sake of argument that fetuses are living human persons

is *not* a premise. Neither is the subordinate clause: "fetuses are living human persons." For these obviously lend no support to the conclusion:

the assertion that fetuses are living human persons surely does not *help* the pro-abortion case. The first sentence merely calls attention to the fact that *this* argument differs from other defenses of abortion in that it does not rely on the usual premise about the status of the fetus—the premise that fetuses are not living human persons. The parenthetical phrase "hence no living human person" was extraneous. It called our attention to a certain consequence of the premise, so it was not an essential *part* of the premise. It was there to remind us that the author is allowing for the sake of argument (although not assuming as part of his argument) that fetuses are living human persons.

Arguments often are mingled with extraneous clauses. The only way to tell for certain whether a clause is a premise is by the role it plays.

Example 8   The materials of nature (air, earth, water) that remain untouched by human effort belong to no one and are not property. It follows that a thing can become someone's private property only if he works and labours on it to change its natural state. From this I conclude that whatever a man improves by the labour of his hand and brain belongs to him, and to him only. (John Locke)

In the first sentence, the phrase "and are not property" is redundant. The second sentence is possibly an intermediate step. Or perhaps it is a mere repetition, an obvious paraphrase of the first sentence. We might formulate the express premise and conclusion this way:

The materials of nature that remain untouched by human effort belong to no one.

∴ Whatever a man improves by the labor of his hand and brain belongs to him, and to him only.

Or we might eliminate strictly stylistic complications so as to bring out a formal connection between premise and conclusion:

Whatever no one has improved by his labor belongs to no one.

∴ Whatever someone has improved by his labor belongs to him, and to him only.

The second standardization is better. Although it alters the original text of the argument, the alteration is strictly stylistic, and it brings out a formal connection between premise and conclusion, simplifying the argument's form and making it more nearly valid (minimizing the number of additional premises needed to make the argument valid).

7.3. COMPOUND ARGUMENTS

A *compound argument* is an argument composed of two or more *sub-arguments*. They constitute a *derivation* (or an attempted derivation) of the argument's conclusion from its premises. Besides premises and a conclusion, every compound argument contains one or more *intermediate steps*, each the conclusion of one subargument and a premise of another.

Example 9   Because standard IQ tests are culturally biased, they are discriminatory. That makes it unconstitutional to use them in public schools.

Express steps:

first subargument {
Standard IQ tests are culturally biased. (premise of whole argument and of first subargument)

Standard IQ tests are discriminatory. (intermediate step of whole argument, conclusion of first subargument, premise of second subargument)

It is unconstitutional to use standard IQ tests in public schools. (conclusion of whole argument and of second subargument)
} *second subargument*

In reconstructing a compound argument, one must distinguish the premises and conclusion of the argument as a whole from the conclusions of its subarguments. And if the argument is sufficiently elaborate, one might have to evaluate it by evaluating its subarguments separately.

For either of these tasks, as well as for that of identifying tacit premises, it helps to construct a *tree diagram* of the given argument. I illustrate with an old friend:

Example 10   Because none but *Carnivora* kill mice, and no cats fail to kill mice, cats are carnivorous. But no animals are carnivorous unless they prowl at night. So cats prowl at night, and thus, since animals that prowl at night always love to gaze at the moon, cats love to gaze at the moon. Consequently, cats are suitable for pets, inasmuch as every animal is suitable for a pet that loves to gaze at the moon. But the only animals in this house are cats. So the only animals in this house are suitable for pets, and thus kangaroos are not in this house, since they are not suitable for pets. No animals ever take to me, however, except what are in this house, whence it follows that kangaroos do not take to me. So I detest them, since I detest animals that do not take to me. And when I detest an animal, I avoid it. Therefore, I always avoid a kangaroo.

This ten-premise argument begins with the two-premise subargument:

None but *Carnivora* kill mice.

No cats fail to kill mice.

∴ Cats are carnivorous.

We can represent this subargument as a *tree*:

None but *Carnivora* kill mice.   No cats fail to kill mice.

Cats are carnivorous.

This is a particularly simple argument-tree. It has just two *branches*. A five-premise argument with no intermediate steps would call for five branches. The upper ends of the two branches—the two *top nodes*, as they are called—are occupied by the two premises. The *bottom node* is occupied by the subargument's conclusion, which is both an intermediate step of the whole kangaroo argument and a premise of the next subargument. The latter is represented by this tree diagram:

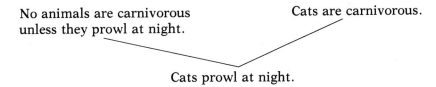

No animals are carnivorous unless they prowl at night.   Cats are carnivorous.

Cats prowl at night.

Combining these two diagrams, we get the more elaborate diagram:

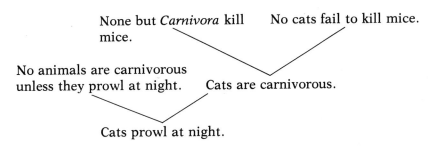

None but *Carnivora* kill mice.   No cats fail to kill mice.

No animals are carnivorous unless they prowl at night.   Cats are carnivorous.

Cats prowl at night.

which represents a compound subargument—compound because it contains two subarguments of its own. By adding the subsequent sub-arguments to the diagram just above, we get a tree diagram of the kangaroo argument as a whole:

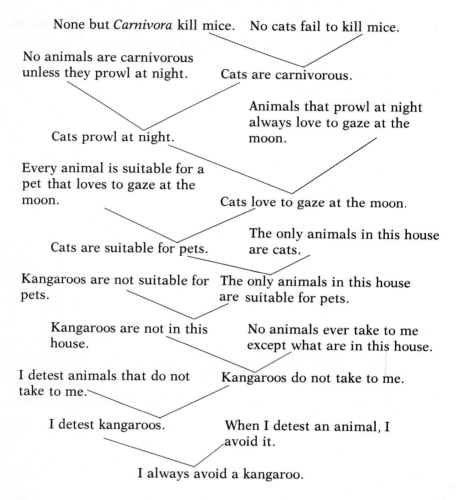

There are ten *top nodes*—ten nodes with no branches leading up from them. Each is occupied by a *premise* of the entire argument. There is one *bottom node*—one node with no branch leading down from it. It is oc-cupied by the *conclusion* of the entire argument. The remaining eight nodes—the *intermediate nodes*—are occupied by *intermediate steps*.

After you "tree" an argument this way, you can spot the premises and conclusion of the entire argument at a glance: The premises occupy the top nodes, the conclusion the bottom node. You also can tell more easily whether the whole argument is valid: It is valid if each subargument is valid (although it is not necessarily true that each subargument is valid if the whole argument is). And you can decide more easily which subarguments, if any, to evaluate.

Example 11   Suppose God existed. Then being omniscient, He would know of every evil. But being omnipotent, He would be able to prevent every evil. And being omnibenevolent, He would prevent every evil He knew of and was able to prevent. So He would prevent every evil, and thus none would exist. But some evil does exist. Consequently, God does not.

"God does not" obviously is elliptical for "God does not *exist*," which is the conclusion. "Some evil exists" is an express premise. ("But" and the emphatic "does" are extraneous.)

Identifying the other express premises requires a bit of care. A pair of sentences of the form:

Suppose A. Then B

amounts to:

If A, then B.

In Example 11, then, the first sentence, "Suppose God existed," amounts to prefixing "If God existed" to the second sentence, and indeed to the third, fourth, fifth, and sixth sentences as well. In the second sentence, the phrase "being omniscient" amounts to "because He would be omniscient." So this sentence, with "If God existed" prefixed, amounts to the subargument:

If God existed, He would be omniscient.

∴ If God existed, He would know of every evil.

The third and fourth sentences, with "If God existed" prefixed, constitute similar arguments. So the whole argument begins with three one-premise subarguments. In the fifth sentence, "So He would prevent every evil, and thus none would exist," the words "So" and "thus" are reliable conclusion-indicators: from the conclusions of the three initial subarguments, another intermediate conclusion is supposed to follow ("He would prevent every evil"), and from that yet another ("No evil would exist"). For the argument as a whole, we get this tree diagram:

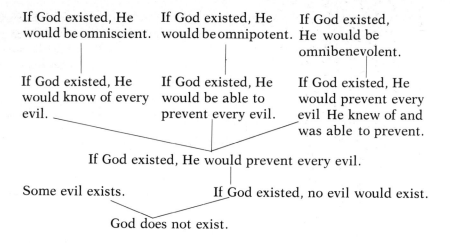

If God existed, He would be omniscient.

If God existed, He would be omnipotent.

If God existed, He would be omnibenevolent.

If God existed, He would know of every evil.

If God existed, He would be able to prevent every evil.

If God existed, He would prevent every evil He knew of and was able to prevent.

If God existed, He would prevent every evil.

Some evil exists.

If God existed, no evil would exist.

God does not exist.

So the argument has four express premises; they occupy the four top nodes.

I could perfectly well have phrased the first premise as: "Suppose God existed. Then He would be omniscient." Similarly for the other steps phrased above with "If"—the other steps governed by "Suppose God existed" in the original text.

Here is an abbreviated tree of the same argument:

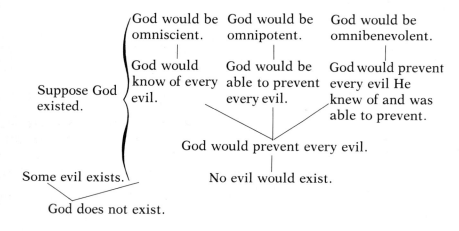

Suppose God existed.

God would be omniscient.

God would be omnipotent.

God would be omnibenevolent.

God would know of every evil.

God would be able to prevent every evil.

God would prevent every evil He knew of and was able to prevent.

God would prevent every evil.

Some evil exists.

No evil would exist.

God does not exist.

The clause "Suppose God existed" plus the brace is tantamount to pre-fixing "Suppose God existed"—or, equivalently, "If God existed"—to every sentence inside the brace. Besides conforming more closely to the original language of Example 11, this tree is simpler and clearer than the first. The reasoning displayed inside the brace is much like a subargument of which "God exists" is an additional premise. But not quite: "God exists" cannot really be a premise, because its truth is not affirmed (indeed it is denied) by Example 11. It is only temporarily assumed in order to draw a consequence from it. Because "God exists" is not affirmed by the argument, its consequence, "No evil exists," is not thereby affirmed either, which is all to the good, inasmuch as this consequence is denied by one of the argument's premises.

Let us call a "suppose" clause followed by a brace a *supposition* of the material inside the brace. A supposition is somewhat like a premise, except that it is not affirmed, but only assumed noncommitally in order to show that certain statements follow from it. It is an abbreviated way of prefixing an "if"-clause to each sentence inside its brace.

Example 12   THEOREM. If xy is odd, then x and y are both odd.
Proof. Suppose, on the contrary, that x and y were not both odd. Say x = 2z. Then xy = 2zy, and thus xy would be even, contrary to our hypothesis. Likewise if y = 2z. That suffices to prove the theorem.

Tree:

Note that the "if" part of the argument's conclusion—of the theorem—functions as a supposition throughout the argument. That often (not always) happens with mathematical theorems. Remember high school geometry, in which you were "given" soandso and told "to prove" suchandsuch? Your proof was an argument; Euclid's axioms, its premises. The conclusion—the theorem you proved—was not suchandsuch—not the sentence labeled "to prove." It was:

If soandso *then* suchandsuch.

Soandso functioned as a supposition throughout—in the statement plus the entire proof of the theorem.

By the way, Examples 11 and 12 illustrate an especially prevalent type of argument: *reductio ad absurdum.* It consists in supposing the opposite ("God exists," "x and y are not both odd") of what one wishes to establish ("God does not exist." "x and y are odd"), then deducing from it a statement that is plainly false ("No evil exists," "xy is even") given one's premises and prior suppositions ("Some evil exists," "xy is odd").

7.4. VALIDITY AND TACIT PREMISES

To complete Step One, *assess* the *validity* of the partly reconstructed argument as it stands, that is, before adding tacit premises. Then *add tacit premises* (if there are such) and reassess validity (if that seems necessary).

Many arguments commonly encountered are obviously valid or obviously invalid—it is obvious, at any rate, to someone with your level of logical acuity. Faced with an argument that is neither obviously valid nor obviously invalid, you should do one or more of the following:

(i) Display the argument's logical form.

(ii) Check whether the discourse from which the argument was extracted contains a convincing derivation (which you might rewrite in tree form).

(iii) Try to construct a derivation.

(iv) Try to find a counter-example to the argument's form— another argument of the same form with obviously true premises and an obviously false conclusion.

(v) Test the argument by diagram. That is, represent all its premises in one diagram and see whether this premise-diagram verifies the conclusion. (The procedure is a bit more complicated if the argument's logical form consists partly of connectives, as I explained in §6.3.)

(vi) Seek help from someone who is good at logic.

(ii) and (v) tend to be especially fruitful tacks.

More often than not, your candidate argument as it stands will be invalid. And more often than not, that will be because some essential premises were left tacit. Add them and reassess validity.

Any argument can be made valid (if not otherwise virtuous) by adding *some* premise. Adding the conclusion as a premise will always ensure validity, after all.

The premises you add should be *reasonable*, though. It should be reasonable to attribute them to the argument's author: they should be compatible with whatever may be known of the author's beliefs and intentions. Beyond that, they should be as plausible as possible— plausible enough, anyway, to lend some credibility to the conclusion.

Problem: You may find an argument to be invalid, without finding any validating premises that it would be *reasonable* to add. Maybe every candidate premise is implausible or otherwise unattributable to the argument's author.

When that happens, stop! Your evaluation is finished. Your verdict: An irremediably invalid argument.

But be generous: Always try to validate an argument by adding reasonable premises before condemning it as irremediably invalid.

Example 13   The bigger the burger, the better the burger.

The burgers are bigger at Burger King.

∴ The burgers are better at Burger King.

Valid as it stands. No additional premises needed.

Example 14   Although I didn't see the stone, I can tell you it must have been green, because, as you know, it was an emerald.

Express premise and conclusion:

The stone was an emerald.

∴ The stone was green.

As it stands, the argument obviously is invalid. No doubt the author was tacitly assuming:

All emeralds are green,

which, added as a premise, makes the argument valid.

Example 14 illustrates a simple, frequently effective strategy for finding tacit premises. The express premise links two terms, "the stone" and "emerald." The conclusion links "the stone" to a third term, "green." To find a validating tacit premise, you could have looked for a plausible statement that closes the circle, linking the two terms, "emerald" and "green," not yet linked. Pictorially:

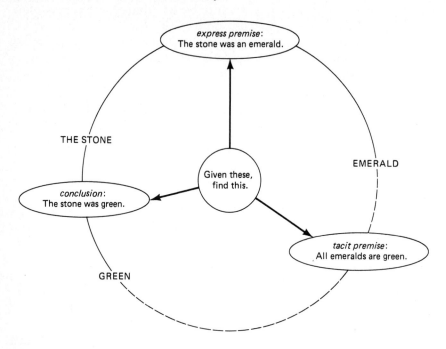

The circle-closing strategy also applies to many arguments containing four or more terms. In each case, one looks for premises that close the circle of term links established by the express premises and the conclusion.

Example 15   He was found dressed in black, on the balcony of the ransacked room, panting and giggling, a sack of the dowager marchioness's jewelry slung over his shoulder.

∴ He's guilty.

Invalid. Tacit premise:

Whoever was found dressed in black, on the balcony of the ransacked room, panting and giggling, a sack of the dowager marchioness's jewelry slung over his shoulder, is guilty.

The express premise links "he" to "found dressed in black, on the balcony of the ransacked room, panting and giggling, a sack of the dowager marchioness's jewerly slung over his shoulder." The conclusion links "he" to "guilty." The tacit premise closes the circle, linking "found dressed ..." to "guilty."

Often your logical intuitions, honed by the hardships of Parts One and Two and aided by the circle-closing strategy, are adequate guides to validating premises. When your intuitions fail, try diagraming the express premises, finding some additional diagrammatic feature (usually shading of a particular region) that would verify the conclusion, then finding some additional premise(s) represented by this feature. In short, try reading tacit premises off the premise-diagram.

Example 16   All Communists are atheists.

　　　　　　　Madalyn is an atheist.

　　　　　　∴. Madalyn is a Communist.

Logical form plus premise-diagram:

　　　All Cs are As.

　　　m is an A.

　　∴ m is a C.

Invalid. Any validating additional premise would have to exclude m from the A - C class. But that would be tantamount to saying:

(*)　Madalyn is not both an atheist and a non-Communist (that is, Madalyn is a nonatheist or a Communist).

A validating premise can be stronger than (*)—as is "All atheists are Communists." But is must be *at least* as strong: (*) must be at least part of what it says. For it must exclude "m" from the A - C region to verify the conclusion. It is unlikely, though, that anything as strong as (*) is a tacit premise of Example 16, for three reasons: First, (*) is implausible. Second, (*) is less plausible than any premise the author troubled to state. Third, if (*) were added to the premises, the first, stated premise would serve no purpose: the argument would be valid without it. It seems more likely that the author simply reasoned badly than that he relied on a tacit premise.

Often, as in Example 16, the diagram of an argument's express premises reveals the weakest additional premise (or set of premises) that would validate the argument. If even this minimal premise is flatly unreasonable, the argument is irremediably invalid. Otherwise, this premise is a candidate for tacit premise. There may be other candidates—a situation I discuss in §7.5.

Example 17   If God existed, He would be omniscient.

If God existed, He would be omnipotent.

If God existed, He would be omnibenevolent.

Some evil exists.

∴ God does not exist.

Invalid. These premises and conclusion came from a compound argument, of which I gave a tree diagram in the last section. That diagram makes it easier to see what additional premises would make the argument valid. Here is the tree diagram again, but with tacit premises added:

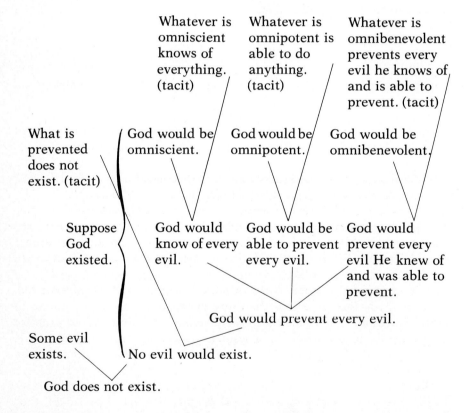

By making all the subarguments valid, the four added premises make the argument as a whole valid.

To find validating tacit premises for a compound argument, it helps to find them for each subargument.

Example 18   Whatever no one has improved by his labor belongs to no one.

∴ Whatever someone has improved by his labor belongs to him, and to him only.

Invalid. Logical form and counter-example:

Whatever no one has I
by his L B to no one.

∴ Whatever someone has I
by his L B to him.

Whatever no one has ingested
by his digestive process causes
heartburn to no one.

∴ Whatever someone has ingested
by his digestive process
causes heartburn to him.

Invalidity also can be proved by diagram:

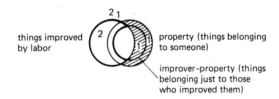

The "1" region represents things no one has improved by his labor. The "2" region represents things belonging to no one. The shading of the "1" region minus the "2" region represents the premise. The conclusion is not verified, because it calls for shading of the heavily outlined subregion. I can find no plausible validating premise—no plausible premise that would shade the heavily outlined region. Here is a candidate:

If something that previously belonged to no one is then improved by one person, it belongs to him.

Adding this as a premise does not quite ensure validity. If we represent it in the diagram above, we get:

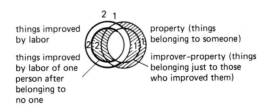

The conclusion is not verified, because the new heavily outlined region is not shaded. Shading this region is equivalent to affirming:

> Whatever is improved by two or more people belongs to them, and whatever has belonged to one person and is then improved by a second person belongs to the latter.

So adding a premise at least as strong as this would ensure validity. And the *only* way to ensure validity is to add a premise at least as strong as this—a premise that at least shades the heavily outlined area. The trouble is that the second clause of this candidate premise is not the least bit plausible. I conclude that the argument's author—the seventeenth-century English philosopher John Locke—just reasoned badly.

7.5. COMPARING CANDIDATE PREMISES

In reconstructing an argument, you may find a number of ways to supply tacit premises—a number of sets of fairly plausible statements, any one of which would make the argument valid if added to the express premises.

Choose among these sets according to the following three criteria:

FIDELITY Add premises that are *faithful to the author's beliefs and intentions,* insofar as these are known. So added premises should neither conflict with the stated argument nor make any stated premise gratuitous.

GENEROSITY Be generous to the author by adding premises that are as *plausible* as possible (relative to the argument's intended audience, insofar as that is known). Added premises should be sufficiently plausible, anyway, to enhance the credibility of the conclusion to some degree.

GENERALITY Add premises that are as *general* as possible, consistent with Fidelity and Generosity.

One statement is *more general* than another if the two say similar things, the first about a wider class, the second about a narrower class. Thus, "Ignatz likes tall blondes" is more general than "Ignatz likes Farrah" and less general than "Ignatz likes blondes." As this example illustrates, adding qualifications to a statement decreases its generality; dropping qualifications increases generality.

Whether Fidelity is important depends on your purposes. If you aim to determine what an author meant, your reconstruction of his argument should of course be as faithful to his beliefs and intentions as you can make it. But if you want to determine how good a particular line of reasoning is, regardless of who authored it or what he had in mind, then Generosity and Generality are far more important than Fidelity.

Why be generous? Not to be polite, but to learn as much as possible. If you find no plausible way to reconstruct an argument so as to make it valid, you have learned something new: that the argument is not only invalid but very likely irreparably so. If you find plausible premises whose addition makes the argument valid, you have found what could well be the author's intended argument, since people are likely to reason validly more often than not; but at any rate you have found a pretty good argument and thereby extended your knowledge.

Suppose you are deciding which of two potential premises to add to an argument, and neither is preferable according to Fidelity or Generosity, but one is more general than the other. According to the Generality criterion, you should choose the more general. Why? Because the more general candidate is a likely reason or justification for the less general one, hence a likelier ultimate reason or justification for the argument's conclusion—a likelier *premise*, in other words.

Example 19   The trouble with censorship is that it stifles creativity.

Standardization:

>   Censorship stifles creativity.
>
> ∴ Censorship is wrong.

Here is a validating premise that apparently satisfies Fidelity and Generosity:

> (1) Censorship is wrong if it stifles creativity.

What about Generality? The most natural way to generalize (1) is the following:

> (2) Any action or policy that stifles creativity is wrong.

But this is *too* general: It violates Generosity, being much less plausible than (1). A policy of preventing medical researchers from experimenting on unwilling human subjects, for example, stifles creativity without being wrong. The reason, of course, is that the virtues of such a policy are sufficiently great to compensate for the fact that the policy stifles creativity. This suggests the following modification of (2):

> (3) Any action or policy that stifles creativity *and does not have compensating virtues* is wrong.

By itself, (3) does not validate the argument. A further premise is needed:

> (4) Censorship is a policy that does not have compensating virtues (virtues sufficient to compensate for stifling creativity).

As a pair, (3) and (4) are more general than (1) and no less plausible. A reasonable way to complete the reconstruction of Example 19, then, is to add (3) and (4).

Example 20   The costs of going to war always outweigh the benefits of going to war.

∴ We should go to war no more.

Invalid. Premise-diagram:

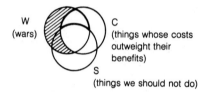

W
(wars)

C
(things whose costs outweight their benefits)

S
(things we should not do)

This fails to verify the conclusion, which calls for shading of the W−S region, because the heavily outlined area is not shaded. So an added premise will validate the argument if, and only if, it shades that area.
Simply shading the heavily outlined area amounts to affirming:

> (1) We should not engage in wars whose costs outweigh their benefits.

Shading the whole upper part of the W circle or the C circle also would shade the heavily outlined area. Shading the upper part of the W circle amounts to affirming:

> (2) We should go to war no more.

Shading the upper part of the C circle amounts to affirming:

> (3) We should do nothing whose costs outweigh its benefits.

So (1), (2), and (3) would each validate the argument.
(3) is best. (2) violates Fidelity: because (2) is just the conclusion, it could not be the premise the author had in mind, else his stated premise

would be gratuitous. (2) is ruled out by Generosity as well: no statement is sufficiently plausible to enhance its own credibility. (1) and (3) are both plausible. But (3) is more general (because less qualified), and there is no evident reason to favor (1) (no evident reason for the qualification), so (3) is preferable according to Generality.

When a premise-diagram reveals several validating premises, choose among them according to Fidelity, Generosity, and Generality, bearing this in mind: A candidate premise that shades a more inclusive region is more general than one that shades a less inclusive region. And a candidate premise that shades some region is more general than one that merely excludes a singular term from the same region. Generality calls for validating premises that shade the widest areas, consistent with Fidelity (to the extent that Fidelity is important) and Generosity.

Example 21   The peculiar evil of silencing the expression of an opinion is that it is robbing the human race, posterity as well as the existing generation. . . . If the opinion is right, they are deprived of the opportunity of exchanging error for truth; if wrong, they lose, what is almost as great a benefit, the clearer perception and livelier impression of truth produced by its collision with error. (John Stuart Mill)

Express premises and conclusion:

If an opinion is right, silencing its expression deprives mankind of the opportunity of exchanging error for truth.

If an opinion is wrong, silencing its expression causes mankind to lose the clearer perception and livelier impression of truth produced by its collision with error.

∴ Silencing the expression of an opinion robs mankind.

In the conclusion, I replaced "the human race" by "mankind." This strictly stylistic modification simplifies the argument's form and makes it more nearly valid, eliminating the need for the additional premise, "Mankind is the human race." The argument is invalid as it stands. We can make it valid by adding either of these two statements to its premises:

(1) To deprive X of Y or to cause X to lose Y is to rob X of Y.

(2) To deprive anyone of the opportunity of exchanging error for truth is to rob him of it, and to cause anyone to lose the clearer perception and livelier impression of truth produced by its collision with error is to rob him of it.

Although more general than (2), (1) is ruled out by Generosity. To be sure, even (2) is debatable. But (2) is a paragon of plausibility compared with the preposterous (1). Does the mailman *rob* me of the letters I have posted when he collects them? Do garbage men, tax collectors, or creditors always rob us?

EXERCISES

Reconstruct the following arguments. Set out your work by listing both express and tacit premises, parenthetically labeling each "express" or "tacit," followed by the conclusion. If an argument is irremediably invalid (a rare occurrence), say so. If an argument is compound, display its premises (express and tacit, labeled as such), intermediate steps, and conclusion in a *tree.*

* 1. I'm opposed to girlie magazines, because they debase women.

 2. Because all conservatives are Republicans, none is a Democrat.

* 3. Capital punishment is justified, because it deters crime.

 4. Capital punishment is not justified, because it does not deter crime.

* 5. Not all Ugandans love Idi Amin, since some are Christian.

 6. He gave no argument, really. He just harangued instead of giving reasons for his conclusion.

* 7. Whoever has an Albanian accent cannot have a proper Irish brogue. So those who do are not Albanians.

 8. Huskies must be mammals. After all, they're dogs. Aren't they?

* 9. Someone is a politician, and someone is greedy. So someone is a greedy politician.

 10. Whether we have free will or not, we certainly *believe* we do, since we deliberate about alternative courses of action.

* 11. Yes, the history of humanity is riddled with episodes of disease, hunger, war, religious persecution, airplane crashes, and other apparent misfortunes. Still, there really are no catastrophes, appearances to the contrary notwithstanding. For God prevents every catastrophe He knows of and can prevent, and that includes every catastrophe whatever.

 12. Not all Texans are liberals, else they'd be happy to have intrastate gas federally regulated.

* 13. Because some folks are enamored of Red China, not everyone is unhappy about breaking relations with Taiwan.

 14. Whoever failed stayed home. So no one who failed came on the picnic.

* 15. We should not outlaw prostitution, because to do so is to legislate morality.

16. We should not outlaw prostitution, because prostitution harms no one with the possible exception of voluntary participants.

* 17. What's wrong with pornography? It serves no purpose but to stimulate lust, that's what.

18. What's so horrible about capital punishment? That's simple: *Capital punishment is irreversible punishment.*

* 19. Because everyone has the right to publish whatever information he wishes to publish, the *New York Times* had the right to publish the *Pentagon Papers.*

20. Because standard IQ tests are culturally biased, they are discriminatory. That makes it unconstitutional to use them in public schools.

* 21. Those term-paper mills do nothing illicit. Cheating on school assignments is entirely the fault of the students who use the service.

22. "Hey! It says 'No Smoking!'," uttered by a student to a professor smoking in class with a "No Smoking" sign.

* 23. Why outlaw pornography? Well, for one thing, we know it does no psychological harm. And surely naked bodies per se are not evil.

24. "When better cars are made, Buick will make them."

* 25. If we really wanted to benefit the underdeveloped countries, we'd give them more food, fewer arms.

26. We've got to crack down on civil disobedience. It's often well-motivated, I admit. And it's unquestionably had some good results. But we can't just let citizens decide for themselves which laws to obey. That would be anarchy.

* 27. *THEOREM.* If $x + y$ is odd, then x or y is even.

    Proof: Suppose x and y were both odd. Then $x - 1$ and $y - 1$ would be even, and thus, since a sum of even numbers must itself be even, $(x - 1) + (y - 1) + 2$ would be even. But $(x - 1) + (y - 1) + 2 = x + y$. So $x + y$ would be even, which is absurd.

28. The whole debate over national health insurance—in particular, over the costs and relative equity of alternative programs—is so much blatherskyte. Let some national health-insurance program be cheap and equitable—cheaper than the laissez-faire status quo and perfectly equitable, if you like: Still it does not follow that this program ought to be adopted. On the contrary, the program would definitely be a mistake. For health-care provision is no part of the federal government's constitutional function.

* 29. To graduate, I'd better take Bosworth's course. For suppose I am going to graduate. Then I'll need another American History course plus Sex Education and Basket Weaving. But there are just two American History courses I can take besides Bosworth's: One conflicts with Sex Education, the other with Basket Weaving.

30. Compared with smoking cigarettes, the failure to have an annual dental examination does trivial harm to one's health. Consequently, no rational person who troubles to have an annual dental exam would ever smoke cigarettes.

* 31. O.K. I'll tell you what's wrong with capital punishment: *People* may not kill one another just for the sake of retribution or deterrence. So what entitles *society* to do so?

32. Because nondrinkers drive safely, Baptists must be good drivers.

* 33. Because some evil exists, God either does not want to prevent or cannot prevent evil. Hence, God is not both omnibenevolent and omnipotent.

34. A company that has discriminated against women in hiring ought now to *favor* women over men in hiring. That way it compensates women for the discrimination they have suffered.

* 35. Prohibitionists and antipornography crusaders are not being unfair (as often is alleged) to those who do not share their views. For they do not propose to impose upon others restrictions they would not gladly have imposed upon themselves.

36. You have the right to engage in homosexual practices, because everyone has the right to engage in *private actions*—actions affecting the legitimate interests of no one but the actors.

* 37. If *I* hadn't bought the stolen fur coat, someone else would have bought it, and the harm (if any) would have been the same—but I wouldn't have gotten the coat. So there really was nothing wrong with my buying it.

* 38. If it were all right to allow congenitally deformed infants to die, it would be no more objectionable to terminate the lives of ill, unwanted elderly people. What's the difference?

* 39. Many people just do not believe, on religious or any other grounds, that homosexuality is wrong. Those who favor anti-sodomy laws are just trying to foist their own controversial religious beliefs on others. That violates the wall of separation between church and state.

40. It is unfair for Hindus to try to outlaw beef consumption, preventing even non-Hindus from eating beef. Would Hindus want their Moslem countrymen to do the same by outlawing pork consumption, preventing Hindus and other non-Moslems from eating pork?

8

Meaning and Ambiguity

8.1. STEP TWO: DOES THE ARGUMENT DEPEND ON AN AMBIGUITY?

Sometimes an argument owes its appeal to an *ambiguity*—a multiple meaning of some word or other piece of language: we judge the argument to be valid *and* to have plausible premises *and* to have an interesting conclusion only if we impute two or more meanings to one expression.

Example 1   Château La Tour is dry.

Whatever is dry is not wet.

Therefore, Château La Tour is not wet.

The first premise is plausible only if "dry" means "not sweet"; the second, only if "dry" means "not wet." But the argument is valid only if "dry" is interpreted the same way—it does not matter which way—in both premises. For it then has the form:

c is D.

Whatever is D is not W.

∴ c is not W.

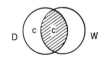

which the accompanying diagram shows to be valid, rather than the *in*valid form:

159

c is D_1.

Whatever is D_2 is not W.

∴ c is not W.

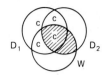

Notice how, in depicting logical form, I treat two occurrences of the same string of letters as two occurrences of the *same expression* only if the two occurrences have the *same meaning.* I do not treat two occurrences of "dry" as the same word if one means "not wet" and the other "not sweet."

Example 2   A law is just if it forbids only what is wrong.

                 To break a law is to do what the law forbids.

                 It always is wrong to break a law.

                 Therefore, every law is just.

If "just" means *"legally* just," or simply "legal," and if "wrong" means *"legally* wrong," or simply "illegal," the premises are plausible and the argument valid. But then the conclusion says that every law is legally just, or simply legal, and that is much less interesting than the conclusion seemed at first to be. Only if "just" means *"morally* just" (or something similar) is the conclusion maximally interesting. But then the first premise is implausible unless "wrong" means "morally wrong," in which case the third premise is far less plausible than it seemed at first to be. And the argument is valid only if "just" and "wrong" are each interpreted in the same way—it does not matter which way—throughout.

An argument *depends on an ambiguity* if it contains one or several expressions meeting these three conditions:

(i)   The expressions are ambiguous; they have two or more meanings each.

(ii) The argument owes its appeal to interpreting at least one of the expressions more than one way. That is, the combination of plausible premises, valid form, and interesting conclusion requires that at least one of the expressions (it might not matter which one) be taken in two or more senses.

(iii) The argument is valid only if each of the expressions has the same meaning throughout.

For an argument to depend on an ambiguity, conditions (i)–(iii) must *all* hold. It is not enough for the argument to contain an expression with two or more meanings, nor even for the argument to owe its appeal to such multiple meaning. The argument also must owe its validity to the expression's having the same meaning throughout.

Step Two of my three-step procedure for evaluating arguments consists in checking whether the argument being evaluated depends on an ambiguity.

When an argument depends on ambiguity, that fact may not be obvious, at least not at first. It was obvious in the case of Example 1, less obvious in the case of Example 2. Among arguments that depend on ambiguities, the important ones are the less obvious ones, those that might deceive because they are more appealing than they would be if the ambiguities in them were more evident.

To say of an argument that it depends on an ambiguity is to give an important criticism of the argument—but not necessarily a devastating criticism. Consider Example 2. To ensure validity plus plausibility of premises, we must interpret "just" throughout as "*legally* just." That makes the conclusion relatively uninteresting but leaves the argument otherwise unscathed.

Example 3   Antipornography laws destroy liberty and therefore promote slavery.

Reconstruction:

Antipornography laws destroy liberty. (express)

To destroy liberty is to promote slavery. (tacit)

∴ Antipornography laws promote slavery.

The first premise is plausible only if "destroy liberty" means to terminate or preclude *some* liberty—perhaps a very trivial liberty. But then the second premise is not so plausible. The second premise is plausible only if "destroy liberty" means to terminate or seriously diminish *most important* liberties, in which case the first premise is implausible. Yet the argument is valid only if "destroy liberty" has the same meaning throughout.

8.2.   VARIETIES OF AMBIGUITY

Ambiguity is *multiple meaning*, very broadly construed: If an expression can be used or understood two or more ways, and if the truth or falsity of some sentence can depend on which way the expression is used or understood, then these ways of using or understanding the expression count as different meanings, so the expression counts as ambiguous. *To resolve* the ambiguity is to specify which way the expression is to be used or understood.

The meaning of a sentence depends on two things: the meanings of its component words, and its syntactic (grammatical) structure. Either can be ambiguous, making the sentence ambiguous. Ambiguity of words is called *equivocation*. Syntactic ambiguity is called *amphiboly*.

"Strike" is equivocal. It means different things in baseball, labor disputes, and bricklaying. "Pipe" also is equivocal. It can mean a hollow cylinder or a smoking device. Here are some more equivocal words: line, base, stock, head, man, case, authority, reason, value, same, care, light.

The sentence:

> Those who jog often catch colds

is amphibolous: it has an ambiguous syntactic structure. It is not clear whether "often" modifies "jog" or "catch." Another example:

> Republicans are more like Tories than Democrats.

Does it mean that Republicans are more like Tories than Democrats are? Or does it mean that Republicans are more like Tories than like Democrats? Some more examples of amphiboly:

> Bertha ran up to Ludmilla, and she cried. (Who cried?)
>
> I had lunch with Ignatz, the chairman, and Bertha. (Are Ignatz and the chairman one person, or two?)
>
> I met a smart professor's wife. (Who is smart, the professor, or his wife?)

The ambiguities on which arguments depend sometimes are rather *subtle*. Compare Examples 1, 2, and 3. The difference between the two meanings of "dry" in Example 1 is greater and more obvious than the difference between the two meanings of "just" in Example 2. And the latter difference is greater and more obvious than the difference between the two meanings of "destroy liberty" in Example 3. You will find the two meanings of "dry" in many dictionaries. Even large, up-to-date dictionaries do not give the two relevant meanings of "just" (although some come close). And none gives both relevant meanings of "destroy liberty"—even when the entries for "destroy" and "liberty" are combined.

The ambiguity of "destroy liberty" is one of *degree*: the two meanings of this phrase differ only in degree—in *how much* destruction of liberty is meant. Ambiguities of degree are quite common. Often they are quite subtle. Words especially liable to this sort of ambiguity are called *vague*.

Thus "bald" is vague because it rarely is clear exactly how bald a head must be to qualify as bald; the distinction between bald heads and other heads is fuzzy.

The meanings of many if not most words and sentences depend to some extent on *context of utterance*, verbal and nonverbal. And it is the context of utterance, normally, that resolves potential ambiguities—that specifies which meaning is the intended one. In "I just bought this," for example, what is meant by "this" depends on what things were previously mentioned, on what the speaker points to, and so on. When such contextual clues are insufficient, "this" is ambiguous.

So much is obvious in the case of pronouns. It is less obvious but nonetheless true of common adjectives, nouns, and verbs. Take "red." When we wish merely to distinguish things with a reddish hue from black, white, green, blue, and other things that are not the least bit red, we use "red" in a wide sense, counting many pink and maroon things as red. But when we are minded to distinguish purely red things from others, including other reddish things, we use "red" in a narrow sense, not counting any pink or maroon things as red. Unless context makes clear which sort of distinction the speaker is making, "red" is ambiguous. The same holds for such nouns as "cat." Someone who uses this word might be distinguishing house cats from all other creatures, including lions and tigers; or he might be distinguishing all members of the cat family, including lions and tigers, from nonfeline fauna. Or consider the verb "to know," as in "Madalyn knows the Pope." Depending on context, a nodding acquaintance with someone might or might not count as *knowing* him. A congressman who says he knows a certain constituent but does not know a certain hoodlum could be using "know" in a broader sense the first time than the second.

Amphiboly, too, normally is resolved by context. I recently read this sentence in a novel: "I don't like managing women." What does the speaker dislike, having to manage women, or women who tend to manage others? The preceding text makes clear that the speaker is expressing his distaste for a particular woman, known for her tendency to run other people's lives, hence that "managing women" means "women who manage others."

Sometimes *common knowledge* resolves a potential ambiguity. "Latin American historian" can mean either "historian who studies Latin America" or "historian who is Latin American." "Invertebrate zoologist" enjoys a similar duality of meaning. While contextual clues are needed to resolve the first ambiguity, common knowledge about the anatomy of those creatures who receive the Ph.D. in zoology suffices to resolve the second.

An expression that is ambiguous out of context ("strike") can be unambiguous in some context (a baseball game). An expression that is ambiguous in one context ("I saw a strike") can be unambiguous in another ("I threw a strike"). And an expression that is ambiguous out of context but unambiguous in some contexts can have different meanings in two such contexts ("I threw a strike," "I went on strike").

8.3. THE SPECIAL AMBIGUITY OF TALK ABOUT CLASSES

Among the ways you can talk about a class are these three: You can say that each member has a certain feature; you can say that the class as a collective unit has a certain feature; or you can say that the members tend to have a certain feature—meaning that they normally or usually have this feature, or that they are more likely than members of other, comparable classes to have it. As a result, a statement of the form:

As are B

sometimes can be interpreted in more than one of these three ways:

Each A is B.

The class of As, taken as a collective unit, is B.

As tend to be B.

Arguments often depend on this sort of ambiguity (an amphiboly, I should say, attributing it either to the "——— are . . ." construction or to the parsing of the subject).

Compare these three arguments:

Timber wolves are furry.
Bertha is a timber wolf.
Therefore, Bertha is furry.

Timber wolves are disappearing.
Bertha is a timber wolf.
Therefore, Bertha is disappearing.

Timber wolves are fierce.
Bertha is a timber wolf.
Therefore, Bertha is fierce.

Grant that Bertha is a timber wolf. Then the first argument is valid and has true premises, so its conclusion is true.

The second argument seems to have the same form as the first. Yet it has true premises and a false conclusion. So it cannot be valid. It depends on an ambiguity. The first premise is plausible only if "timber wolf" is parsed as a *singular term*, designating the *class* or *species* of timber wolves. But the argument is valid only if "timber wolf" is parsed throughout as a *general term*, so that the first premise means *"Every timber wolf is disappearing."* In other words, when we read the argument so that the premises are plausible, it has the form:

t are D.

b is a T.

∴ b is D.

which the accompanying diagram shows to be invalid. But when we read the argument so that it is valid, it has the form:

T are [each] D.

b is a T.

∴ b is D.

which makes nonsense of the first premise.

In the third argument, the first premise is plausible only if it means that timber wolves *tend* to be fierce. But the argument is valid only if the first premise means that *every* timber wolf is fierce.

Here are two arguments that depend on similar ambiguities:

The Germans are efficient.
Bertha is German.
Therefore, Bertha is efficient.

The Republicans are to blame for Watergate.
Ignatz is a Republican.
Therefore, Ignatz is to blame for Watergate.

8.4.   HOW TO SAY WHAT SOMETHING MEANS

There are many ways to convey an expression's meaning. One is by *defining* it. That cannot be the only way. You did not learn most of the English you know from definitions. But it is one important way.

Here are a few things you should know about definition:

Thing 1. To define an expression is to formulate its meaning. There are different ways to do this, different styles of definition. They have this in common: Each equates the meaning of the expression defined, called the *definiendum*, with that of another expression, called the *definiens*.

The standard meaning of "brother" can be formulated any of these ways:

A brother is a male sibling.

"Brother" means "male sibling."

Brother = df. male sibling.

Brother means *male sibling*.

"Brother" means male sibling.

BROTHER: (noun) *male sibling*.

Something is a *brother* if, and only if, it is a male sibling.

"Brother" is defined as "male sibling."

"Brother" is used in English to refer to male siblings.

Male siblings are called brothers.

Each formulation equates the meaning of "brother," the definiendum, with that of "male sibling," the definiens.

Thing 2. A *successful* definition *makes clear* the meaning of the definiendum, hence is *illuminating*, hence is neither *obscure* nor *circular*. Taken by itself, the definition of "God" as "the ground of being" is too obscure to be illuminating. Although not obscure, the definition of "carpenter" as "one who does carpentry," unless coupled with a satisfactory definition of "carpentry," is *circular*. That means it defines an expression ("carpenter") in terms of itself or a close cousin ("carpentry"). One who does not know the meaning of "carpenter" is not likely to know the meaning of "carpentry."

Thing 3. A good definition conveys the *meaning* of the expression defined, not any factual or evaluative contention about things to which the expression applies. The definition of "airplane" as "the Wright brothers' famous invention" is poor. Yes, the Wright brothers invented the airplane. But that is an historical fact about the Wright brothers and the airplane, not part of the *meaning* of "airplane."

A *loaded* definition embodies some controversial contention about the things to which the defined expression applies, a contention that clearly is not part of the expression's meaning. Example: "A bureaucrat is a mealy-mouthed, pointy-headed pinko who works for the government."

Thing 4. A good definition is *not too broad* and *not too narrow*. It does not require the definiendum to apply to too many things or to too few. Its definiendum and definiens are related this way:

NOT TOO BROAD, NOT TOO NARROW

not in any of these ways:

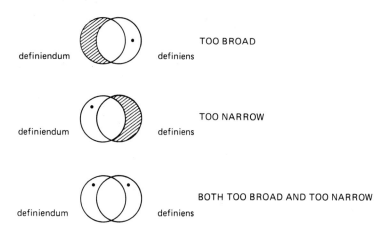

TOO BROAD

TOO NARROW

BOTH TOO BROAD AND TOO NARROW

Compare:

A bachelor is an unmarried person.

A bachelor is an unmarried man who is unhappy without a wife.

A bachelor is an unhappy man.

A bachelor is an unmarried man.

As a definition, the first is too broad, the second too narrow, the third both too broad and too narrow, the fourth just right.

Thing 5. In a good definition, definiendum and definiens are *grammatically similar*—everywhere interchangeable without violence to grammar. Replace "bachelor" in any grammatical sentence with "unmarried man," and you get another grammatical sentence. But suppose someone defined "strike" thus:

A *strike* is when workers collectively withhold their labor.

This is poor, because definiendum and definiens are not grammatically similar. Replace "strike" in the grammatical sentence "They went on strike" with "when workers collectively withhold their labor," and you get the gibberish: "They went on when workers collectively withhold their labor."

Thing 6. Definitions customarily are classified into two basic types, based on the jobs they are designed to do:

> LEXICAL or REAL definitions *report* (or explain) the *conventional* meanings of the expressions they define. Example:
> "A bachelor is an unmarried man."

> STIPULATIVE or NOMINAL definitions are not reports of conventional meaning, but acts of *legislating* meaning. Unlike a lexical definition, a stipulative definition does not report the way an old expression has been used. It introduces a new expression or assigns a new meaning to an old expression. Examples:

> Let "gluck" mean "portable, inflatable, amphibious truck."

> Let "duck" mean "portable, inflatable, amphibious truck."

Especially in science, one often finds *hybrid* definitions. Partly lexical, partly stipulative, they partly preserve and partly alter the standard meanings of the expressions they define. Example: "Force is mass times acceleration."

You know the meanings of numerous English words but cannot define them all. Many simply cannot be defined. Take "red." You know perfectly well what it means. You use it and read it correctly. But try to define it! My dictionary offers "of red color." But that is circular. And citing the frequency of red light will not convey the *meaning* of "red," because people knew the meaning before the advent of modern physics, and most English speakers today know the meaning but not the frequency. Or consider "chair." My dictionary defines it as "a seat, usually with a back, for one person." This is too broad: bar stools and bucket car seats are not chairs.

The trouble with "red" is that the property *redness* cannot be analyzed in any illuminating way into other properties, as *bachelorhood* can be analyzed into manhood and nonconnubiality. "Chair" resists definition for a different reason: There are *clear* or *paradigm* cases of chairs. Each is a one-person, normal-size, movable piece of seating furniture with a back and with a horizontal seat supported on four rigid, vertical legs. Over time, we have come to apply the word "chair" to items that *resemble* paradigm chairs but do not have *all* the features just listed. Had we not done this, we should have ended up with too many names or too many things without names, so rich is the variety of actual and potential pieces of seating furniture.

Definition, I have said, is only one way to convey an expression's meaning. Here are four others:

> OSTENSION   Cite the expression and point to that for which it stands. Example:

Red is that color (pointing to several red things) but not that one (pointing to several nonred things).

LISTING   List all or some of the things to which the expression applies. Examples:

Apostle: Peter, Andrew, James (the Greater), John, Philip, Bartholomew, Matthew, Thomas, James (the Less), Jude, Simon the Cananaean, and Judas Iscariot.

President: Washington, Adams, Jefferson, Madison, etc.

PARTIAL DEFINITION   Narrow the expression's meaning without fully or precisely defining it. Example:

Rock-'n'-roll: a contemporary form of popular music.

Red: of the color red.

The first of these is too broad to be a proper definition, the second circular. But each gives some useful information about the meaning of the expression in question. Often dictionary definitions are just partial definitions.

DESCRIPTION OF USAGE   Describe or explain how the expression is used, without giving an equivalent expression. Example:

"Ouch!" is an English expletive used to express pain.

To *identify an ambiguity*, one must distinguish two or more meanings of one word, sentence, or other locution. Sometimes one can formulate each meaning with a definition. But this is not always possible. And it is not necessary even when possible. One need not fully characterize each meaning. One need only say *enough* about each meaning *to distinguish* it from the others. Example: One can distinguish two meanings of "strike" simply by calling them the baseball sense and the labor sense.

A common way to distinguish two meanings of one expression is to give two nonambiguous *paraphrases*—two nonambiguous expressions, each equivalent to one of the expression's two meanings. Examples:

"Dry" means either "not sweet" or "not wet."

"Just" means either "legally just" or "morally just."

The two paraphrases of "dry" are pretty good definitions. The two paraphrases of "just" are at best poor definitions (perhaps we should not even call them definitions), because they are circular. But they do their job perfectly: they clearly distinguish the two meanings.

8.5. MORE ARGUMENTS

Example 4   Only men are rational, so no woman is.

Reconstruction:

> Only men are rational. (express premises)
>
> No woman is a man. (tacit premise)
>
> ∴ No woman is rational.

The first premise is plausible only if "man" means "human." But then the second premise is implausible. The second premise is plausible only if "man" means "male human." But then the first premise is implausible. Yet the argument is valid only if "man" has the same meaning in both premises.

Example 5   Capital punishment is wrong, because it is killing human beings.

Reconstruction:

> Capital punishment is killing human beings. (express)
>
> It is wrong to kill human beings. (tacit)
>
> ∴ Capital punishment is wrong.

The argument is valid only if the second premise means that *all* killing of human beings is wrong. But that is at best debatable; it is less plausible, certainly, than the second premise seemed at first to be. That premise is maximally plausible only if it means something like "It is *normally* wrong to kill human beings." But then the argument is not valid.

Example 6   The government of Alabama has the right to enforce the laws of Alabama.

The laws of Alabama include Jim Crow laws.

∴ The government of Alabama has the right to enforce Jim Crow laws.

The first premise is most plausible only if "laws" means something like "legitimate legislative enactments," or "legislative enactments that should be enforced," so that the premise means:

If an Alabama legislative enactment is legitimate (if it should be enforced by *some* agency), then it is the government of Alabama (rather than another agency) that has the right to enforce it.

But the second premise is plausible only if "laws" means "legislative enactments." And the argument is valid only if "laws" has the same meaning throughout.

Example 7   Lawbreakers are criminals. So if owning guns is outlawed, only criminals will own guns.

Reconstruction:

Lawbreakers are criminals. (express)

Whoever does what is outlawed is a lawbreaker. (tacit)

∴ If owning guns is outlawed, only criminals will own guns.

The second premise is plausible only if "lawbreaker" means "one who breaks some law," in which case the first premise is plausible only if "criminal," too, means "one who breaks some law." But that makes the conclusion trivial. It is when we construe "criminal" as something like "chronic, serious, professional lawbreaker" that we find the conclusion interesting. But this reading makes the first premise false unless "lawbreaker" has the same meaning, in which case the second premise is false. And a dual reading of either "criminal" or "lawbreaker" makes the argument invalid.

Example 8   It is impossible to eradicate poverty, because there must always be someone at the bottom of the economic ladder.

Reconstruction:

There must always be someone at the bottom of the economic ladder. (express)

Whatever is eradicated no longer exists. (tacit)

Poverty consists in someone being at the bottom of the economic ladder. (tacit)

∴ It is impossible to eradicate poverty.

The conclusion is interesting only if "poverty" is interpreted in absolute rather than relative terms—as the nonattainment of a specified income or standard of living. But in that sense, the third premise is flatly false: a society could be so wealthy and egalitarian that the bottom of its economic ladder were above the specified poverty line. Yet the argument is valid only if "poverty" has the same meaning throughout.

Example 9   Everyone, in the last analysis, is selfish, inasmuch as everyone—even the so-called altruist—does only what he thinks will give him the greatest gratification in the end.

This argument defends the doctrine known as *psychological egoism*. Reconstruction:

Everyone does only what he thinks will give him the greatest gratification in the end. (express)

It is selfish to do only what one thinks will give one the greatest gratification in the end. (tacit)

∴ Everyone is selfish.

The first premise is plausible only if "gratification" is interpreted broadly, so that it applies even to the gratification some people get from helping others. With "gratification" interpreted this way, however, the second premise is plausible only if "selfish" is so interpreted that anyone who seeks maximum gratification is perforce selfish, even if his gratification comes entirely from helping others at the expense of his own health, wealth, safety, and physical comfort. But that makes the conclusion uninteresting. We find the conclusion interesting only when we think of the selfish person as one who tends *not* to be willing to help others at the expense of his own health, wealth, safety, and physical comfort. Yet the argument is valid only if "gratification" and "selfish" are each interpreted uniformly.

EXERCISES

Explain the ambiguity of these words by specifying two or more meanings of each:

*   1. line

     2. base

*   3. care

4. stock

* 5. head

6. men

* 7. case

8. run

* 9. authority

10. same

* 11. reason

12. value

Explain the ambiguity of each of these sentences:

* 13. They talked about going fishing frequently.

14. I looked in the classroom and saw a smoking professor.

* 15. You will save time and cut fingers with a sharpened saw.

16. Gilligan, Goldberg, and Gonzales are French chefs.

* 17. John Rawls's *Theory of Justice* is the most important contribution to moral philosophy since the Second World War.

18. I hired a Mexican exterminator.

* 19. People who eat sweets normally don't get fat.

20. He stopped a minute.

* 21. $3 \cdot 2 + 1 = 9$.

22. He spoke about enduring inflation.

* 23. I found a large dog's bone.

24. There is a sermon tonight about drug abuse in the church.

Criticize each of these (putative) definitions:

* 25. A descendant is an offspring or an offspring's descendant.

26. LOGIC: (noun) *the subject that teaches you to think.*

* 27. *To preach:* What clergymen do when they give uplifting speeches during church services.

' 28. A *Democrat* is one who advocates big spending in the public sector.

29. Love is never having to say you're sorry.

30. A *democrat* is one who advocates the American form of government.

Apply Steps One (*reconstruct* the argument) and Two (check whether it depends on any *ambiguity*) to each of these arguments:

* 31. Because they are light, feathers dispel darkness.

32. The Russians are numerous. So Brezhnev must be numerous.

* 33. All angles of a triangle are equal to two right angles. ABC is an angle of a triangle. So ABC is equal to two right angles.

34. Whoever fails to lead a good life is no Christian. So every Christian leads a good life.

* 35. It is the government's job to care for national resources. But people's health is a national resource. So it is the government's job to care for people's health.

36. Bertha always turns in her cars after two years. Today she bought a new car. So in two years she will turn in a new car.

* 37. Because he aided the enemy, Daniel Ellsberg is a traitor.

38. All capitalists are not artists. So businessmen are not artists, since they are capitalists.

* 39. Senator Klaghorn represents his constituents, so his feelings must be much like theirs.

40. Being a Republican, Senator Klaghorn must have lost prestige after Watergate.

* 41. A miser can't be rich, because he doesn't have enough money.

42. Lars must be Protestant because he's a Swede.

* 43. A company that has discriminated against women in hiring ought now to *favor* women over men in hiring. That way it compensates women for the discrimination they have suffered.

44. Many people just don't believe, on religious or any other grounds, that homosexuality is wrong. Those who favor anti-sodomy laws are just trying to foist their own controversial religious beliefs on others. That violates the wall of separation between church and state.

* 45. Everyone, ultimately, is a hedonist—a pleasure-seeker. For everyone—even the so-called ascetic—does only what he thinks will give him the most satisfaction in the end. (This argument defends the doctrine known as psychological hedonism.)

46. Because they are obligated to shareholders to maximize profits, corporate managers should not pursue social responsibilities that conflict with the maximization of profits.

* 47. Young women who dress provocatively invite rape. So they have only themselves to blame when that is what happens.

9

Evaluating Premises

9.1. OVERVIEW OF STEP THREE: EVALUATE THE PREMISES

Since any statement about any subject could be a premise of an argument, you would be omniscient if you could tell the truth or falsity of every premise of every argument you might ever encounter. Whenever you study or otherwise learn about a subject, you extend the class of premises whose truth you are able to judge. There is no set of rules or criteria, no test or procedure for deciding the truth or even the plausibility of premises generally. With rare exceptions (such as inconsistent premises), you cannot say much about the truth or plausibility of premises without *some* knowledge of their subject matter.

All the same, if you are fairly typical of the audience to whom an argument is addressed, you are likely to know enough about the subject matter of its premises to find them plausible. Otherwise, the author has argued poorly: his premises are not sufficiently plausible relative to his intended audience. But that fact is itself a strong criticism of the premises.

To evaluate a premise, in most cases, you must both know something about its subject matter and apply your knowledge to that premise. The procedure I shall describe for evaluating premises does not tell you how to acquire the relevant knowledge; it tells you how to apply whatever knowledge you have.

Designed to help you uncover premises that are either false or not sufficiently plausible to support the conclusions drawn from them, the procedure consists of four tasks:

First, *read* each premise *critically*. This instruction is elaborated in §9.2.

Second, check whether the premises are *self-defeating* and whether any of them is *question-begging*—two especially blatant cases of premises not sufficiently plausible to support the conclusion drawn from them. These defects are explained in §9.3.

The third and fourth tasks normally are the most important: To every general premise, apply the tests of *immunity from counter-example* and *sufficient generality*. In effect, the first test requires of a premise that it not be too general; the second, that it be general enough. Explanations and illustrations of these tests are given in §§9.4 and 9.5.

Many faulty premises can be criticized without resort to the techniques just listed. Often you will come across premises that simply are debatable or questionable or obviously false or incompatible with some special knowledge you happen to have. If, at any point and for any reason, you find a premise to be false or at least questionable, you should say so.

9.2. READ CRITICALLY

The task of reading each premise critically consists of six subtasks:

One Carefully read a separate, complete formulation of each premise, stripped of extraneous matter. This includes tacit premises. Dwell a moment on each premise. Think about what it says, ignoring catchy, felicitous, or authoritative style and ignoring (for the moment, anyway) the source of the premise.

Most of the work involved in this subtask has already been accomplished at Step One (reconstruction). This subtask may be combined with Step One.

Made explicit, fully and separately formulated, and stripped of extraneous matter, a premise can appear problematic although it did not appear so (if it appeared at all) in the original text of the argument in question, witness Example 19 of Chapter 7.

Two Check whether you understand each term. If you do not, consult a dictionary or other source. This subtask is conveniently combined with Step Two.

Three Demand a tolerable measure of *clarity*. Without further explanation, a premise like "God is the ground of being" or "It is undemocratic to deny human rights" communicates nothing.

Technical jargon is common in mathematics, science, law, and elsewhere. It can enhance clarity, but only if it is clearly explained.

Work at understanding each premise, but do not be taken in. If someone advances a premise you do not understand, the fault is more likely his than yours. It is his job to convey his thoughts intelligibly. Do not automatically assume he is so intelligent his thoughts are over your head. His thoughts might be over his own head.

The importance of clarity is that its absence detracts from plausibility. It does this two ways: First, the less clear a premise is, normally, the less clearly true it is. Second, the less clear a premise is, the more likely it is that its author either is confused or else is trying to deceive his audience (and possibly himself) by wrapping a questionable contention in a cloak of obscurity.

Four Look carefully for partly *hidden assertions*. "Bertha has stopped beating her husband" obviously asserts that Bertha does not now beat her husband. Slightly less obviously, it also asserts that Bertha *used* to beat her husband. "The spy François Abdul Benito Wahrhaftig may get a new trial" asserts not only that Wahrhaftig may get a new trial but that Wahrhaftig is a spy. Make sure you notice *all* the assertions packed into each premise.

Often an apparently subtle change in one term packs a whole new *evaluational* assertion into a premise. Compare:

My opponent's proposed solution would cost $5 billion.

My opponent's panacea would cost $5 billion.

Both statements tell us that the opponent's proposed solution would cost $5 billion. The second adds that his proposal is unrealistic. Or compare:

Ignatz is very conservative politically.

Ignatz is a reactionary.

Both sentences tell us that Ignatz is very conservative politically. The second adds that it is bad to be that conservative.

Five Classify each premise as general or nongeneral. A *general statement* says something about all the members of some specified class. These statements are general:

All ravens are black.

No one loves a tax collector.

Except in unusual circumstances, it is wrong to break a promise.

These are *not* general:

Bertha drank the pitcherful.

The American Revolution occurred at the end of the eighteenth century.

Generality admits of degree. The wider the class to which a statement applies, or the fewer the particular entities it specifies, the more general it is. "Farrah loves professors" is less general than "All blondes love professors" but more general than "Farrah loves Tom," which is not general at all.

Relatively general statements merit special attention for three reasons: First, tacit premises normally are general. Second, there are simple but fruitful techniques for critically evaluating general premises of all sorts, regardless of subject matter; I discuss them in §§9.4 and 9.5. Third, it is good strategy to aim critical scrutiny at general principles that serve as tacit premises, linking express premises to conclusions; these tend to be comparatively unspecialized in subject matter, hence to require only comparatively general knowledge for their appraisal.

Six Fit each general premise, *when possible*, into one of these four fundamental categories:

> EMPIRICAL STATEMENTS purport to describe, predict, or explain observable phenomena. Examples: "All ravens are black." "E = mc²." Scientific knowledge consists largely of very general empirical statements.

> NORMATIVE STATEMENTS prescribe or evaluate behavior, character, procedures, institutions, art-works, and other things. Examples: "Hoarding fuel is morally wrong." "Saint Francis was a good person." "One should open a good Bordeaux four hours before drinking." "His data failed to verify the hypothesis, owing to insufficient controls in his experiment."

> MATHEMATICAL STATEMENTS concern properties of numbers, functions, and other mathematical objects. Examples: "$2 + 2 + 6$." "Every Boolean algebra is isomorphic to a field of sets."

> VERBAL STATEMENTS purport to be true (whether or not they really are true) by virtue of their *logical form* or the *meanings* of their component words. (Recall that a statement true by virtue of its logical form alone is a *logical truth*.) Examples of verbal truths: "Every bachelor is a bachelor." "No bachelor is married." Example of a false verbal statement: "By definition, every Republican is conservative." (This is clearly a verbal *statement*, even though not a verbal truth, thanks to the "by definition." Rarely are we blessed with such a clear clue.)

Classifying a premise this way helps one decide what type of knowledge one must possess to determine its truth.

Some statements probably fit none of the four categories. Example: "God loves you." Of these, some are hybrids. Example: "All ravens are black, and 2 + 2 = 4, and fuel-hoarding is wrong, and murder is perforce wrong." (Note that the last clause is verbal.)

Sometimes it is unclear whether a statement is empirical, normative, or verbal, because its author's intention is unknown. Example:

All democratic governments respect freedom of speech.

Bertha could have any of three reasons for making this statement: (1) She *defines* "democratic" to mean, among other things, "respectful of freedom of speech," making the statement a verbal truth. (2) She does not define "democratic" this way, but she believes that all democratic governments do, historically speaking, respect freedom of speech; this makes the statement empirical. (3) Using "democratic" as a fairly general term of political approbation, she makes the above statement in order *to voice her approval* of freedom of speech, so that the statement is normative.

Mathematical truths, such as "2 + 2 = 4," and verbal truths, such as "Every bachelor is a bachelor" and "No bachelor is male," have this in common: Their truth does not depend on what happens out in the world. They are *necessarily* true. They could not possibly have been false. Empirical truths, such as "All crows are black," are not thus necessary. Neither are most normative truths, such as "Hitler was evil."

Certain high-level normative generalizations, such as "It is wrong to break a promise made freely when keeping it would do no serious harm to anyone and would conflict with no other moral obligations," are arguably necessary: their truth does not seem to depend on what happens out in the world. But their necessity is not that clear: Some philosophers (noncognitivists) deny that such assertions are either true or false at all, let alone necessarily true, contending that they merely express feelings or attitudes or the like and do not state facts. Others say the truth of such statements is not necessary, contending that they could conceivably be false—depending, in the case of the so-called utilitarians, on what sorts of behavior tended to maximize aggregate happiness, or in the case of the so-called intuitionists, on what sorts of behavior possessed certain intuitively apprehensible right-making properties.

There seems to be less agreement about the truth of normative statements—especially moral and aesthetic judgments—than there is about the truth of statements of other sorts. Unlike scientific knowledge, normative knowledge does not constitute a growing, widely understood, generally accepted corpus. This often leads students to feel it is nearly pointless to *reason* about normative issues, that there is no reward in doing so. I hope to convince you, by example, that the three-step method of argument analysis not only applies to normative issues but takes us very far toward separating good from bad normative arguments, even if this method does not decisively determine which conclusions are true.

9.3. SUFFICIENT PLAUSIBILITY: SELF-DEFEATING AND QUESTION-BEGGING PREMISES

As a minimum test of sufficient plausibility, check whether the premises of the argument you are evaluating are *self-defeating* and whether any of them is *question-begging*.

Self-defeating premises *refute themselves:* assuming they are true, they must be false. Any *inconsistent* set of premises is perforce self-defeating. So is any set of premises that can be turned into an inconsistent set by adding some *platitudes*—some especially simple, glaring, uncontroversial truths.

Because consistency is determined by logical form, you do not have to know anything about the subject matter of the following argument to tell that its premises are inconsistent:

Example   1   Angelo the barber is a man who lives in Austin, Texas. He shaves all and only those men who live in Austin, Texas, and do not shave themselves. Therefore, Angelo the barber does not shave himself.

In case the inconsistency is not obvious, I can make it so by deducing an explicit contradiction from the two premises. Assume those premises. Then Angelo is a man who lives in Austin. So he cannot shave himself. For if he did shave himself, he would not be one of those whom Angelo shaved, which is to say he would not shave himself after all. But because, as just shown, Angelo does not shave himself, he must be one of those whom Angelo shaves. So Angelo both shaves himself and does not.

Nontechnical arguments with inconsistent premises are so rare that I do not recall ever having encountered a serious one. More common are arguments with *consistent but self-defeating* premises, such as this one:

Example   2   Those who would prohibit pornography in the name of morality forget that morality is a matter of private judgment. Everyone, even the opponent of pornography, has the right to do what he thinks is morally right, and no one has the right to stop him. Consequently, while those who think pornography is evil have every right not to read pornography, those who do *not* think pornography is evil also have the right *to read* it, and no one has the right to stop *them*.

Reconstruction:

Everyone has the right to do what he thinks is morally right. (express)

No one has the right to stop anyone from doing what the latter thinks is morally right. (express)

Not to think a thing is evil is to think it is morally right. (tacit)

∴ Those who do not think pornography is evil have the right to read it, and no one has the right to stop them.

Although the premises are consistent, we get an inconsistent set when we combine them with the following platitude:

Some people think it is morally right for them to read pornography, while others think it is morally right for them to stop anyone from reading pornography.

The combined set of statements is inconsistent, because it has the following inconsistent consequence: Someone has the right to read pornography, and no one has the right to stop him, and someone has the right to stop him. For assume the combined set. Then someone—call the person X—thinks it is morally right for him to read pornography, and thus, by virtue of the first and second premises, X has the right to read pornography and no one has the right to stop him. But by virtue of the platitude, someone else thinks it is morally right for him to stop X from reading pornography, so by the first premise, he has the right to stop X from reading pornography.

To be self-defeating, it is not enough for a set of premises to be inconsistent with some truth or other. *Any* false premise is inconsistent with *some* truth, notably its own negation. Rather, a *self-defeating* set of premises must be *inconsistent with some set of platitudes*—some set of especially simple, glaring, uncontroversial truths. In other words, a self-defeating premise-set falls at most slightly short of being formally inconsistent.

A *question-begging* premise dogmatically asserts a point at issue, a point that is closely related to the conclusion and ought to be proved, not merely asserted. (Question-begging premises are so-called because they "beg" or ask the speaker's opponents to grant or concede a question at issue.)

If this point is the very conclusion, or a patent paraphrase thereof, the argument is called *circular*: reasoning proceeds in a circle, from conclusion back round to itself. This argument is patently circular:

Example   3   Busing supporters are all Communists, because only a Communist would support busing.

More common and more interesting are arguments that are question-begging without being strictly circular. In such an argument, no premise is the *same* as the conclusion, yet some premise *closely related* to the conclusion *merely asserts* a point that *should be argued for,* because the intended audience are no more willing to grant the author this point than they are to grant him the conclusion itself.

Example 4   A Communist-sympathizer, Alger Hiss was doubtless willing and eager to betray his country to the Comintern. Therefore, he had a motive for committing espionage.

Reconstruction:

Alger Hiss was a Communist sympathizer. (express)

Every Communist sympathizer is (was, will be) willing and eager to betray his country to the Comintern. (tacit)

To be willing and eager to betray one's country is to have a motive for committing espionage. (tacit)

∴ Alger Hiss had a motive for committing espionage.

This argument is not quite circular—no premise is a patent paraphrase of the conclusion—yet its first premise is question-begging. For it blatantly asserts that Hiss's loyalty was to international Communism rather than to his country, and that is about as controversial as the conclusion, to which it is closely related in most people's minds. Whether it is so is a question that should not be begged—not simply given a "yes" or "no" answer—if one wants to enhance the credibility of the conclusion to any significant degree.

Example 5   You ought to believe that God exists, because it says so in the Bible.

Reconstruction:

It says in the Bible that God exists. (express)

Whatever it says in the Bible is true. (tacit)

∴ God exists.

This does not beg the question whether God exists. It does beg the closely related question whether what the Bible says is true. No one who doubts the conclusion would believe the tacit premise. Many people, indeed, believe the conclusion but not that premise.

For a premise of an argument to be question-begging, it must, in the minds of the argument's intended audience, be closely associated with the conclusion and about as debatable as the conclusion. How closely associated, and how debatable? I am afraid I cannot say exactly. To be question-begging is to have a trait that admits of degree and is therefore imprecise. But that does not mean one cannot tell whether arguments are question-begging. It just means there are likely to be many border-line cases. We often have little trouble classifying people as tall, short, fat, and thin, even though these traits are imprecise.

9.4. IMMUNITY FROM COUNTER-EXAMPLE

In this section and the next, I formulate two *tests* to apply to *general premises* of all sorts.

The first test is that of IMMUNITY FROM COUNTER EXAMPLE: Are there plausible counter-examples to the premise—situations in which what the premise says is plainly false?* If so, the premise evidently is false.

Example   6   We saw an interesting-looking bird at the San Diego Zoo last week. The sign said it was a swan. But that must have been a mistake, because the bird was black.

Reconstruction:

The interesting-looking bird we saw at the San Diego Zoo last week was black. (express)

No swan is black. (tacit)

∴ The interesting-looking bird we saw at the San Diego Zoo last week was not a swan.

Counter-example to the tacit premise: Black swans have been found in Australia.

Because the tacit premise is *empirical*, a merely *hypothetical* counter-example—an imagined rather than an observed case of black swans—would not have refuted this premise. In general, a counter-example to an *empirical* generalization must be an actual situation known to have occurred, not a mere hypothetical case. Reason: An empirical statement describes or explains the way the world actually is.

---

*This use of the expression "counter-example" is different from that introduced in Chapter 2. The two uses are related, though: A counter-example (in the sense of Chapter 2) to an *argument-form* is a counter-example (in the sense I am now introducing) to the *general statement* that every argument of that form with true premises has a true conclusion.

Qualification: A merely hypothetical counter-example can *weaken* (although it cannot conclusively refute) an empirical generalization, so long as it is more or less realistic—similar, that is, to actual cases. The more realistic it is, the more it weakens the generalization. Example: Someone conjectures that all wooden pencils are yellow. Quite certain that he is wrong but unable to produce a nonyellow wooden pencil or to cite a specific example of one, I describe the hypothetical case of a pencil manufacturer who wishes to distinguish his pencils from those of his competitors by painting his heliotrope. Because this example is quite realistic—because businessmen tend to reason in the manner described—the example casts doubt on the generalization, although it does not conclusively refute it.

Example 7   "You had suspected, my lord, that the late countess was killed right here, at Plywood Manor, by her girdle," said Chief Inspector Hornfby-Thifflesnwhyte to Reuben, Earl of Sandwich. "And you've been proved correct, by Jove! But I'm curious about your contention that you knew it all along. You had your suspicions, of course. Still, how could you really have *known* more than the Yard?"

"Well, why not, Inspector?" his lordship replied. "Unlike yourself, I believed very strongly that my wife was killed at Plywood Manor by her girdle. I was quite certain of it, as you realized. And I was right. Isn't that what it means *to know* something?"

Reconstruction:

I was quite certain that my wife was killed at Plywood Manor by her girdle. (express)

I was right that my wife was killed at Plywood Manor by her girdle. (express)

To know that something is so means to be quite certain that it is so and to be right that it is so. (express)

∴ I knew that my wife was killed at Plywood Manor by her girdle.

Counter-example to the third premise: Ignatz answered "yes" to an examination question, although he was totally unfamiliar with its subject matter, because he had answered "no" to the previous question and was quite certain that every "no" answer was followed by a "yes" answer. But he was wrong to believe that every "no" was followed by a "yes." He also was wrong to answer "no" to the preceding question. He was lucky, though: his "yes" answer was correct. So he was quite certain that the correct answer was "yes" and right about that. Yet he can hardly be said to have *known* that the correct answer was "yes." His reason, after all, was totally wrong.

As this illustrates, a counter-example to a *verbal* generalization can be merely hypothetical. It can be an imagined case rather than an actually observed one. That is because a verbal statement purports to tell us, not merely what *is* the case, but what *must be* the case, given the meanings of the words it contains. It therefore purports to characterize *all possible* cases, hypothetical as well as actual. So if it fails to hold in some merely hypothetical case, it is false. That is, a merely hypothetical counter-example is enough to refute it.

Example   8   They say publication of inside information about the C.I.A. is dangerous. Maybe so. Still I strongly oppose the use of court injunctions to prevent publication of such information. This is a free country, after all. Everyone has the right to publish any information he wishes about the government. *Dangerous* information is no exception. (Isn't "danger" always the censor's excuse?)

Reconstruction:

Everyone has the right to publish any information about the government. (express)

Information about the C.I.A. is information about the government. (tacit)

If someone has the right to do something, any action by the government to prevent him from doing it would be wrong. (tacit)

A court injunction is an action by the government. (tacit)

∴ A court injunction to prevent someone from publishing inside information about the C.I.A. would be wrong.

Counter-example to the first premise: During wartime, the enemy sympathizer François Abdul Benito Wahrhaftig would publish the departure times of troop ships, virtually ensuring their destruction and making an enemy victory much more likely, unless he were prevented by government censors. Because such censorship surely is justified, Wahrhaftig has no right to publish the information.

In this argument, the errant premise is *normative*, and the counter-example to it is *hypothetical* (though fairly realistic). Hypothetical counter-examples often suffice to refute normative generalizations. Because, for the most part, the latter tell us how the world *should be* rather than how it *is*, they tend not to depend very much on the way the world actually happens to be. They usually are meant to prescribe for all or at least a wide range of possible situations, hypothetical as well as actual.

Sometimes, though, a normative generalization is supposed to hold only in actual situations, or at least situations that are realistic in certain respects. A counter-example to such a statement must be an actual one, or at least one that is realistic in the relevant respects. Example:

> One should do nothing that is likely to benefit the Ku Klux Klan.

You cannot refute this normative generalization by citing an hypothetical example in which the K.K.K. is a good rather than an evil organization. For the statement obviously is meant to depend on the fact that the K.K.K. is the evil organization we know it to be. You can, however, cite as a counter-example a hypothetical situation in which some widely beneficial deed (a tax cut, say) is likely to benefit the K.K.K. along with a large number of deserving people and in which there is no feasible way to exclude the K.K.K. from the benefits.

When in doubt, keep your counter-examples to normative generalizations as realistic as possible.

Some people are puzzled by the use of merely hypothetical examples, especially ones that seem highly contrived, to test normative principles. We only use such principles to guide or evaluate actions (or whatever) in actual situations. So why demand that they yield plausible results in other situations?

The reason is this: If a normative principle yields no anomalous prescriptions even in hypothetical situations contrived for the purpose of refutation, it is all the more worthy of our confidence in actual situations. On the other hand, if the principle yields an anomalous prescription in some merely hypothetical situation, that increases the danger that it will yield unacceptable prescriptions in actual situations too. Testing normative generalizations against hypothetical examples is much like testing empirical generalizations against experimental (as opposed to observational) evidence: If an empirical generalization yields no false prediction even in laboratory situations created for the purpose of falsification, it is all the more worthy of our confidence in less contrived situations. And if it yields a false prediction in some laboratory situation, that increases the danger that it will yield false predictions in noncontrived situations too. Think of hypothetical counter-examples as experiments conducted in the laboratory of one's imagination.

The relation of a normative principle to actual and hypothetical situations (or of an empirical generalization to observational and experimental situations) is depicted thus:

	confirming situations (positive cases, paradigm examples)	unclear situations	disconfirming situations (negative cases, counter-examples)
actual situations	test cases	intended applications	test cases
hypothetical situations	test cases	////////	test cases

We *use* the principle to guide us in *actual but unclear* situations—ones in which we have more confidence in a well-conceived, well-tested principle than in our concrete normative judgments. We *test* the principle by applying it to *clear* situations—ones in which we have more confidence in our concrete normative judgments than in any principle. These include *confirming* situations, in which what the principle says is plausible, and *dis*confirming situations (counter-examples), in which what the principle says is implausible. Of course, if the principle is a good one, there are no situations of the latter type. We get a tougher test if we broaden the class of clear situations to include merely hypothetical ones. The advantage of doing this is that our confidence in the principle is enhanced if it passes the test. The likely objection to doing this—to allowing merely hypothetical examples to count against the principle—is that we need never *apply* the principle in such situations. But the same is true of the clear, actual situations. Both are needed only for testing. They are no less important on that account.

Whether something is a counter-example to a general premise can be debatable—as debatable as the premise itself.

Example 9   Despite grave provocations, it would be wrong for Lesotho to go to war with Liechtenstein, because it always is wrong to wage war.

Reconstruction:

It always is wrong to wage war. (express)

∴ It would be wrong for Lesotho to wage war against Liechtenstein.

Putative counter-example to the premise, which is normative: It was not wrong for the United States to wage war against Japan and Germany in World War II.

The trouble is that the likely proponents of the premise are thorough-going pacifists. They simply would not agree that the cited case really is a counter-example. They would contend that it *was* wrong for the United States to wage war against Japan and Germany in World War II.

Even when a putative counter-example to a general premise is not universally accepted as a counter-example, it can still *weaken* the premise: although it did not decisively refute the premise, it could diminish the premise's plausibility.

9.5. SUFFICIENT GENERALITY

The second test is that of SUFFICIENT GENERALITY: Is there some natural way to make the premise in question *more general*—to apply it to a wider class of cases, to replace some noun, verb, or adjective therein by a more general one? If so, is there any good reason not to do so? In other words, is there some *relevant difference* between the cases to which the premise already is applied and the others in the wider class—some difference that would justify applying the premise to the former cases only? If not, the premise fails the Sufficient Generality test.

This does *not refute* the premise. What it does is give us grounds for insisting that the author is committed to a more general premise. The more general premise extends the original premise to a more inclusive class of cases; the original premise restricts the more general version to a less inclusive class of cases. Because there is no evident reason for the restriction—no evident difference between the cases in the less inclusive class and the others in the more inclusive class that would justify apply-ing the premise to the former cases only—there is no evident reason for asserting the original premise except that one accepts the more general version: the generalized premise is the author's likely reason for assert-ing the original.

The test of Sufficient Generality is useful as a critical tool because the more general of two statements often is the easier to criticize. Applying the test is much like trying to discover tacit premises If there is a natural way to generalize a given premise and no evident reason not to do so, then the generalized premise is a likely reason for asserting the original premise, hence a likely unstated assumption of the author's. It differs from a tacit premise this way: A tacit premise is an unstated *linking* assumption—an unstated logical link between express premises and conclusion. A generalization of an express premise is an unstated *supporting* or *underlying* assumption—an unstated reason for asserting the express premise.

If an author does not accept a generalization of one of his premises, he must either have a reason for not generalizing his premise that way or else give up or modify his premise.

To apply the test of Sufficient Generality to the premise:

The Podunk Anthropology Department should hire more men,

you should ask: Why *men* rather than *people*? What relevant difference is there between men and women—what difference that would justify hiring more men but not more women? An answer might be that men make better anthropologists. But if that is implausible, the premise must either be found suspect or else made more general—which could impair the argument in which it occurs.

Again, faced with the premise:

By and large, a politician will advocate practically any position if he thinks that will help him win elections,

you should ask: Is there any reason not to ascribe similar hypocrisy to other vocations? Maybe there is. Maybe there is a somewhat plausible explanation of why politicians are peculiarly hypocritical. But if not, the premise must be generalized to other vocations (certain ones, anyway) or rejected. This does *not* mean there is *anything wrong* with the premise or the argument in which it occurs. It just means we may reasonably attribute a generalized version of the premise to the argument's author and that any good criticism of the generalized premise counts as a good criticism (not necessarily a devastating one) of the argument.

Or consider:

One should keep a promise made freely and with full knowledge, unless one is released by the promisee, or else keeping the promise turns out, unexpectedly, to be extremely costly or difficult.

Why not generalize this to the requirement that *all* promises be kept? Is there a relevant difference between those promises that this statement requires one to keep and other promises? Yes. Compare, for example, a promise made to a villain under threat of torture and death, hence not made freely, with an ordinary promise. Only in the latter case did the promisor *voluntarily incur* an obligation. Surely that is a relevant difference. Surely that is a reason for saying that only in the second case does the promisor *have* any obligation.

Example 10   There is no god. For if there were, it would be perceived by the five senses. But none is thus perceived.

Reconstruction:

> If there were a god, it would be perceived by the five senses. (express)
>
> No god is perceived by the five senses. (express)
>
> ∴ There is no god.

There is no evident reason not to generalize the first premise this way:

> Whatever there is must be perceived by the five senses.

That is, there is no evident difference between gods and other things that would explain why gods must be perceived by the five senses while other things need not be. If anything, it is the other way round. But the generalized premise runs afoul of this counter-example: There is a prime number between five and eleven. Because it is a number rather than a material object or event or a perceptual attribute, it cannot be perceived by the five senses.

This illustrates how to *combine* the tests of Sufficient Generality and Immunity from Counter-Example. The first premise of Example 10 is hard to criticize directly and decisively. But there is a natural way to generalize it, no evident reason not to generalize it that way, and a decisive counter-example to the generalized version. The idea behind the combined test is that one cannot immunize one's premises from counter-examples by restricting their generality unless there is a plausible reason for the restriction. So if there is no plausible reason not to generalize a premise a certain way, a counter-example to the generalized version refutes the original.

Example 11   *Of course* we should hire Ignatz in preference to Bertha. True, they're equally qualified candidates. But Ignatz is a *man*.

Reconstruction:

> We should hire a man in preference to a woman when the two are equally qualified candidates. (tacit)
>
> Ignatz is a man. (express)
>
> Bertha is a woman. (tacit)
>
> Ignatz and Bertha are equally qualified candidates. (express)
>
> ∴ We should hire Ignatz in preference to Bertha.

In the absence of a relevant difference between men and women—a difference that would justify giving job-preference to any man over any equally qualified woman—the first premise must be rejected or generalized. The simplest generalization extends the premise to women, so that it applies not just to men but to all people:

> We should hire any person in preference to any other person when the two are equally qualified candidates.

But this is open to an obvious counter-example: Say two or more people apply for the job in question. According to the generalized statement, each should be given preference over every other, hence none should be hired.

A less simple generalization extends the original statement not to *all* women but to those who are heads of households, restricting the general "women" category to those who are not heads of households:

> We should hire any man, or any woman who is head of a household, in preference to any woman who is not head of a household whenever the two are equally qualified candidates.

Is this sufficiently general? Is there a relevant difference between men and female household heads, on the one hand, and women who are not household heads, on the other? True, those in the latter category are not heads of households. But some men in the former category are not heads of households either. So *that* is not a relevant difference. A relevant difference between A's and B's must be a difference between *each* A and *each* B.

We might save a version of the original premise by a combination of generalizing and ungeneralizing:

> We should hire any household head in preference to anyone who is not a household head when the two are equally qualified candidates.

But then we destroy the argument's validity unless we add premises to the effect that Ignatz is a household head while Bertha is not—premises that could well be false, depending on who Ignatz and Bertha are.

9.6. EXAMPLES

The time has come to put the pieces together and apply the whole three-step procedure to some arguments of familiar sorts.

Example 12   Without legal sanctions, almost no one would pay taxes, because almost no one would pay taxes unless it were in his self-interest to pay.

Reconstruction:

> Almost no one would pay taxes unless it were in his self-interest to pay taxes. (express)
>
> Without legal sanctions, it would be in (almost) no one's self-interest to pay taxes. (tacit)
>
> ∴ Without legal sanctions, almost no one would pay taxes.

Two generalizations of the first premise:

> Almost no one would do *anything* that was not in his self-interest.
>
> Almost no one would do anything *of a public-spirited character* that was not in his self-interest.

I see no reason not to generalize the premise one of these ways—no reason to suppose that tax-paying is *peculiarly* self-interested.

Especially in political, economic, and philosophical discussions, the relational expression:

(*)   —— is in . . .'s self-interest

can be *ambiguous*. We might construe it in a narrow, colloquial way, so that it stands for one among several reasons or motives for action. Then both generalized premises, which are empirical, are open to numerous counter-examples: People who vote, who work for political campaigns and causes, who give to charity, or who stop to help accident victims normally are not acting in their own self-interest.

We can save the generalized premises by construing (*) much more broadly and less colloquially, so that it means something like:

—— would satisfy (please, gratify) . . .

But this makes the second premise less plausible—not hopelessly implausible, just less plausible than it seemed at first to be. For all I know, many people pay taxes from a sense of civic duty more than a fear of sanctions. A dual interpretation of (*) makes the argument invalid. So whichever way we interpret (*), the argument is weaker than it seemed at first to be.

Note once again that my three-step method sometimes uncovers an argument's *weaknesses* without yielding a knockdown *refutation*. That is to be expected. Although some arguments are thoroughly bad, many are not. But of these, hardly any is airtight if it has an interesting conclusion.

Example 13   It was wrong to hit Bertha back, Ignatz, because two wrongs don't make a right.

Reconstruction:

It is not right to respond to one wrong with another wrong. (express)

Ignatz's hitting Bertha back was responding to one wrong with another wrong. (tacit)

∴ It was wrong for Ignatz to hit Bertha back.

I rewrote the highly abbreviated express premise to make the argument's form clearer and more nearly valid, minimizing the number and complexity of additional validating premises. Thus reconstructed, the argument is *circular*. The tacit premise baldly asserts, among other things, that Ignatz's hitting Bertha back was a wrong. If the circularity was not obvious at first, that is because the errant premise is tacit—a common occurrence.

We can eliminate the circularity by weakening the tacit premise thus:

Ignatz's hitting Bertha back was responding to one wrong act with an act of a sort that *normally* is wrong (wrong when not a response to some wrong act).

But this invalidates the argument.

We can restore validity by construing the first premise as shorthand for the following:

It is wrong to respond to one wrong act with an act of a sort that is normally wrong (wrong when not a response to some wrong act).

But counter-examples beset this new premise: Almost every case of justified self-defense, criticism, complaint, blame, or punishment is a case of responding to a wrong act with an act of a sort that is normally wrong (wrong when not a response to some wrong act).

Example 13 illustrates a common trait of arguments: Often an argument has one of several defects, depending on how exactly we interpret it. We can construe Example 13 as circular, or we can remove the circularity and construe it as invalid, or we can construe it as noncircular and valid but with a premise that fails the test of Immunity from Counter-Example.

Example 14   Head Start programs have been reasonably effective, I
               think, and that justifies their continuance. Oh, I
               realize some people disagree. But if they are right—if
               Head Start programs have been *in*effective—then that
               reflects an inadequate level of funding.

Reconstruction:

If Head Start programs have been effective, that justifies their
continuance. (express)

If Head Start programs have been *in*effective, that shows that their
level of funding has been inadequate. (express)

To show that a program's level of funding has been inadequate is
(among other things) to justify the program's continuance (at a
higher level of funding). (tacit)

∴ The continuance of Head Start programs is justified.

No significant ambiguities are evident. Generalization of the second
premise:

If a government program has been ineffective, that shows that its
level of funding has been inadequate.

Maybe there is a reason not to generalize the premise this way; maybe
there is something special about the Head Start programs that makes
any ineffectiveness in *them* the result of inadequate funding. But that is
by no means obvious. In the absence of a further argument to this effect,
we have every right to attribute the more general premise to the argument's author. We have been given no reason to apply the premise *just*
to Head Start programs. But the generalized premise is implausible:
surely *some* government programs have been ineffective for reasons
other than inadequate funding. Any such program is a counter-example.

Example 15   If *I* hadn't bought the stolen fur coat, someone else
               would have bought it, and the harm (if any) would
               have been the same—but I wouldn't have gotten the
               coat. So there really was nothing wrong with my buy-
               ing it.

Reconstruction:

The harm from my not buying the stolen fur coat would have been
the same as the harm from my buying it. (express)

> If the harm from not doing something would have been the same as the harm from doing it, then there is nothing wrong with doing it. (tacit)

∴ There was nothing wrong with my buying the stolen fur coat.

No significant ambiguities are evident. Counter-example to the second premise: I borrow your car and promise to return it by Friday. Come Friday, I find I still need the car. Unfortunately, so do you. Our needs are equal. So the harm (to you) from my not returning it would be the same as the harm (to me) from my returning it. Still, it obviously would be wrong not to return your car.

Example 16   It is wrong for the law to interfere with voluntary sexual activities, because they concern no one but their participants.

Reconstruction:

> Voluntary sexual activities concern no one but their participants. (express)
>
> The law should not interfere with any voluntary activity that concerns no one but its participants. (tacit)

∴ The law should not interfere with voluntary sexual activities.

"Concerns" is ambiguous. In the *psychological sense,* to say that X concerns Y is to say that Y *cares about* X. In the *normative sense,* to say that X concerns Y is to say that X is Y's *proper business*—that Y has a *right to interfere with* X.

In the normative sense, the second premise is plausible. But the first is question-begging: It says no one has a right to interfere with voluntary sexual activities. And that not only is very similar to the conclusion; it is stronger and more debatable than the conclusion.

In the psychological sense of "concerns," the second premise says the law should not interfere with voluntary sexual activities that nonparticipants do not care about. Arguable counter-example: Suppose no one cared about voluntary sexual relations between adults and young children, or about voluntary experimentation by young children with dangerous drugs. Such activities would plausibly still be wrong. Therefore, the second premise, so interpreted, is not too plausible.

With "concerns" interpreted psychologically, the first premise says no one cares about voluntary sexual activities except participants. I think you will agree that there are many counter-examples to this empirical generalization.

The first premise can be *generalized*, thus:

> Voluntary *activities* concern no one but their participants.

Is there any reason not to generalize the first premise this way—any relevant difference between voluntary *sexual* activities and other voluntary activities? None is evident. So it seems reasonable to attribute the more general version to the argument's author. But that version is even more open than the original to counter-examples. The world teems with busybodies.

Example 17   Because everyone has the right to publish whatever information he wishes to publish, the *New York Times* had the right to publish the *Pentagon Papers*.

Reconstruction:

> Everyone has the right to publish whatever information he wishes to publish. (express)
>
> The *Pentagon Papers* is information. (tacit)
>
> The *New York Times* wished to publish the *Pentagon Papers*. (tacit)
>
> ∴ The *New York Times* had the right to publish the *Pentagon Papers*.

"Information" is ambiguous. The second premise is plausible only if "information" is interpreted broadly, so that information includes specific texts, not just facts reported therein. But then the first premise is false: any copyrighted text is a counter-example.

We can avoid this objection by interpreting "information" so that information includes both facts and publicly owned texts but not copyrighted texts. Thus, the argument does not *depend* on the ambiguity of "information."

Still, there are problems with the first premise. It can be generalized thus:

> Everyone has the right to *disseminate* whatever information he wishes.

There are obvious counter-examples to this—yelling fire in a crowded theater, for one. Publishing the times of troop-ship departures during a war is a counter-example to the original premise as well as the generalized version.

Example 18   If Turkey wants to use U.S. foreign aid to finance a program whereby homosexual relations are encouraged as a means of curbing population growth, then the United States has no right to prevent this. For any country has the right to act according to its own moral beliefs, however opposed those beliefs may be to our own.

Reconstruction:

> Any country has the right to act according to its own moral beliefs. (express)
>
> For Turkey to use U.S. foreign aid to finance a program whereby homosexual relations are encouraged as a means of curbing population growth is for Turkey to act according to its own moral beliefs. (tacit)
>
> Turkey is a country. (tacit)
>
> The United States is a country. (tacit)
>
> If a country has the right to do something, no country has the right to prevent the former from doing it. (tacit)
>
> ∴ If Turkey wants to use U.S. foreign aid to finance a program whereby homosexual relations are encouraged as a means of curbing population growth, then the United States has no right to prevent this.

"Prevent" is ambiguous. If it is interpreted so that the mere refusal to finance some activity counts as preventing that activity, then the fifth premise is false: every case of another country pursuing a policy that it plainly has a right to pursue (building roads, say) but that the United States has no obligation to finance and indeed has refused to finance is a counter-example. If, on the other hand, "prevent" is so interpreted that the mere refusal to finance an activity does not count as *preventing* it, then the conclusion is a good deal less interesting than it seemed at first to be. So the argument depends on an ambiguity.

It also has a *self-defeating* set of premises. We get an inconsistent set when we combine the first and fifth premises with this platitude:

> In some cases, for the United States to prevent other countries from acting according to *their* own moral beliefs is for the United States to act according to *its* own moral beliefs.

Example 19   Here's what's wrong with laws against pornography: To enforce such laws is to prevent some people from reading what they want. But those who would do this would thereby do unto others what they would not have others do unto them.

Reconstruction:

To enforce laws against pornography is to prevent some people from reading what they want to read. (express)

Those who would enforce laws against pornography would not want to be prevented by others from reading what they want to read. (tacit)

It is wrong for anyone to do something to others that he would not want those others to do to him. (tacit)

∴ It is wrong for anyone to enforce laws against pornography.

Counter-example to the third premise: Dr. Krankheit, whose health is perfect, performs a needed surgical operation on Ignatz, a nondextrous grade-school dropout who swoons at the sight of blood. But Dr. Krankheit would not want their roles reversed.

I took the language of the third premise from the third sentence of Example 19, a sentence that functions as an intermediate step. But perhaps that language is just shorthand for the following, more generous formulation of the Golden Rule:

It is wrong for anyone to do something to others if he would not want them to do a *morally similar* thing to him *in morally similar circumstances.*

Altering the third premise this way invalidates the argument. We can restore validity by adding the following premise:

To enforce laws against pornography and to prevent those who would enforce such laws from reading what they want to read are to do morally similar things in morally similar circumstances.

But this premise weakens the argument considerably, making it question-begging or nearly so. What is at issue, in a way, is whether preventing people from reading pornography *is* morally similar to preventing people from reading nonpornographic literature.

EXERCISES

Evaluate the following arguments. In setting out your work, *reconstruct* each argument according to Step One, but mention only those subsequent steps or parts thereof that yield criticisms. It is quite possible in some cases for two students to come up with different criticisms, the arguments in question being quite good.

* 1. We should not outlaw prostitution, because to do so is to legislate morality.

  2 We should not outlaw prostitution, because prostitution harms no one with the possible exception of voluntary participants.

* 3. What's wrong with pornography? It serves no purpose but to stimulate lust, that's what.

  4. More and more, nowadays, doctors are allowing terminally ill patients who are wracked by unbearable pain or are hopelessly comatose to die, making little or no attempt to save their lives. Why is this practice allowed to go on? *Mercy* killing is still *killing*, after all. And there is no justification for doctors' killing their patients.

* 5. To allow every person unbounded freedom of speech must always be, on the whole, advantageous to the state; for it is highly conducive to the interests of the community that each individual should enjoy a liberty, perfectly unlimited, of expressing his statements. (Whately, *Elements of Logic*)

  6. Why must you find Ignatz guilty? Because his crime was an especially dastardly and heinous one.

* 7. Democratic governments are naturally more popular than others, because they are popularly elected.

  8. The Vietnamese government is not democratic, because it does not protect individual rights.

* 9. Because no evil should be allowed that good may come of it, punishment should be abolished.

  10. He who believes himself always to be right in his opinion lays claims to infallibility. But you always believe yourself to be right in your opinion. So you lay claims to infallibility. (Whately, *Elements of Logic*)

* 11. Not everyone has the right of private judgment in religious matters, because it is not possible for everyone to be right in his judgment.

  12. The western window through which he had stared so intently has, I noticed, one peculiarity above all windows in the house—it commands the nearest outlook onto the moor. There is an opening between two trees which enables one from this point of view to look right down upon it, while from all other windows it is only a distant glimpse which can be obtained. It follows, therefore, that Barrymore, since only this window would serve his purpose, must have been looking out for something or somebody upon the moor. (Arthur Conan Doyle, *The Hound of the Baskervilles*)

* 13 I oppose laws against "abnormal" sexual practices, because such laws prevent people from leading their lives as they please.

  14. Those who refuse to indulge in a practice should not make its rules. So Catholic bishops should not tell people how to have sex.

* 15. In a democracy like ours, the government should do whatever a majority want. So if a majority want prayers in the public schools, that's what we should have.

16. My opponent, Alderman McGraft, is a liar. He said the rate of increase of violent crime in Metropolis decreased this year. But recently released FBI statistics show that the rate this year is as high as last year.

* 17. People should not be allowed to allocate their Social Security contributions to the retirement program they think is best, else many will make poor choices.

18. The peculiar evil of silencing the expression of an opinion is that it is robbing the human race, posterity as well as the existing generation. . . . If the opinion is right, they are deprived of the opportunity of exchanging error for truth; if wrong, they lose, what is almost as great a benefit, the clearer perception and livelier impression of truth produced by its collision with error. (John Stuart Mill)

* 19. A woman has the right to have an abortion, because everyone has the right to perform *private actions*—actions affecting the legitimate interests of no one but the actor.

20. Many people do not believe, on religious or other grounds, that mercy killing is wrong. Those who favor laws against mercy killing are just trying to foist their own controversial religious beliefs on others. That violates the wall of separation between church and state.

* 21. It's unfair for Hindus to try to outlaw beef consumption, preventing even non-Hindus from eating beef. Would Hindus want their Moslem countrymen to do the same to them by outlawing pork consumption, preventing Hindus and other non-Moslems from eating pork?

22. Laws against pornography and blasphemy do not violate freedom of speech. Freedom of speech is the freedom to say what you want so long as that is not opposed by a majority.

* 23. In a way, even Hitler was a moral person, because he did what *he* thought was morally right.

24. Alimony is unreasonable. That a man has supported his wife thus far is no reason for him to have to support her for the rest of her life.

* 25. We've got to crack down on civil disobedience, because we cannot allow each citizen to decide for himself which laws he'll obey.

26. You can't really condemn term-paper-writing companies. The actual wrongdoing is not by them but by the students who use their services.

* 27. It would be better for management to allow theft by employees than to crack down. For the crackdown, even if effective, would likely be more costly than the theft itself.

28. Compared with smoking cigarettes, the failure to have an annual dental examination does trivial harm to one's health. Consequently, no rational person who troubles to have an annual dental exam would ever smoke cigarettes.

* 29 A company that has discriminated against women in hiring ought now to *favor* women over men in hiring. That way it compensates women for the discrimination they have suffered.

30. Prohibitionists and antipornography crusaders are not being unfair (as often is alleged) to those who do not share their views. For they do not propose to impose upon others restrictions they would not gladly have imposed upon themselves.

10

Argument and Explanation

10.1. ARGUING, EXPLAINING, AND ARGUING BY EXPLAINING

This homely piece of reasoning could be an argument to show that Ignatz's windows are closed:

Example   1   Ignatz's windows are closed because he is running his air conditioner.

More likely it is an *explanation* of *why* Ignatz's windows are closed. Either way, we can reconstruct it as follows:

Ignatz is running his air conditioner. (express premise)

Whenever Ignatz runs his air conditioner, he closes his windows. (tacit premise)

∴ Ignatz's windows are closed.

Arguments and explanations are much alike. Like an argument, an explanation gives a reason ("Ignatz is running his air conditioner") for something ("Ignatz's windows are closed"). It reasons, let us say, from one or more *explanatory premises* to an *explanatory conclusion*. Like an argument, an explanation involves the contention (usually implicit) that its conclusion follows from its premises—often deductively, sometimes in an appropriate nondeductive sense. Like an argument, an explanation can have tacit premises or a tacit conclusion. Like an argument, an explanation can be evaluated, up to a point, by means of my three-step procedure.

For all their similarities, arguments and explanations are meant to do different jobs, a difference that begets others. An argument is meant to *show that* its conclusion is true; an explanation, to *explain why* its conclusion is true. An argument is meant to get some target audience to believe its conclusion. An explanation usually is addressed to an audience who already believe the conclusion but wish to know why it is true. An argument aims at conviction; an explanation, at understanding.

For this reason, the premises of a good argument must be plausible enough to support the conclusion—to enhance its credibility—while those of a good explanation need not be. Such is not the purpose of explanation. Typically, the conclusion of an explanation already is known to be true; the explanation, if successful, explains why it is true. Often this involves premises also known to be true—laws of physics, for example. But often it does not. Often, indeed, explanatory premises are less plausible than the conclusions they explain. Far from *lending* credibility *to* their explanatory conclusions, they *draw* credibility *from* those conclusions. Take Example 1: As an explanation, it would likely be offered to someone who knew that Ignatz's windows were closed but wondered why. Unlike the conclusion, the stated premise would not have been known to be true. It would gain credibility precisely from being a good explanatory premise. The statement that Ignatz is running his air conditioner, that is, would gain credibility from its success in explaining Ignatz's closed windows.

Sometimes, to be sure, a belief gains credibility when a sufficiently plausible explanation of its truth is produced. Example: Having heard what sounds like a lion's roar coming from a railroad train, I remain skeptical of my own perception until a disembarking passenger, made up and attired as a clown, explains the roar by pointing out that the train is carrying a circus. And sometimes a belief loses credibility when no sufficiently plausible explanation of its truth is produced. Example: Having long taken for granted that girls are born intellectually inferior to boys, Ignatz wonders why. Unable to find a plausible explanation in terms of genetics, fetal development, or anything else, he comes to give up his explanatory conclusion in favor of another. Instead of trying to explain why girls are born intellectually inferior to boys, he now tries to explain *why he believed* that girls are born intellectually inferior to boys. In this he has greater success.

Good explanatory premises must enjoy some measure of plausibility. The more plausible they are, other things equal, the better. Still, they need not meet the standards of plausbility appropriate to the premises of an argument: they need not be plausible enough to enhance the credibility of the conclusions they are used to explain. They need only be plausible enough to be accepted by dint of their explanatory value— plausible enough not to be rejected in the face of explanatory success.

An explanatory premise not previously accepted as true is an *hypothesis*—a conjecture or speculation provisionally assumed to see what follows from it. To the extent that an hypothesis is a good explanatory premise, we have reason to believe it: explanatory success bestows credibility on it. The explanatory premise that Ignatz is run-

ning his air conditioner was a mere hypothesis. A conjecture or speculation not previously accepted as true, it gained credibility from being a
good or reasonable or likely explanation of why Ignatz's windows are
closed.

Although to explain something is not to argue for it, one often argues
by explaining. The conclusion of one's argument, in such a case, is not
the *explanatory* conclusion; it is an explanatory *premise*. The explanatory conclusion is rather a premise of one's argument. In explaining that
soandso is the case because suchandsuch is the case, one thereby argues
that suchandsuch is the case because soandso is. One defends an
hypothesis ("Ignatz is running his air conditioner") on the ground that
it best explains something ("Ignatz's windows are closed") previously
accepted. The latter is regarded as *evidence for* the hypothesis. Where A
is the hypothesis and E the previously accepted statement, the picture is
the following:

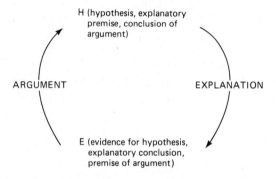

When there are additional, nonhypothetical explanatory premises, P_1,
..., P_n, they serve as premises of the argument as well as the explanation. One contends that E and P_1, ..., P_n are true and that H together
with P_1, ..., P_n best explain E and concludes that H is true. Let us call P_1,
..., P_n *background premises*. Here is the general picture.

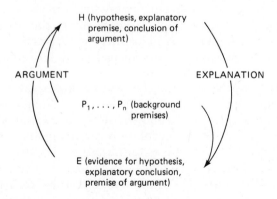

To cover situations in which there seem to be more than one *hypothetical* explanatory premise, let us regard H as the conjunction of them all. Example:

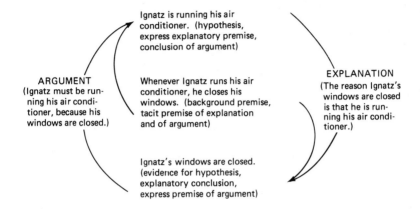

You have doubtless observed that Example 1 (including the tacit premise) is deductively valid as an explanation but not as an argument. Having read §1.4, you know, of course, that we can make any argument deductively valid by adding as a premise:

$$\text{If}\underline{\hspace{2cm}}\text{then} \ldots,$$

filling the first blank with the other premises and the second with the conclusion. This lets us treat the argument as deductive without any impairment, but without any improvement either: the added premise does not enhance the conclusion's credibility. So let us keep things simple by construing arguments of this sort as nondeductive.

Example 2   We know that all the swans examined so far are white. This is best explained by the hypothesis that all swans are white.

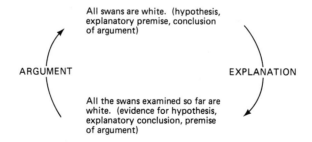

This example could be intended as either an argument or an explanation or (most likely) both.

Construed as an argument, Example 2 is *inductive* in the *narrow sense* explained in § 1.5: the conclusion ("All swans are white") *generalizes* the information contained in the premise ("All the swans examined so far are white"). All inductive arguments in the narrow sense can be regarded as reverse explanations (broadly but usefully construed). But not all arguments of the reverse-explanation variety are inductive in the narrow sense. Not all have conclusions that generalize the information contained in their premises, witness the argument from "Ignatz's windows are closed" to "Ignatz is running his air conditioner." (The important category, practically and theoretically, is not that of inductive arguments, but that of reverse-explanation arguments, so long as the word "explanation" is construed broadly enough to encompass the likes of "All swans are white.")

Construed as explanations, Examples 1 and 2 are deductively valid. But not all acceptable explanations are deductively valid.

Example   3   Senator Julep voted against the 1965 Voting Rights Act because he represented a Southern state (a one-time Confederate state).

Reconstruction:

Senator Julep represented a Southern state. (express explanatory premise)

Most senators who represented Southern states voted against the 1965 Voting Rights Act. (tacit explanatory premise)

∴ Senator Julep voted against the 1965 Voting Rights Act.

This obviously is invalid, although objectionably so only if construed as deductive. We can make it valid by strengthening the tacit premise as follows:

Every senator who represented a Southern state voted against the 1965 Voting Rights Act.

But this is too strong. It happens to be false. Even if you did not know that, you would probably find it questionable. Generosity counsels reconstructing the explanation the first way and construing it as nondeductive.

Although an argument of the reverse-explanation type might consist of nothing more than an explanation in reverse, it also might contain some explicit argumentation to the effect that the explanatory hypothesis is the right or best or most reasonable one.

Example 4   Ignatz's windows are closed. There are three likely explanations of this: Either Ignatz is away on a trip, or he finds it too cold to open his windows, or he is running his air conditioner. Because Ignatz's lights are on and his car is in the driveway with the garage door open, the first hypothesis is unlikely. And because it has been very warm all day, the second is implausible. That leaves the third: Ignatz must be running his air conditioner.

10.2. EVALUATING EXPLANATIONS AND EVALUATING ARGUMENTS

You can evaluate a reverse-explanation argument by evaluating the explanation it involves. And up to a point, you can evaluate an explanation the way you evaluate a deductive argument: by going through Steps One, Two, and Three, although without demanding validity of nondeductive explanations and without demanding that explanatory premises be plausible enough to enhance the credibility of the conclusions drawn from them. Sometimes this reveals important shortcomings.

Example 5   Not many people would have jumped into the gator-infested bayou to save a strange child, as Ignatz did. Still, Ignatz's action can be explained fundamentally the same way as all human behavior: like the rest of us, Ignatz acted selfishly. Oh, I know it seems otherwise. But look at it this way: Ignatz would not have done what he did had he not expected to get maximum satisfaction from his action.

This is an explanation. Here is its reconstruction:

Everyone acts selfishly. (express)

Whoever acts selfishly does whatever he expects will give him maximum satisfaction. (tacit)

Ignatz expected that his jumping into the gator-infested bayou to save the strange child would give him maximum satisfaction. (express)

∴ Ignatz jumped into the gator-infested bayou to save the strange child.

If "acts selfishly" is interpreted colloquially, the first premise is plainly false. People often act unselfishly, deliberately helping others at the expense of their own health, wealth, safety, or physical comfort. Some soldiers really have thrown themselves on live grenades to save their fellows. The very action imputed to Ignatz is a counter-example.

We can save the first premise by construing "acts selfishly" very broadly (and contrary to standard usage), so that pursuing one's own objectives automatically counts as acting selfishly, even if those objectives are of a sort we should normally regard as self-sacrificing. But then, for the second premise to be true, the phrase "maximum satisfaction" must mean something like "the feeling of having accomplished one's achievable objectives, whatever those objectives happen to be." For the explanation to be valid, though, "maximum satisfaction" must have the same meaning in the third premise as in the second. As a result, the third premise comes to differ little from the following:

Ignatz expected that his jumping into the gator-infested bayou to save the strange child would accomplish his achievable objectives.

But this differs little from the explanatory conclusion. It is question-begging or nearly so.

Just as an argument with a question-begging premise fails to enhance conviction, so an explanation with a question-begging premise fails to enhance understanding. You can no more explain a conclusion merely by stating it or a close cousin than you can defend a conclusion that way. The statement that someone thought his action would accomplish his achievable objectives, without any specification of those objectives, tells us little more than that he willingly did what he did, and that does not enhance our understanding of why he did what he did.

With "acts selfishly" construed broadly, a more common way to criticize Example 5 is to say that the first premise is empty, or vacuous: it is trivial, says nothing, has no content. Such premises are paragons of plausibility; the reason they are regarded nevertheless as *bad explanatory hypotheses* is that nothing much follows from an empty hypothesis, so explanations based on such hypotheses tend to rely on question-begging background premises.

In applying Steps One, Two, and Three to explanations (including those involved in reverse-explanation arguments), most of the effort usually is focused on ascertaining the truth and plausibility of hypothetical explanatory premises. When such premises are *general* (as is often the case), the effort consists mainly of looking for *counter-examples*. To the extent that the cases one examines turn out not to be counter-examples, they are said to *confirm* the hypothesis at issue. Counter-examples *disconfirm* the hypothesis.

A *strictly* general hypothesis purports to hold *without exception*. Examples:

All swans are white.

No swan is black.

Everyone acts selfishly.

A *weakly* general hypothesis *allows exceptions.* Examples:

Swans tend to be white.

Hardly any swan is black.

Ninety percent of all people act selfishly.

A single counter-example refutes a strictly general hypothesis, despite a large number and variety of confirming cases. Thus, a single black swan refutes the hypothesis that all swans are white. Usually a single counter-example does not refute a weakly general hypothesis, although a large enough number does, and even a few detract from its plausibility; the more numerous, varied, or typical they are, the more they detract. Thus, a single black swan does not refute the hypothesis that hardly any swan is black, but it detracts from the plausibility of this hypothesis, and a large enough number or variety of black swans would refute it.

In rare cases, a single counter-example refutes a weakly general hypothesis. If a single swallow from a newly opened bottle of whiskey is not bourbon, that is enough to refute the weakly general hypothesis that *most* swallows from the bottle are bourbon. For we know in advance that this particular hypothesis holds either without exception or not at all—that either every swallow is bourbon or none is.

So long as an hypothesis remains unrefuted, confirming cases enhance its credibility. The more numerous, varied, or typical they are, the more they enhance its credibility, because the less likely it is that counter-examples lurk.

The evaluation of explanations differs from the evaluation of arguments two ways:

First, in applying Step Three, one should not automatically reject an explanatory premise, or a candidate for the role of tacit explanatory premise, just because it is not plausible enough to support the conclusion drawn from it.

Second, the evaluation of explanations involves an additional step:

Step four

Check whether there is any reasonable alternative explanation—any other reasonable explanation with the same explanatory conclusion.

When we seek an explanation of something, we seek the *correct* or the *best* explanation. We criticize (possibly refute) the position that a particular explanation is the correct or best one when we produce a good or reasonable or likely alternative. We support the position when we rule out alternative explanations. The author of Example 4 entertained three hypotheses, each designed to explain why Ignatz's windows are closed:

(H$_1$) Ignatz is away on a trip.

(H$_2$) Ignatz finds it too cold to open his windows.

(H$_3$) Ignatz is running his air conditioner.

To support his contention that H$_3$ is the correct or best explanation, the author showed it to be better or more reasonable or more likely than H$_1$ or H$_2$; he ruled out H$_1$ and H$_2$.

Ignatz's closed windows could conceivably have been best explained by a *combination* of factors (his desire to keep out flies plus his desire to keep out drafts), not just one. But if so, an explanation in terms of this combination would be the best one; it would be better than any alternative explanation, including any based on a single factor.

Unlike the author of an explanation, the author of an argument does not maintain that his reasoning is uniquely good or correct. There can be many good or correct arguments for the same conclusion; the more, the better. As a result, one does not criticize an argument when one shows that there are better alternative arguments, as one criticizes an explanation by showing that there are better alternatives. Neither does one support an argument when one rules out alternative arguments, as one supports an explanation by ruling out alternative ones.

How to show that one explanation is better than another? Two main ways:

Way 1 By showing that the first has more *plausible* premises than the second.

Way 2 By showing that the first has more *economical* premises than the second.

I elaborate and illustrate Way 1 in §10.3, Way 2 in §10.4.

10.3. PLAUSIBILITY

One of the most common ways to criticize an explanation is to produce a plausible alternative explanation—one with plausible premises. The more plausible it is, in most cases, the stronger the criticism.

In most cases; not all. Sometimes even a much more plausible alternative explanation has no critical force. Plausibility is a virtue of explanations, but not the only virtue. The more plausible of two explanations can be sufficiently defective in other ways to be the inferior explanation. Consider any perfectly good explanation with an hypothetical premise and a conclusion already known to be true. Any alternative explanation with a blatantly circular set of premises would be more plausible but no better, indeed no good.

Still, you level a strong criticism at an explanation when you produce an alternative explanation equally good in other respects and no less plausible. When you make such a criticism, you are using plausibility as a measure of explanatory merit. But as you know, explanatory merit is one measure of plausibility. So when comparing explanations in terms of plausibility, you must establish relative plausibility on grounds other than relative explanatory merit.

Example 6   Did you know that the average college student is much more likely to flunk Freshman English than Advanced Nuclear Physics? I guess the old idea that the natural sciences are tougher for students than the humanities is a myth; if anything, the reverse is true.

This is a reverse-explanation argument. Explanatory hypothesis (and conclusion of argument):

The humanities are tougher for students than the natural sciences.

Explanatory conclusion (and premise of argument):

The average college student is much more likely to flunk Freshman English than Advanced Nuclear Physics.

The reasoning is poor, because the suggested hypothesis is much less plausible than this alternative one:

The number of college students who *take* Freshman English is very many times greater than the number who take Advanced Nuclear Physics.

Example 7   He must have been shot shortly before we found his body, because the blood near his wound was still wet.

Hypothesis:

He was shot shortly before we found his body.

Explanatory conclusion:

The blood near his wound was still wet when we found his body.

Alternative explanatory hypothesis:

He was a hemophiliac (one whose blood does not clot).

Barring additional information, the *original* hypothesis is more plausible, because most people are not hemophiliacs. Still, the alternative hypothesis is worth noting, in case further investigation rules out the original hypothesis or increases the likelihood that the subject was a hemophiliac (which Lord Peter Wimsey's investigation did do in Dorothy Sayer's *Have His Carcase*).

Example 8   Testimonial from a satisfied customer: "My self-confidence increased eightfold after just one bottle of Dr. Krankheit's Armadillo Extract."

This is a reverse-explanation argument. The express premise of the argument is the explanatory conclusion:

The testimonial writer's self-confidence increased eightfold after one bottle of Dr. Krankheit's Armadillo Extract.

The unstated conclusion of the argument is the explanatory hypothesis:

Dr. Krankheit's Armadillo Extract tends in general to increase self-confidence.

Alternative hypotheses:

Dr. Krankheit's Armadillo Extract increases self-confidence *in certain people*, including the testimonial writer.

Some other specifiable factor or combination of factors, present in the testimonial writer's case, tends in general to increase self-confidence.

Many people, including the testimonial writer, tend to benefit in certain ways when they ingest things they believe will benefit them in those ways, independently of the composition of those things. ("placebo effect")

Barring further information, the alternative hypotheses, especially the third, are about as plausible as the original. At all events, they are plausible enough to diminish the plausibility of the original hypothesis.

Example   9   My, what yummy-looking strawberries! I'll take a
basket.

Because all one can see of a basket of strawberries is the top layer, the
speaker has evidently accepted the reverse-explanation argument from
the explanatory conclusion:

> The top layers of strawberries in those baskets are yummy looking

to the hypothesis:

> On the whole, the strawberries in those baskets are yummy
> looking.

Here is an alternative, more plausible hypothesis:

> To attract customers, the top layer of each basket was filled with
> yummy-looking strawberries.

This argument is inductive in the narrow sense: its conclusion (the
hypothetical explanatory premise) generalizes the information contained in its premise (the explanatory conclusion). In any such argument, what the premises say about a small class, called the *sample*, the
conclusion says about a more inclusive class, the *population*. In the case
at hand, the sample comprises the top layers of strawberries; the population, all the strawberries. The argument is poor, one would usually
say, because the sample is *biased*, or *unfair*, meaning that it is not typical of the whole population, or at least not typical enough to warrant
attributing the specified feature of the sample to the population as a
whole. In my terms: There is, or could well be (for all we know), a
plausible explanation of why the sample, but not necessarily the whole
population, has the feature in question.

The simplest *fair* or *un*biased sample is a *random* one—a strictly
random selection from the entire population. The distinguishing mark
of unbiased samples generally is that they are so constructed as to make
alternative hypotheses extremely implausible. Thus, if a reasonably
large random sample of strawberries (random by virtue of a blind drawing from a revolving drum containing all the strawberries, say) looked
yummy, any explanation other than that all the strawberries are
yummy looking would be most implausible.

Whether a sample is fair can depend on background knowledge about
the population or the hypothesis being evaluated. If we are judging a
basket of strawberries for yummy appearance, the top layer is a biased
sample. So is a single, randomly chosen berry. But if we are examining a
bottle for whiskey type (bourbon, Scotch, Canadian, and so on), a single
swallow is a fair sample (even if it does not a summer make). And a

single drop of blood is a fair sample for many medical tests. For we know that one swallow from a bottle of whiskey or one drop of a man's blood is much like another.

Example 10   In 1936 the *Literary Digest* polled 10 million voters chosen at random from telephone directories, motor-car registrations, and the list of *Digest* subscribers. Of the 2,300,000 responses, only about 40 percent favored President Franklin D. Roosevelt, the Democratic candidate, in the forthcoming presidential election. The conclusion drawn was that the Republican candidate, Governor Alfred M. Landon of Kansas, probably would win the election.

This is a reverse-explanation argument. Explanatory conclusion:

A large majority of a sample of 2,300,000 responding voters out of 10 million voters chosen at random from telephone directories, motor-car registrations, and the list of *Literary Digest* subscribers preferred Landon to Roosevelt.

Explanatory hypothesis:

A majority of all voters preferred Landon to Roosevelt.

In fact, Roosevelt won with 60 percent of the vote. What went wrong? Did all that many voters change their minds between the time of the poll and election day? No, the proffered hypothesis just was not as plausible as an alternative:

Relatively prosperous voters tended to prefer Landon to Roosevelt.

In 1936 only relatively prosperous Americans had telephones, motor cars, or subscriptions to the *Literary Digest*.
One can make much the same point by saying that the sample was biased in favor of the minority who, in 1936, were sufficiently prosperous to have telephones, cars, or *Literary Digest* subscriptions. The bias is particularly bad (and the original hypothesis particularly implausible compared with the suggested alternative) because it was reasonable to suppose that relatively prosperous people were more inclined than others to vote Republican. But even if we had no reason to believe this, the sample would still be biased (diminishing the hypothesis' plausibility somewhat) unless we had positive reason to believe that those who had cars, telephones, or *Literary Digest* subscriptions (and were inclined to respond to mail polls) typified the wider electorate.

10.4. ECONOMY

Other things equal, one of two explanations with the same conclusion is better than the other if it has more economical premises.

Economy is a combination of two virtues: *simplicity* and *explanatory power*, simplicity being the opposite of *complexity*. Of two equally powerful explanatory premises, the simpler is the more economical. Of two equally simple premises, the more powerful is the more economical. One judges the economy of an hypothesis or other premise by judging how powerful it is for its level of complexity. That is,

$$E \text{ (economy)} = \frac{P \text{ (explanatory power)}}{C \text{ (complexity)}}$$

where

$$C = \frac{1}{S \text{ (Simplicity)}}$$

The explanatory power of a premise is measured (roughly) by the number and variety of the conclusions it explains. The complexity of a premise is measured (roughly) by its length, the number of words and clauses it contains, and the like. When an explanatory premise is a mathematical equation representable by a curve in a two-dimensional coordinate system, smoothness of that curve is a good measure of the premise's simplicity, as is the degree of any polynomial expression therein. I am afraid this is much less clear than I should have liked. Tolerably good definitions of power and simplicity (or complexity) are yet to be found.

A certain town has two barber shops, Angelo's Unisex Coiffures in the north and Ignatz's Institute of Tonsorial Aesthetics in the south. Fifteen townsmen were asked the barber shop they used and the neighborhood in which they lived—northeast, southeast, southwest, or northwest. The results:

	NEIGHBORHOOD	BARBER SHOP
1	NW	Angelo's
2	NE	Angelo's
3	SW	Ignatz's
4	SW	Ignatz's
5	NW	Angelo's
6	SE	Ignatz's
7	SE	Ignatz's
8	NE	Angelo's
9	SE	Ignatz's
10	NW	Angelo's
11	NE	Angelo's

	NEIGHBORHOOD	BARBER SHOP
12	NE	Angelo's
13	NW	Angelo's
14	SE	Ignatz's
15	SW	Ignatz's

How to explain these data? Five hypotheses:

(H_1) Northeasterners use Angelo's; southeasterners, Ignatz's; southwesterners, Ignatz's; and northwesterners, Angelo's.

(H_2) Northerners use Angelo's, while southerners use Ignatz's.

(H_3) Townsmen use the barber shops closest to where they live.

(H_4) Townsmen tend to minimize distance from home when using services.

(H_5) People tend to minimize distance from home when using services.

Each successive hypothesis explains the data better than its predecessor, because each successive hypothesis is more economical and not significantly less plausible. $H_1 - H_3$ explain exactly the same behavior, so they are equal in explanatory power. But H_2 is simpler than H_1, and H_3 is simpler still. H_4 is about as simple as H_3—certainly it is not much more complex—but it has much greater explanatory power, since it explains many actions other than going to the barber shop. H_5 is at least as simple as H_4, and it has greater explanatory power, because it applies to all people, not just male denizens of the town in question.

Later hypotheses in the list of $H_1 - H_5$ are better than earlier ones because more economical. Still, earlier ones are not *incorrect* on that account. They are just less than the best. The reason is evident enough: The later hypotheses explain the earlier ones. So if a later one is true, any earlier one is true as well. And a true hypotheses can hardly be called incorrect.

In many cases, we regard the inferior of two alternative explanations as incorrect, not just less than the best. But when the superior explanation explains the inferior one (along with the common explanatory conclusion), we do not regard the inferior one as incorrect on that account. We just feel that it does not go as far or as deeply as it could.

Notice how, in my example, the hypotheses that attribute underlying mechanisms, processes, causes, or motivations to the occurrences they purport to explain are more economical than those that do not. That tends in general to be the case, since what we regard as underlying explanatory factors (as opposed to more superficial ones) are what give unity to diverse phenomena, both simplifying and extending our account of the world.

Compare explanatory economy with fuel economy. Of two cars, the one that burns less gasoline is not necessarily more economical, else a poorly tuned Cadillac limousine that was hardly ever used would be an economy car. Neither is the car that goes farther more economical, else an overloaded Land Rover with flat tires that was frequently driven across the Gobi Desert would be an economy car. A car's fuel economy is measured, not by how little gasoline it uses, nor by how far it goes, but by how far it goes on how little gasoline. Likewise, explanatory economy is measured, not by how much is explained, nor by how simple are the premises being used, but by how much is explained using how simple a set of premises. Economy of every sort is output per input— how much you get out for what you put in.

Example 11   Blanche is white all over because all polar bears are.

Explanatory conclusion:

Blanche is white all over.

Explanatory premise:

All polar bears are white all over.

Here is a more economical explanatory premise:

Predators tend to have characteristics that make it hard for their prey to see them.

Not quite as simple as the original premise, this one is vastly more powerful. Here is an even more powerful one:

Species tend to have characteristics that maximize their chances of survival.

Example 12   After the Civil War, the Radical Republicans, who controlled Congress, instituted Military Reconstruction of the South, disenfranchising white Southerners, because the Radical Republicans wanted to punish white Southerners for rebelling and to protect newly freed Negroes.

Explanatory conclusion:

After the Civil War, the Radical Republicans, who controlled Congress, instituted Military Reconstruction of the South, disenfranchising white Southerners.

Hypothetical explanatory premise:

> The Radical Republicans wanted to punish white Southerners for rebelling and to protect newly freed Negroes.

Alternative hypothesis:

> Political parties tend to try to increase their percentage of the vote, especially in ways that seem justifiable on other, nobler grounds.

Because white Southerners were Democrats, disenfranchising them increased the Republican percentage of the vote. Barring further information, the second hypothesis is preferable because it is more economical and no less plausible, and it is more economical because it is much more powerful and about as simple.

Example 13   According to the Student Health Service, 542 students reported severe stomach cramps yesterday afternoon. In a joint letter to the editor of the student newspaper, 34 of the afflicted students demanded an investigation of the Campus Food Service, noting that they had all eaten the enchiladas served that day in the student cafeteria. Therefore, every afflicted student either ate the enchiladas and signed the letter or else did not sign the letter but caught a stomach virus.

Explanatory conclusion:

> The students who signed the letter had all eaten the enchiladas and gotten stomach cramps.

Explanatory hypothesis:

> Every afflicted student either had eaten the enchiladas and signed the letter or else had caught a stomach virus and not signed the letter.

Alternative hypothesis:

> Every afflicted student had eaten the enchiladas.

The alternative hypothesis is better because it is more economical, and it is more economical because it is equally powerful but much simpler.

In cases like this, we find the simpler hypothesis *more plausible* as well, suggesting to some that we tend to believe the world to be simple (or uniform). But the reason we find the simpler hypothesis more plausible is that it explains the evidence better. Remember: Explanatory merit partly determines plausibility, and simplicity partly determines explanatory merit. Simpler hypotheses tend to be more plausible because they explain better, not necessarily because we believe the world to be especially simple—unless this apparent profundity just means that we find simpler explanations to be better and therefore more plausible.

Example 14   "Why does your watch tick, Daddy?"

"Because there is an invisible cricket inside, Ignatz."

This is a perfectly terrible explanation, because the profferred hypothesis is less simple but no more powerful or plausible than the question-begging hypothesis:

Something inside the watch makes the watch tick.

Although the cricket hypothesis has consequences that the question-begging hypothesis lacks (for example, "There is a cricket in the watch"), none is an *explanatory* consequence: none describes an occurrence we should ever notice and want explained, owing to the invisibility of the putative cricket. That is why the cricket hypothesis has no greater explanatory power than the question-begging one.

Example 15   We've found that salesmen who dress better sell better. So I guess customers are more willing to buy from well-dressed salesmen.

Alternative explanation:

People tend to dress as well as they can afford to dress.

Because better salesmen make more money, they can afford to dress better. From this plus the alternative hypothesis, it follows that they tend to dress better. The alternative hypothesis is better because more economical, and it is more economical because more powerful: it explains the sartorial standards of a more inclusive class of people.

10.5. PARADOX LOST (optional)

Among inductive arguments in the narrow sense (arguments whose conclusions generalize the information contained in their premises), the simplest have this form:

All As examined so far are B.

∴ All As are B.

As noted in §1.5, some arguments of this form are bad, despite unimpeachable premises. These anomalous cases, first remarked by the distinguished philosopher Nelson Goodman, are regarded as paradoxes.

One such problematic argument comes from Quine and Ullian's *Web of Belief*:

Every moment of my life examined so far has been followed by further living.

∴ Every moment of my life is (was, will be) followed by further living. (H_1)

The problem is that H_1 conflicts with the far more plausible conclusion of another, apparently better inductive argument:

Everyone examined so far has lived no more than 170 years.

∴ Everyone lives (lived, will live) no more than 170 years. (H_2)

Although H_1 and H_2 are conflicting hypotheses, not alternative ones, we can still choose between them according to which is the better explanation. H_2 is far more plausible. But that restates the problem instead of solving it. Why do we find H_2 more plausible?

Because it is more *economical*. It is as simple as H_1; and it is far more powerful, since it applies to all people. (H_1 could be extended to all *present and future* people, but not to *all* people.)

Now for Goodman's famous example, given in §1.5. To call something *grue*, you may recall, is to say that it is either green (all over) and examined before now or else blue (all over) and not yet examined. All emeralds examined so far are green, hence grue. So these inductive arguments both have true premises:

Every emerald examined so far is green.

∴ Every emerald is green. (H_3)

Every emerald examined so far is grue.

∴ Every emerald is grue. (H_4)

H_3 and H_4 conflict. According to H_3, every emerald not yet examined is green. According to H_4, every emerald not yet examined is grue, hence blue, hence not green.

No doubt H_3 is true and H_4 false. But the question, as before, is: Why?

The same cases (emeralds examined before now) confirm both. None disconfirms either.

I suggest that H_4 should be rejected because it conflicts with H_3, which is *more economical*. To compare two hypotheses in respect of economy, we must first replace each explicitly defined term ("grue") with its definiens ("green [all over] and examined before now or blue [all over] and not yet examined"), else we could turn the most complex hypotheses into startlingly simple ones by introducing new words as definienda for old complex phrases. Replacing "grue" with its definiens in H_4, we get:

> Every emerald is either green (all over) and examined before now or else blue (all over) and not yet examined.

And this clearly is less economical than H_3, because it is equally powerful but less simple.

Objection: Call a thing *bleen* when it is either blue (all over) and examined before now or else green (all over) and not yet examined. Then just as we defined "grue" and "bleen" in terms of "blue" and "green," we can as well define "blue" and "green" in terms of "grue" and "bleen":

> "Green" means "grue and examined before now or bleen and not yet examined."

> "Blue" means "bleen and examined before now or grue and not yet examined."

If we replace "green" in H_3 by its new definiens, we get:

> Every emerald is either grue and examined before now or else bleen and not yet examined,

which is no more economical than H_4.

Reply: The objection just shows that H_4 *would* have been as economical as H_3 *if* "blue" and "green" had been expressly introduced into English by definition in terms of "grue" and "bleen" instead of the reverse, hence that H_4 *could* have been as economical as H_3. But my point was that H_3 is *in fact* more economical than H_4.

True, I thereby attached some importance to which words were in fact expressly defined, hence to the linguistic status quo. But such conservatism is itself a kind of economy, linguistic change being costly. In a way, the really significant bias in my approach is toward formulating hypotheses in terms of those attributes for which we have common words, hence those we most readily *notice* (green and blue as opposed to grue and bleen). But this makes it easier to frame, test, and apply hypotheses. It also increases the number and variety of confirming and disconfirming cases we are aware of, thereby increasing the likelihood of refuting false hypotheses while increasing our confidence in those that go unrefuted. Besides, the bias in favor of our present vocabulary is unavoidable if we are to use simplicity as a criterion of explanatory merit, since without this bias (as noted earlier) we could make any explanatory premise as simple as you please by replacing complex phrases with newly defined single words.

EXERCISES

Each of the following pieces of reasoning is either an explanation or a reverse-explanation argument. Each involves an hypothetical explanatory premise. In each case, formulate the explanatory conclusion and the hypothesis (either of which might be tacit). Then formulate one or several of the most likely alternative hypotheses you can think of. If an alternative hypothesis is either more economical than the original or else plausible enough to refute or weaken the original explanation—which is true in most cases—say so and say why. And if not, say so and say why.

* 1. Bertha must have been at Ignatz's house because, when he opened the door, I saw a woman disappear into the bedroom.

2. Miss Persimmon polled her ninth-grade class and found that ninety percent of them smoke. So most teen-agers smoke.

* 3. I saw her coming out of the firehouse with a license plate on her bicycle. Because it is the Fire Department that registers bicycles and gives out license plates, she must have just gotten her bicycle's license plate.

4. Although he had the chance, he did not flee. So it could not have been he who committed the crime.

* 5. The alarm rang because someone pulled a fire-alarm switch somewhere in the city.

6. He studied harder for Jones's course than for Smith's because it took more effort to pass Jones's course than Smith's.

* 7. "Female students often come to see me and talk to me in a sweet, sexually suggestive way," said Professor Chalkdust. "I guess I'm irresistible to women."

8. There's a puddle on the kitchen floor. I guess the refrigerator was unplugged without proper defrosting.

* 9. The fire started in his bedroom. He must have been smoking in bed.

10. The chances of a married man becoming an alcoholic must be double that of a bachelor, since 66 percent of all souses are spouses.

* 11. Once a staunch segregationist, Senator Julep recently voted for the constitutional amendment to give the predominantly black District of Colum-

bia Congressional representation. I guess he's had a change of heart regarding black people.

12. Birds build nests to lay their eggs.

* 13. Those who use seat belts have a lower automobile fatality rate than nonusers. I guess seat belts do save lives.

14. Spouses tend to have similar tastes in food and entertainment. I guess people tend to marry others with similar tastes in food and entertainment.

* 15. A trail of crumbs leads from the living room to the front porch, where the cookie box lies crumpled under the rocking chair. It must have been opened in the living room, then carried to the porch.

16. This pill will help you sleep because it contains a soporific substance.

* 17. The car moved because the gas pedal was depressed.

18. At long last, a really effective way to stop smoking! Fifty percent of those who have tried Dr. Krankheit's Rhinoceros-Horn Capsules have stopped smoking.

* 19. Most letters received by legislators concerning the Equal Rights Amendment support passage. So I guess a majority of citizens of this state favor passage of the ERA.

20. Although Ignatz owned his house outright, he just took out a mortgage on it. Poor chap. Must've had some financial misfortune.

* 21. In a recent election, a majority opposed a law forbidding discrimination against homosexuals in employment. A majority of our citizens, it seems, oppose equal employment opportunities for gays.

22. A Mexican-American Government professor active in Chicano politics was turned down for tenure. He had worked hard, published a number of articles, and taught courses students liked. You see, the university is still racist.

* 23. Klaghorn got 53 percent of the vote. So 53 percent of his constituents must favor Klaghorn.

24. We offer a money-back guarantee: If you are not absolutely delighted with Dr. Schwartz's Armadillo Extract, send us the unused portion and we will send you a full refund of the purchase price.

* 25. The average car in the United States is traded in every 3¼ years. In Sweden, Volvos last an average of 11 years. And more than 95 percent of all Volvos sold in the United States in the last 11 years are still on the road.

26. When they met, they fell deeply in love and ignored each others' faults. Now that they are married, they are less openly and continually amorous. They bicker occasionally. Perhaps living together engenders dislike.

* 27. "I cured my warts with my genuine Swiss Army Knife," writes a satisfied customer.

28. The top layers of strawberries in those baskets are yummy looking because, to attract customers, the grocer filled the top layers with yummy-looking strawberries.

PART·4
APPLICATIONS

Matters of Life and Death

11.1. TWO ARGUMENTS AGAINST CAPITAL PUNISHMENT

You can use my three-step procedure, not only to evaluate arguments with which you are presented, but to help decide issues—to help decide whether this or that position on a given issue is true or plausible or reasonable. You do this by jotting down, briefly and informally, the most plausible or prominent reasons you can think of for the position in question, then reconstructing and evaluating each reason according to Steps One, Two, and Three. In this chapter and the next, I show you how I have applied this approach to some issues I find especially interesting.

One such issue is that of capital punishment. There are two arguments against this practice that I have encountered more often than others. Both struck me, at first, as reasonable. Here is one of them:

> I oppose capital punishment because it has not been shown to be an effective deterrent.

This has just one express premise:

> Capital punishment has not been shown to be an effective deterrent.

"Effective deterrent" means, of course, "deterrent that is significantly more effective than the alternative, lesser deterrents" rather than "deterrent that is more effective than no deterrent at all." The conclusion, unstated, is something like:

> Capital punishment is unjustified.

Or replace "unjustified" with another negative epithet; it will not affect my discussion.

This argument, like most, in invalid as it stands. It becomes valid when any of these statements is added as a premise:

(1) *Capital* punishment is unjustified if it has not been shown to be an effective deterrent.

(2) *Any* punishment is unjustified if it has not been shown to be an effective deterrent.

(3) Any *severe* punishment is unjustified if it has not been shown to be an effective deterrent.

Statements (2) and (3) are each preferable to (1) according to Generality: they are more general than (1), and there is no apparent reason to accept (1) except that one accepts the more general (2), or at least (3). There is no apparent difference between capital and other punishments—other severe ones, anyway—that would warrant demanding demonstrated deterrence only of *capital* punishment.

But the argument with (2) or (3) as a premise depends on an ambiguity. Let us interpret:

. . . has been shown to be ———

as:

. . . has been definitely and directly proved to be ———.
(strong interpretation)

Then (2) says that *any* punishment is unjustified if it has not been *definitely and directly proved* to be an effective deterrent; (3) says the same of any *severe* punishment. But surely some punishments, indeed some severe ones, such as lengthy prison sentences, are justified; yet none, or virtually none, seems to have been definitely and directly proved to be an effective deterrent.

We avoid the objection by giving

. . . has been shown to be ———

a weaker interpretation, something like:

it has been made reasonably plausible that . . . is ———. (weak interpretation)

But then, the express premise says it has not been made reasonably plausible that capital punishment is an effective deterrent. This is questionable. Does not attaching a relatively high cost to an action of any sort—to buying coffee, for example—ordinarily deter people, to some significant degree, from performing that action? And does not this fact make it reasonably plausible that capital punishment is an effective deterrent?

Now the second argument against capital punishment:

> The trouble with capital punishment—the really terrifying thing about it—is that it is *irreversible*. When you send someone to jail, then find he is innocent, you can release him. But when you execute someone and then find he is innocent, you cannot undo his punishment; you cannot even pay him compensation for his ordeal.

Reconstruction:

> Capital punishment is irreversible. (express)
>
> No irreversible punishment is justified. (tacit)
>
> ∴ Capital punishment is not justified.

If to call a punishment *reversible* is to say that it can somehow be undone, or at least that the punished person can be compensated, then the tacit premise is arguably open to counter-example. Surely many long prison terms are justified. But none, or virtually none, is reversible. If Ignatz spent his life in prison, then died, how can we undo his punishment or compensate him for it? If Bertha has spent twenty years in prison and is still alive, we can release her. But how can we undo the punishment she has already incurred? We cannot give her back the twenty years. And there probably is no feasible way to compensate her for the time spent—her prime years, perhaps. The same is true even of five years in prison. When you take somone's life, you cannot give it back or compensate him for it. When you take a *significant part* of someone's life, the same often is true.

This, of course, is just the beginning of the story. There are other arguments against capital punishment, as well as various arguments *for* capital punishment. You might enjoy citing some and applying Steps One, Two, and Three to them.

11.2. ABORTION: SEPARATING THE LEGAL FROM THE MORAL ISSUE*

Opponents of legalizing abortion consider abortion a serious moral offense, roughly comparable to murdering you. Many who would

*My discussion benefits from that of Baruch Brody, "Abortion and the Law," *The Journal of Philosophy* **68** (1971).

legalize abortion disagree. They say abortion is not a serious moral offense, that it is nothing like murdering you.

Other proponents of legalizing abortion take a different tack. They try to separate the *moral* issue from the *legal* one (better described, perhaps, as the political issue of legalization). They contend that *abortion should be legal whether or not it is moral.* Their task is to defend the legalization of abortion without using any premise that denies the immorality of abortion, implicitly or explicitly. Their task, in other words, is to defend the legalization of abortion using only premises acceptable to those who consider abortion a serious moral offense.

Some common arguments for legalization:

> Outlawing abortion leads to death and suffering at the hands of quack abortionists.
>
> Outlawing abortion is unfair to the poor, who alone cannot afford competent abortions, domestic or foreign, when abortion is illegal.
>
> Outlawing abortion leads to the birth of unwanted children.
>
> Outlawing abortion leads to the birth of too many children.
>
> Outlawing abortion, like outlawing alcoholic-beverage consumption, engenders disrespect for the law.
>
> Outlawing abortion interferes with the right of women to do what they want with their bodies.
>
> Outlawing abortion restricts freedom of religion, and partly destroys the separation of church and state, by imposing the views of one religion on everyone.
>
> Outlawing abortion legislates morality, imposing highly controversial moral strictures on everyone.

Each of these arguments involves one stated premise:

> (P$_1$) Outlawing abortion leads to X,

where X is any of a number of apparently bad or unjust or unfortunate or otherwise condemnable states of affairs—harm from quack abortionists, unfairness to the poor, the birth of unwanted children, the birth of too many children, disrespect for the law, interference with the right of women to use their bodies as they see fit, restriction of religious freedom, or the legislation of morality. In each case, the conclusion is to this effect:

> (C) Abortion should not be outlawed.

The argument obviously is not valid as it stands. What additional premises would make it valid? Something like the following seems to be involved:

(P₂) X is bad [unjust, unfortunate, objectionable, or whatnot].

Adding (P₂) alone does not make the argument valid. One more premise is needed:

(P₃) If doing something leads to a bad state of affairs, it should not be done.

But (P₃) is a piece of cake for Counter-Example Man: Necessary dental treatment sometimes leads to pain, and pain is bad, but it is false that necessary though painful dental treatment should not be done.
More plausible than (P₃) is:

(P₃′) If doing something leads to a *worse* state of affairs than *not* doing it, then it should not be done.

But replacing (P₃) with (P₃′) invalidates the argument. We restore validity if we also replace (P₂) with a premise to the effect that X is worse than any state of affairs to which not outlawing abortion leads. Here, then, is the full argument:

(P₁′) Outlawing abortion leads to X.

(P₂′) X is worse than any state of affairs to which not outlawing abortion leads.

(P₃′) If doing something leads to a worse state of affairs than not doing it, then it should not be done.

∴ (C)   Abortion should not be outlawed.

The trouble is, *if* abortion is a serious moral offense, like murdering you, *then* (P₂′) is flatly false. For if abortion is a serious moral offense, then not outlawing abortion (that is, legalizing abortion) presumably leads to mass murder, which presumably is worse than X—worse than the harm from quack abortionists, unfairness to the poor, the birth of unwanted children, the birth of too many children, disrespect for the law, interference with the right of women to use their bodies as they see fit, the restriction of religious freedom, or the legislation of morality.
So the abortion-legalization advocate has failed to separate the legal from the moral issue of abortion. He has failed to support (C) with premises acceptable to those who find abortion immoral. His defense of (C) uses a premise, (P₂′) or something similar, that implicitly denies the immorality of abortion.

11.3. ATTACKING ABORTION BY APPEAL TO THE STATUS OF THE FETUS

Opponents of abortion commonly argue that a human fetus shares with you and me a certain protective *status*—that it is living or human or a person or a possessor of the right to life. Those who would permit abortion typically argue that a human fetus enjoys no such status.

Instead of debating the anti-abortion premise concerning the fetal status, let us temporarily grant this premise and ask whether it really supports the conclusion that abortion is wrong. What we want to examine, then, is this argument:

(P₁) Normally a human fetus has the status S [that of a living creature, a full-fledged human being, a person, a possessor of the right to life, or whatnot].

∴ (C) Normally it is wrong deliberately to abort a human fetus.*

Remember: I am conceding the single stated premise in order to examine whether the argument is otherwise good. If we find it is, we can go back and debate the status of the fetus. If we find it is not, we save ourselves the trouble of debating this obscure, possibly intractable issue.

I inserted the vague word "normally" because most opponents of abortion are willing to grant that there are exceptional cases, in which it would *not* be wrong to abort a human fetus. If we find the argument otherwise good, we can go back and try to replace "normally" with something more precise.

Opponents of abortion differ in their formulation of the protective status, which I abbreviated simply as "S." Common formulations are unclear and otherwise poor. In a standard sense, human fetuses are *of course* human beings (they are not armadillos), they are *of course* living rather than nonliving (they are not rocks), and they are *of course* living rather than dead unless they have died. Used colloquially, "person" is not very clear, and even children are not full-fledged persons in the more precise legal sense—they cannot make contracts, for instance. "Possessor of the right to life" probably is the best of the above formulations.

Still, it is far from clear what the right to life consists of. It includes your right not to be assassinated. It does not include Count Dracula's right to keep himself alive by sucking your blood. So one's right to life is the right to certain but not necessarily all the things one needs to stay alive. It is not clear whether a fetus' right to life (assuming it has one)

---

*It is for ease of formulation that I speak, barbarously, of *aborting a fetus* rather than *aborting a pregnancy*.

includes the right to live off its mother's body. Is a fetus like a potential assassination victim, or is it like Dracula?

The argument above is invalid as it stands. The most obvious way to make it valid is to add these two premises:

(P₂) It is wrong deliberately to bring about the death of anything that has the status S.

(P₃) Deliberately to abort a fetus, normally, is deliberately to bring about its death.

Some would object to (P₂) in some or all of these three ways: (1) It is not always wrong deliberately to bring about the death of a full-fledged adult human person who *deserves* death—a condemned murderer, for example. (2) It is not always wrong deliberately to bring about the death of a full-fledged adult human person who is threatening someone's life, health, or safety—an enemy soldier, for example. (3) It is not always wrong to bring about the death of a full-fledged adult human person whose continued existence would be worthless or worse for himself—a half-conscious, pain-crazed terminal-cancer patient whose life and torture would be shortened by the removal of an I.V. bottle, for example.

(P₂) is easily modified to take account of these objections:

(P₂') It is wrong deliberately to bring about the death of anything that has the status S, is innocent, is nonthreatening, and whose future life (if not terminated) is likely to be worthwhile for itself.

To accept (P₂'), you do not have to agree with the objections to (P₂). Because (P₂') follows from (P₂), if you accept (P₂) without qualification (or without all the suggested qualifications), you have to accept (P₂') as well.

Replacing (P₂) by the weaker (P₂') invalidates the argument. But validity is restored if we add a premise to the effect that a human fetus normally is innocent and nonthreatening and has a future life that (if not terminated) is likely to be worthwhile for itself.

Here, then, is the argument in full:

(P₁) Normally, a human fetus has the status S.

(P₂') It is wrong deliberately to bring about the death of anything that has the status S, is innocent, is nonthreatening, and whose future life (if not terminated) is likely to be worthwhile for itself.

(P₃) Deliberately to abort a fetus, normally, is deliberately to bring about its death.

(P_4) Normally a human fetus is innocent and nonthreatening and has a future life that (if not terminated) is likely to be worthwhile for itself.

∴ (C) Normally a human fetus is innocent and nonthreatening

(P_2) runs afoul of the following counter-example, which we owe the philosopher Judith Thomson*: A society of music lovers kidnaps you in the night, drugs you unconscious, and spirits you to a hospital, where you awake the next day strapped to a bed and attached by catheters to a distinguished violinist, afflicted with kidney failure, who will die forthwith unless he can use your kidneys. The hospital administrator apologizes for your situation, in which he had no hand, and assures you the music lovers will be punished. But he cannot release you, he says, because that would bring about the violinist's death, and the violinist is a full-fledged living human person with a right to life (in my jargon, he has the status S), and he is innocent and nonthreatening and is certain to have a worthwhile future life if you stay put. But you will be comfortable, the administrator promises, and the situation will be terminated as soon as the violinist's kidneys recover—in about nine months. Although it would be decent of you to stay and save the violinist's life, it seems you have every *right* to leave, to unplug yourself from the violinist, thereby deliberately (if somewhat regretfully) bringing about his death.

We avoid this counter-example to (P_2'), while preserving validity, by restricting (P_2') to human fetuses:

(P_2'') It is wrong deliberately to bring about the death of any *human fetus* that has the status S, is innocent, is nonthreatening, and whose future life (if not terminated) is likely to be worthwhile for itself.

But (P_2'') fails the test of Sufficient Generality. Among creatures that have the status S and are innocent, etc., there is no evident relevant difference between human fetuses (if, indeed, human fetuses belong to this class) and nonfetuses—no difference that would explain why it is wrong to bring about the death of human fetuses but not, say, adult humans; if anything, it is the other way round.

To sum up: One cannot argue from (P_1) to (C). The necessary linking premises are unacceptable. Even granting that human fetuses are full-fledged living human persons with the right to life (or whatever), it does not follow that it normally is wrong to abort them.

*"A Defense of Abortion," *Philosophy and Public Affairs* 1 (1971). This article has become a classic.

11.4.   RIGHTS, DESIRES, AND ABORTIONS

Some philosophers have defended abortion without denying that a fetus has a right to life, or a right not to be killed.* What justifies abortion, they argue, is that a fetus has *no desire* not to be killed:

> It is my right that you not walk on my lawn. But you do not violate that right by crossing my lawn unless I *want* you *not* to cross it. In general, you cannot violate a *right* to something without violating a *desire* for it. That is, doing something does not violate anyone's right unless he wants the thing not to be done. But no fetus wants anyone not to kill it; fetuses are not capable of such desires. Hence, killing a fetus does not violate any right it may have not to be killed.

The argument has two stated premises:

(P₁) If doing something violates X's right that the thing not be done, then X wants the thing not to be done.

(P₂) Never does a fetus want not to be killed.

The conclusion, unstated, is something like:

(C)   Aborting a human fetus normally is not wrong.

Although invalid as it stands, the argument becomes valid upon the addition of these two premises:

(P₃) Normally, killing a human fetus is wrong only if doing so violates the fetus' right not to be killed.

(P₄) Normally, to abort a fetus is to kill it.

(P₁) is open to any number of counter-examples: Imagine someone who lacks the desire not to be killed only because his desires have been distorted by hypnosis, drugs, brainwashing, or whatnot. Surely, killing him would violate his right not to be killed, even though he lacks a corresponding desire. Or suppose an immigrant from some primitive country does not mind being served food prepared in an unhygienic

---

*Richard Brandt, "The Morality of Abortion," *The Monist* **56** (1972). Michael Tooley, "A Defense of Abortion and Infanticide," *Philosophy and Public Affairs* **2** (1972). Brandt attributes the underlying idea to William James. Tooley seems not to be fully aware that his argument, if otherwise successful, allows him not to take a stand on the questions of fetal personhood and the right to life.

restaurant kitchen because he is ignorant of hygiene. Surely, serving him such food violates his right not to be served unwholesome food in a restaurant, despite his indifference.

We can avoid these counter-examples by restricting (P₁) to cases in which the subject does not suffer from distorted desires or ignorance. And to avoid trouble of other sorts, let us keep the premise weak by leaving the *time* of the subject's desire unrestricted. We end up with this modification of (P₁):

> (P₁′) If doing something violates X's right that the thing not be done, then there is, was, or will be a time at which X wants the thing not to be done, or would want the thing not to be done but for distorted desires or ignorance.*

Weakening (P₁) to (P₁′) turns a valid argument into an invalid one. We can restore validity by strengthening (P₂) this way: If a fetus is killed, then there neither is nor was nor will be any time at which it wants not to be killed, or would want not to be killed but for distorted desires or ignorance.

Here is the whole argument:

> (P₁′) If doing something violates X's right that the thing not be done, then there is, was, or will be a time at which X wants the thing not to be done, or would want the thing not to be done but for distorted desires or ignorance.

> (P₂′) If a fetus is killed, then there neither is nor was nor will be any time at which it wants not to be killed, or would want not to be killed but for distorted desires or ignorance.

> (P₃) Normally, killing a human fetus is wrong only if doing so violates the fetus' right not to be killed.

> (P₄) Normally, to abort a fetus is to kill it.

> ∴ (C) Aborting a human fetus normally is not wrong.

Although weaker and more plausible than (P₁), (P₁′) still is unacceptable. Here are three counter-examples to it:

1. You hit my car with yours, causing $500 worth of body damage to my car but leaving it functionally unimpaired. You are entirely at fault. So you owe me $500 for having damaged my car. That being the case, you must have violated my right that you not damage my car.

But I never desired that you not damage my car. Before I owned the car, I did not care what happened to it. Since I have owned it, my financial situation has made me prefer $500 to an unblemished car

*Brandt and Tooley expressly recognize the need for these qualifications.

body; so badly do I need the $500 that I am glad you damaged my car. And in the future, looking back on my current situation, I shall continue to feel I was right about this. Nor is my lack of desire that you not cause body damage to my car due to distorted desires or ignorance. It is a perfectly rational, well-informed response to penury.

Hence, you violated my right that you not cause body damage to my car, and yet, contrary to (P_1'), there never has been and never will be a time at which I want you not to cause body damage to my car or would want you not to do this but for distorted desires or ignorance.

2. To catch a mugger who has been terrorizing a neighborhood, Lieutenant Kojak strolls through the neighborhood, undistinguished from its residents. As hoped, the mugger attacks Kojak, who easily subdues him. Charged with assault, the mugger is found guilty.

Because he is guilty of assaulting Kojak, the mugger must have violated Kojak's right not to be assaulted. Yet Kojak is glad he was assaulted. He wanted the mugger to assault him so he could make the arrest, thereby protecting the residents of the neighborhood.

3. In the heat of an argument, Bertha, my hot-tempered business competitor, shoots me in the leg, which I did nothing to justify. I press criminal charges against her.

Because I obviously have a just complaint against Bertha, she must have violated my right not to be shot. Yet I wanted to be shot and I am glad she shot me because my business situation makes the imprisonment of my competitor well worth a bullet in the leg.

Although I have a right against others that they not trespass on my property, my legitimate visitors do not violate that right. Although I have a right to the food on my table, my dinner guests do not violate that right. Although I have a right to my car, my friend does not violate that right when I lend him my car. It is from examples like these that (P_1) and (P_1') acquired their initial plausibility. The reasoning from these examples to (P_1) or (P_1') is inductive in the narrow sense. (P_1') seemed a reasonable hypothesis to explain such cases.

But it is a poor explanatory hypothesis, because a better one is available:

> If A has the right that B not do X, but if A also has the right to give B permission to do X, and if A does give B permission to do X, then B's doing X does not violate A's right.

In the cases cited, each right against others that they not do a certain thing included the right to give them permission to do it. The conventions that determine when permission has been given are a varied lot. Unless I post a sign to the contrary, I automatically give blanket permission to anyone with legitimate business to enter my property and walk up to my front door. On the other hand, permission to my friend to use my car has to be more explicit.

The permission hypothesis is clearly superior to the desire hypothesis. It is no less economical and far more plausible. It obviously is true, I should say. We accept it even apart from the examples above.

11.5. THE FETAL STATUS AND THE DEFENSE OF ABORTION

As you saw, opponents of abortion cannot show that abortion is immoral by showing that fetuses have the status S—that they are living or human or persons or possessors of the right to life or whatever. But can *pro*ponents of abortion appeal to the status of the fetus? Can they successfully defend the morality of abortion by showing that fetuses *lack* the status S?

If they can, this is a good argument as far as it goes (assuming the express premise, that is):

(P₁) No human fetus has the status S.

∴ (C) Normally it is not wrong to abort a human fetus.

Although (P₁) is questionable, let us grant this premise to the proponent of abortion and see whether his argument is otherwise good— whether he can get from (P₁) to (C) using only widely accepted linking premises.

The most obvious way to make the argument valid is to add these two premises:

(P₂) If it is wrong to bring about the death of something, it has the status S.

(P₃) To bring about a fetus' death is to abort the fetus.

But (P₂) runs afoul of several counter-examples: It would be wrong for you to kill my dog, even though she lacks the status S. It would be wrong for a zookeeper to kill a rare panda in his charge, although the panda lacked the status S. Also it is wrong to kill members of endangered species, and it is wrong to kill beasts for recreation when this requires inflicting severe, sustained pain.

One might try to skirt these counter-examples by weakening (P₂) as follows:

If it is wrong to bring about *a fetus'* death, then *that fetus* has the status S.

But this suffers from insufficient generality. There appears to be no difference between fetuses and other creatures that would explain why (P₂) should apply only to fetuses.

Or one might weaken (P₂) this way:

> If it is wrong to bring about *a fetus'* death, then *that fetus* has the has the status S, *or* it belongs to someone who does not want it dead, *or* bringing about its death would be painful, *or* it is the job of him who would bring about the thing's death to protect the thing's life, *or* . . . .

But this invalidates the argument.

We can restore validity by adding another premise:

> (P₄) A human fetus belongs to no one who does not want it dead, *and* bringing about its death would not be painful, *and* it is not the job of anyone to protect the fetus' life, *and.* . . .

But this premise is question-begging or nearly so. It is no more plausible than (C). Opponents of abortion would generally disagree with it, contending among other things that it *is* someone's job—the expectant mother's—to protect a fetus' life.

True, I have granted (P₁), which is no more plausible and no more acceptable to abortion opponents than (P₄). But I granted (P₁) just for the sake of argument, to see whether proponents of abortion could get from (P₁) to (C) using only premises that beg no *other* big questions. They cannot.

11.6.   THE REAL ABORTION ISSUE

Opponents of abortion usually argue that human fetuses have the status S—a protective status variously formulated and shared with all or most human adults. But as you saw, they cannot get from this contention to the conclusion that abortion normally is morally wrong. *Pro*ponents of abortion usually argue that human fetuses lack the status S. But they cannot get from this contention to the conclusion that abortion normally is *not* morally wrong. So the morality of abortion does not turn principally on the status of the fetus. The abortion issue usually is misconceived. It is not a status-of-fetus issue. What exactly *is* the real issue?

Consider a person W and a creature F related to W as follows:

(i)   F is temporarily using W's body to support F's life.*

(ii) W had no obligation to let F *begin* using W's body to support F's life.

*"Using" does *not* mean "*deliberately* using" or "*consciously* using" or any such thing. In my broad sense, a green leaf *uses* sunlight to make carbohydrates, for example.

(iii) If W stops letting F use W's body to support F's life (thereby bringing about F's death), that will not make F any worse off than F would have been had F never begun using W's body to support F's life.

A pregnant woman is related to her fetus this way. In the counter-example of §11.3, you were related to the violinist this way.

Ignoring the case of a pregnant woman and her fetus, it seems safe to generalize the violinist example thus: Normally, when (i)−(iii) hold, W has every right to terminate W's support of F's life.

But, of course, if opponents of abortion are right, then a pregnant woman and her fetus constitute an exception to this rule. This means there is some *special relationship* between a pregnant woman and her fetus that obliges the woman to let her fetus use her body to support its life, a relationship that does not obtain in other situations of the (i)−(iii) variety.

What sort of relationship could this be? Three possibilities:

A *promissory* relationship. By getting pregnant, willingly or not, the woman implicitly promised someone—her fetus, its father, God, society, or whomever—to carry her fetus to term. Implausible.

A *proprietary* relationship. The woman's body partly and temporarily belongs to the fetus as well as to herself. It is the fetus' for the same reason it is hers, for the same reason your nose is yours: nature gave it to the fetus, who is naturally attached to it, needs it, and in the normal course of events would have and use it. Not implausible.

An *official* relationship. Protection of fetal life is one of the duties, jobs, or responsibilities that constitute the office or role of motherhood. Most of us would grant that there *is* such an office, with some duties more onerous and no more voluntary than carrying a normal fetus. Most of us also would grant that this office exists before birth: a pregnant woman is obliged by her maternal role to eat properly and avoid drugs and physical activities hazardous to her fetus, for example, at least if she is not about to have an abortion. Plausible.

Properly understood, the abortion issue is not whether human fetuses share a certain protective status with human adults; it is whether human fetuses bear a special protective relationship to their mothers. Abortion is morally wrong if a fetus has a proprietary claim to its mother's body or if the protection of fetal life—like that of infant life—is one of the duties that constitute the office of motherhood. Otherwise, abortion is not wrong. What should be debated is not the fetus' human-

ity or right to life or the like, but the constitution of "natural" proprietary rights, specifically that of a fetus to its mother's body, and the
constitution of "natural" offices or roles, specifically motherhood.

11.7. KILLING AND LETTING DIE

Mercy killing—euthenasia—is not an accepted practice. Mercy killings occur, sometimes with medical connivance. But the practice is
officially condemned by the medical profession and is against the law.
Yet more and more, nowadays, doctors do something similar: they
withdraw or withhold respirators, I.V. bottles, and other therapeutic
devices and treatments from terminally ill patients who are hopelessly
comatose or in agony, thereby bringing about or at least hastening
death. The justification doctors give is that they are merely *letting* these
patients *die, not killing* them. Applied to a given case, that of patient P,
their reasoning takes this form:

> To withdraw or withhold the device or treatment from P is to let P
> die, not to kill P.
>
> Withdrawing or withholding the device or treatment from P (or
> another like P) is wrong only if doing so is a case of killing rather
> than letting die.
>
> ∴ It is not wrong to withdraw or withhold the device or treatment
> from P.

(Conceivably one might give a similar defense of abortion, contending
that abortion is better described as a case of letting die than as a case of
killing and that letting fetuses die is normally permissible even if killing them is not. What do you think?)

The first premise is plausible only if there really is a difference between killing and letting die, not just some difference or other, but a
morally relevant difference. Is there? The second premise is plausible
only if the death-hastening actions (or failures to act) in question really
are cases of letting die, not of killing. Are they? The answers to these
questions depend on the answer to another: Just what is the difference
between killing and letting die?

Maybe this:

> To let P die (as opposed to killing P) is (deliberately) to refrain from
> prolonging P's life when one is in a position to prolong it.

Counter-example: Bertha (deliberately) smothers you, pressing a pillow to your face for a period of several minutes. Once the pillow is in
place, she is in a position to do something that would prolong your

life—to wit, lift the pillow—but she deliberately refrains from doing so. Contrary to the proposed analysis, though, she plainly has killed you, not merely let you die.

To be sure, Bertha has not only refrained from prolonging your life, but has brought about the conditions leading to your death. This suggests the following modification:

> To let P die, as opposed to killing P, is (deliberately) to refrain from prolonging P's life when one is in a position to prolong it and one has not (deliberately) brought about the conditions leading to P's death.

But consider the case of a doctor who mercifully removes a life-lengthening I.V. bottle from a dying patient whose few remaining days have become a mix of drugged stupor and unbearable pain. Not only does this action deliberately bring about conditions leading to the patient's death, but the doctor's very purpose is to hasten death. Yet such actions are commonly described nowadays as letting die rather than killing.

True, current usage might just be a rhetorical camouflage of a questionable practice. Let us treat this usage generously, though, trying to make sense of it, before concluding that the kill/let die distinction comes to naught.

Sometimes the kill/let die distinction is thought of as an instance of the active/passive distinction:

> Killing is active; letting die, passive.

The respirator example lately cited is a counter-example to this proposal. Many cases of letting die—those of the plug-pulling variety—are active rather than passive. There also is a passive species of killing. Suppose an anesthesiologist deliberately fails to make the necessary, routine, expected adjustments in the life-support and monitoring systems attached to a patient undergoing surgery, thereby deliberately ensuring that the patient dies, although the surgery would certainly have been successful otherwise. Such inaction is passive. Yet it would be natural to accuse the anesthesiologist, not merely of letting the patient die, but of killing the patient. Or suppose Ignatz is a deep-sea diver; it is Bertha's job to pump air to him; and one day she decides to stop pumping in order that Ignatz die. Although Bertha has brought about Ignatz's death passively—by inaction—it is clear, I think, that she has killed Ignatz, not merely let him die.

These cases suggest that what makes something a case of killing rather than letting die is not that it is active, but that it alters the normal course of events (actively *or* passively):

To *kill* P is (deliberately) *to alter the normal course of events* in a way that leads to P's death (either by actively intervening in the normal course of events or by refraining from actions that are part of the normal course of events); to *let* a patient *die* is (deliberately) *not* to alter the normal course of events that is leading to P's death (either by refraining from actively intervening in the normal course of events or by terminating some prevailing intervention in the normal course of events or by continuing to participate in the normal course of events).

Although they brought about death passively, the anesthesiologist and Bertha altered the normal course of events. To refrain from active resuscitation in an essentially hopeless case is to refrain from intervening in the normal course of events. To remove a respirator in such a case is to terminate a prevailing intervention in the normal course of events. If the case is not so hopeless, active resuscitation or the continued use of a respirator might fairly be deemed part of what is expected of physicians and therefore part of the normal course of events.

Another suggestion:

To *kill* P is (deliberately) to deny P some essential life-support instrumentality to which P has a *right;* to *let* P *die* is (deliberately) to deny P some essential life-support instrumentality to which P has no right.

Whether killed or allowed to die, a patient is in either case (deliberately) denied some essential life-support instrumentality, actively or passively. What distinguishes the "kill" case, according to this analysis, is that the patient has a right to the instrumentality. In short, killing differs from letting die in being a kind of *taking.*

Most cases of killing a person involve invading the person's body. And if one has a right to anything, it is to one's own *body.* Farmers once owned grazing land in common, and some property still is owned in common. An example is the air around us. When you kill a person by smothering, although you do not invade his body, you deny the person the use of the air he owns in common with everyone. A hospital patient's right to medical services is conditional on those services being of some value to him. So if the patient's remaining days of life clearly would be worthless or worse for him, then removing, say, a life-lengthening I.V. bottle would deny the patient no instrumentality to which he had a right. As a result, according to the proposal just above, it would be a case of letting die, not killing.

I have suggested two analyses of the kill/let die distinction. Neither is crystal clear. But then, the distinction was murky to begin with.

Can you think of a counter-example to either analysis?

Does either analysis make the kill/let die distinction a *morally relevant* one, thereby sustaining the credibility of the first premise?

Does either count all the usual death-hastening actions (or failures to act) by doctors as cases of letting die, thereby sustaining the plausibility of the second premise?

EXERCISES

1. Find and reconstruct an argument in defense of legalizing some morally controversial act. Is it open to my criticisms of abortion-legalization arguments?

   In a newspaper editorial, a political speech, barroom discussion, or wherever, find and evaluate an argument for or against each of these practices:

2. Abortion.

3. Capital punishment.

4. Euthanasia.

5. Answer the question posed at the end of §11.7.

   Evaluate the following arguments. Although none is airtight, some might not be thoroughly bad.

* 6. Capital punishment is just, because it has been shown to be an effective deterrent.

* 7. Capital punishment is unjust, because it is unjust for anyone ever to take a human life except when necessary to defend another human life.

* 8. Abortion should be legalized, because people should be allowed to do anything they want so long as they do not harm others.

* 9. Abortion is morally wrong, because infanticide is, and there is no relevant difference between abortion and infanticide.

10. If a dying patient has minimal brain activity or if his life is a hopeless mix of drugged stupor and unbearable pain, he is virtually a vegetable. Still, to withhold essential life-support measures from him is to end his life. And that cannot be right.

* 11. The Civil War was not worth the cost. In fact, it was a moral outrage. A few more years of slavery would have been bad. Dissolution of the Union would have been bad. But not bad enough to justify killing hundreds of thousands of people, including conscripts and noncombatants.

12. Women have a right to have abortions, because everyone has the right to use his body as he pleases.

* 13. Capital punishment is unjust, because it discriminates against the poor.

14. Societies are subject to the same ethical standards as individuals. What is wrong for the individual is wrong for society. But individuals may not kill others except in self-defense. Specifically, they may not kill others just for the sake of retribution or deterrence. So it is wrong for society to use capital punishment.

* 15. Capital punishment does not work. After all, countries that do not use capital punishment have fewer murders per population than those that do.

16. If a woman not yet prepared to raise a child becomes pregnant, she should have an abortion if she wants, and bear a child later, when she is more prepared. That way her children will be better off.

* 17. Organizations that purvey hate—the Nazis, the K.K.K., and so on—should not be prevented from organizing and voicing their beliefs. For everyone has the moral right—and ought to have the legal right—of free speech and association, however odious his views.

18. It is reasonable to suppose that capital punishment prevents more killings than it brings about. So how can you say it is wrong?

* 19. When you have an abortion, your fetus dies. But neither you nor your doctor has killed it; you have just let it die. So even if we cannot admire your action, we can hardly condemn it as morally wrong.

20. Everyone—even the anti-abortionist—has the right to do what he thinks is morally right, and no one has the right to stop him. Consequently, while those who think abortion is wrong have the right not to have abortions, those who do *not* think abortion is wrong also have the right *to have* abortions, and no one has the right to stop *them*.

12

Society and the Individual

12.1. PREFERENTIAL HIRING AS COMPENSATION

Many advocates of so-called *preferential hiring* feel that employers should make up for past discrimination by discriminating in reverse. They advocate giving minority-group and female job candidates at least some preference over nonminority male candidates. Their reasoning goes something like this:

> Normally it is unjust to discriminate between job candidates on the basis of sex, race, or national ancestry—to favor some candidates over others on account of their sex or race or national ancestry. But there are exceptions. *Just because* it normally is unjust to discriminate on the basis of sex, race, or national ancestry, justice requires that the *victims* of such discrimination be compensated for the injustice they have suffered, hence favored because of their sex or race or national ancestry. By giving some preference to female and certain minority job candidates over white male candidates, we do not discriminate in any morally objectionable way; we merely compensate the victims of injustice. Other things equal, justice requires that we give women and the members of certain minority groups at least some preference over white males when filling jobs.

You have doubtless heard similar arguments in defense of preferential university admissions.

Reconstruction:

> (P₁) White male job candidates have been unjustly favored over minority-group and female job candidates. (express)

246

(P$_2$) If one group of candidates for something have been unjustly favored over a second group, then, other things being equal, justice requires that some preference be given to the second group of candidates over the first. (tacit)

∴ (C) Other things equal, justice requires that some preference be given to minority-group and female job candidates over white male job candidates.

Ambiguities lurk. Take the phrase:

(*)   some preference be given to ——— over . . . .

We can interpret it two ways:

some preference be given to *every* ———
over *every* . . .   (strong interpretation)

or

some preference be given to *some* [many]
——— over *some* [many] . . . .   (weak interpretation)

Under the weak interpretation, (C) says this: Other things equal, justice requires that some preference be given to *some* [many] minority and women job candidates—maybe just those who were once discriminated against—over *some* [many] white male candidates—just those who profited from onetime discrimination, perhaps. But that is less interesting and controversial than (C) seemed at first to be. It is not the preferential-hiring or reverse-discrimination position that exercises people nowadays.

(C) is most interesting and controversial when (*) is given the strong interpretation. For (C) then says the following: Other things equal, justice requires that some preference be given to *all* minority and female job candidates (regardless of whether they ever were victims of discrimination) over *all* white male job candidates (regardless of whether they ever profited from discrimination).

But under the strong interpretation of (*), (P$_2$) seems very unreasonable unless we further interpret:

(**) . . . candidates have been unjustly favored over——— candidates

as:

all . . . candidates have been unjustly favored over *all* ——— candidates   (strong interpretation) rather than:

> *some* [many] ... candidates have been
> unjustly favored over *some* [many]
> ——— candidates [*because* the former
> were ... and the latter ———].   (weak interpretation)

For with (*) interpreted the strong way and (**) the weak way, (P₂) amounts to:

> If some [many] candidates of one group have been unjustly favored over some [many] candidates of a second group, then, other things equal, justice requires that some preference be given to *every* member of the second group of candidates over *every* member of the first.

But this demands, in effect, that *non*victims of discrimination be *compensated* for the discrimination suffered by *others*.

If we interpret (**) the strong way in (P₂), however, we must interpret (**) the strong way in (P₁) also, else the argument will not be valid. But if we interpret (**) the strong way in (P₁), then (P₁) says the following: *All* white male job candidates (present ones included) have been unjustly favored over *all* female and minority job candidates (past and present). And this is patently false.

So the argument depends on an ambiguity. This weakens the argument, but does not destroy it. The weak interpretation of (*) makes (C) somewhat less interesting than it seemed to be, but still not trivial, and it leaves the argument otherwise unimpaired.

And there might be other, better arguments for preferential hiring. Can you think of one?

12.2.   POPULATION POLICY AND FUTURE POPULATIONS*

Many policies are defended nowadays on the ground that they would benefit our posterity, remote as well as near—not just the next few generations, but our distant descendants. Examples include policies of population control, environmental cleanliness, protection of genetic health and variety, and natural-resource conservation. Applied to the issue of population control—to the choice, let us say, between a severely *restrictive* population policy and a more or less *laissez-faire* policy—the argument is likely to run as follows:

*In this section, I borrow from my paper, "Welfare Judgements and Future Generations," *Theory and Decision* **11** (1979).

The standard of living in the distant future would be much higher under the restrictive policy than under the laissez-faire policy.

If the standard of living in a certain period would be much higher under one policy than under another, then the population of that period would be significantly better off under the former than under the latter.

∴ The population in the distant future would be significantly better off under the restrictive policy than under the laissez-faire policy.

Conceivably some persons who would exist under one of two alternative policies would not exist under the other. So for the second premise to be plausible, the form of words:

(*)   the X population would be better off under policy Y than under policy Z

must mean:

> those who would belong to the X population under Y would be better off under Y than those who would belong to the X population under Z would be under Z.

And for the argument to be valid, (*) must have the same meaning in the conclusion, so that the conclusion means:

> Those who would be our distant descendants under the restrictive policy would be better off under the restrictive policy than those who would be our distant descendants under the laissez-faire policy would be under the laissez-faire policy.

Properly understood, this conclusion is less interesting than it seemed at first to be. It does not say of anyone that the laissez-faire policy would make him worse off, in any way, than he would otherwise be. It does not say of even a single individual that he would be worse off under the laissez-faire policy than he would be under the restrictive policy. For *none* of our distant descendants under the laissez-faire policy would in fact also be one of our distant descendants under the restrictive policy; none would exist under the restrictive policy.

To see why, suppose the laissez-faire policy has been adopted. Consider those of our distant descendants whose lives will have been significantly affected thereby. Let X be any one of them. I shall show that X would *not have existed* had the restrictive policy been adopted.

For X to be one of those possible individuals, say Y, who would have existed under the restrictive policy, it is not enough that Y would have had X's name, else I should be identical to all the Thomas Schwartzes in the world. Nor is it enough that Y would have had X's ancestry, else my son and daughter would be identical. What *would* ensure that Y would have been the same person as X—that X would have been Y, had the restrictive policy been adopted?

That is notoriously controversial. Happily, we have no need to enter the controversy. For it is quite certain that no one born under the restrictive policy would have been the same person as X by *any* plausible criterion of personal identity.

The restrictive policy would have brought about a future world different from that of the laissez-faire policy, and X is one of those significantly affected by the adoption of the laissez-faire policy. So the circumstances of X's life would not have been fully replicated under the restrictive policy. One or both of X's parents might not have existed under that policy. Had they both existed, they might not have met. Had they met, they might not have mated. Had they mated, they might not have procreated. Even had they procreated, their offspring, Master Z, would have been conceived under conditions at least a little different from those of X's conception.

But that makes it virtually impossible for Z to have developed from the *same pair of gametes* as X, hence virtually impossible for Z to have had the *same genotype* as X. After all, trivial circumstantial differences could easily have determined the precise time of any of the events involved in sexual intercourse leading up to conception. And the most minute circumstantial differences—a difference of one degree in temperature, say, or of one drop of some chemical—would have determined *which particular spermatazoon fertilized the ovum* and *what particular pattern of meiosis was involved in the production of either gamete.* Let the circumstances surrounding Z's conception be as similar to those surrounding X's conception as one can realistically suppose. Still, Z would have been no more likely than X's nontwin sibling to have had X's genotype.

The combination of a different genotype and a different environment ensure all manner of further difference: Z would not have been composed of the same matter as X; he would not have looked the same as X; and he would not have had the same perceptions, the same memories, the same beliefs or attitudes, the same capacities, the same character, or the same personality as X. As a result, Z would not have had the same psyche as X—by any sensible standard of sameness of psyche. Neither would Z have fulfilled just the same social roles and relationships as X.

In sum, Z would have differed from X in *origin* (different gametes), in *content* (different matter, different mind), and in *basic "design"* (different genotype), and Z would have been shaped by a different environment to perform different functions. We have no more reason to identify Z with X than we have to identify siblings reared apart with each other.

Although the conclusion of the argument we are examining does not say that any individual would be better off under the restrictive policy than that very individual would be under the laissez-faire policy, do you think that it nevertheless provides some support for a restrictive policy? And can you think of other ways to defend a restrictive population policy?

12.3.   WHY COOPERATE?

Political organizers and advocates often try to persuade people to help achieve specified goals by arguing that it is to their mutual advantage to do so: if all members of a given class contribute to achieving the specified goals, these goals will (probably) be achieved, and all members will (probably) be better off.

For example, a union organizer wishing to persuade me to join a university-faculty union and contribute to the unionization effort in various costly or burdensome ways might argue this way:

> The benefit to you (to each professor, really) of unionization is likely to be considerable—far greater than the cost to you of joining the union and otherwise contributing to unionization. But to achieve this benefit, and to achieve it to the greatest degree possible and as quickly as possible, all or at least a majority of professors must contribute to unionization. So each professor is likely to be far better off if all—including himself—contribute to unionization than if many—himself included—do not contribute. In short, it is mutually advantageous for professors to contribute to unionization. So you *help yourself* by contributing.

Standardized, the argument looks like this:

(P$_1$) Each professor would be better off if all professors—including himself—contributed to unionization than if many—himself included—did not contribute.

∴ (C) Each professor would be better off contributing to unionization than not doing so.

This argument is invalid. We can make it valid, easily enough, by adding a premise:

(P$_2$) Assuming each member of a class would be better off if all members did a certain thing than if many—himself included—did not do it, then each member would be better off doing the thing than not doing it.

But (P_2) succumbs to counter-examples. There are examples, indeed, in which every member of a class would be better off if all or most members did a certain thing than if many members, himself included, did not do it, yet *each* member would be better off *not* doing the thing than *doing* it, *regardless of what others might do.* Two such examples:

1. The world is ruled by two superpowers, X-onia and Y-land. Each must decide whether to disarm. The choices facing them are depicted in this table:

X-onia

		disarms	does not disarm
Y-land	disarms	second best for X-onia second best for Y-land	best for X-onia worst for Y-land
	does not disarm	worst for X-onia best for Y-land	second worst for X-onia second worst for Y-land

There are four possible outcomes, corresponding to the four boxes in the table: Either both countries disarm (upper left box), or X-onia disarms but Y-land does not (lower left), or Y-land disarms but X-onia does not (upper right), or neither disarms (lower right).

If both countries disarm, neither can benefit by taking advantage of the other; still, both fare pretty well, since neither can be taken advantage of by the other and each cuts its defense budget. If neither country disarms, neither can be taken advantage of by the other, yet both fare rather poorly because of the cost of arms. Finally, if one disarms but the other does not, the second can dictate terms to the first.

If both countries disarm (upper left box), the outcome is second best for each, while if neither disarms (lower right), the outcome is second worst for each. So if both disarm, each is better off than it would be if neither disarmed.

Even so, each is better off not disarming than disarming. Take X-onia. If Y-land disarms, X-onia can, by not disarming, achieve an outcome (upper right) that is best for itself rather than second best (upper left). And if Y-land does not disarm, X-onia can, by not disarming, achieve an outcome (lower right) that is second worst for itself rather than worst.

So *whatever* Y-land does, X-onia is better off not disarming. Likewise, whatever X-onia does, Y-land is better off not disarming. Although mutually advantageous for the two superpowers, disarmament is not individually advantageous for either of them.

2. One thousand people have bought houses along the newly developed shores of Limpid Lagoon. Each must choose between emptying his sewage in the water and installing a septic tank. A septic tank costs one hundred dollars per year. A single homeowner polluting Limpid Lagoon with his sewage for one year does about one thousand dollars' worth of harm, divided pretty evenly among the thousand homeowners, hence about one dollar's worth of harm to each homeowner, hence about one dollar's worth of harm to himself. That is, each homeowner would be willing to pay about one dollar per year to eliminate his share of the pollution caused by any one homeowner, hence about one dollar per year to eliminate his share of the harm he does to himself by polluting.

If some homeowners pollute, each homeowner suffers one dollar's worth of harm for each polluter. So if all pollute, each suffers one thousand dollars' worth of harm. If even one-quarter pollute, each suffers fully two hundred fifty dollars' worth of harm. But if no one pollutes, each incurs just the one-hundred-dollar cost of a septic tank. So each homeowner would be better off if all homeowners installed septic tanks than he would be if many—himself included—polluted.

Yet each would be better off polluting than installing a septic tank, regardless of what the others did. Although the cost of a homeowner's polluting is one thousand dollars and the cost of his installing a septic tank only one hundred dollars, the former cost would be divided among the thousand homeowners, but he alone would bear the latter cost.

The choice facing each homeowner, say Homer Houseman, is depicted as follows:

	Homer pollutes.	Homer installs a septic tank.	All 1,000 home-owners pollute.	All 1,000 home-owners install septic tanks.
Cost to Homer	$1	$100	$1,000	$100
Cost to all 1,000 home-owners	$1 × 1,000 = 1,000	($100 × 1) + (0 × 999) = $100	$1,000 × 1,000 = $1,000,000	$100 × 1,000 = $100,000

Any argument of this form is a bad argument:

> Each P would be better off if all Ps did U than he would be if many Ps—himself included—did not do U.
>
> ∴ Each P would be better off doing U than not doing U.

It is invalid as it stands, and the obvious validating premise, (P₂), is not true. The faculty-unionization argument is just one bad argument of this form. Other examples involve disarmament and pollution. Still others involve voting, tax-paying, littering, walking on lawns, and keeping promises.

Just because arguments of the specified sort are bad, mutual advantage by itself provides no reason for the members of a class to cooperate—to contribute to a common objective. What is *mutually* advantageous need not be *individually* advantageous.

Sometimes mutually advantageous activity can be *made* individually advantageous by instituting rewards and penalties—fines for polluting Limpid Lagoon, for instance. Such is an often-heard justification for government and an often-heard explanation of government's existence. Government provides rewards and (mainly) penalties, the story goes, to make it individually advantageous to contribute to mutually advantageous objectives.

12.4. COOPERATION AND FAIRNESS

Having failed to persuade me to contribute to unionization by appeal to my self-interest, our friend the union organizer might try appealing instead to my sense of *fairness*:

> In the pollution example, it would be *unfair* for a homeowner to benefit from clean water without doing his part to keep it clean. In a similar way, it would be unfair for a citizen not to pay taxes, for a member of a tug-of-war team to feign pulling, or for a professor to benefit from unionization without working to achieve unionization—to share the benefits of unionization without sharing the costs. It would therefore be unfair for you not to join the union and otherwise contribute what you reasonably can to the unionization effort.

Reconstruction:

> (P₁) If someone stands to benefit significantly from the participation of others in some cooperative endeavor, then it would be unfair for him not to participate in it if he can do so. (tacit or 'semiexpress')

(P₂) Each professor stands to benefit significantly from the participation of others in the cooperative endeavor of unionization.
(tacit)

∴ (C) It would be unfair for any professor who can participate in the
unionization endeavor not to do so.

(P₁) is a general principle, of which the original passage gives several
examples. You can regard those examples either as a vivid way of expressing the principle or as the premises of a reverse-explanation argument for the principle.

Counter-examples beset (P₁): Think of cooperative endeavors that
benefit their participants by inflicting significant, undeserved costs on
nonparticipants. If, for example, petroleum companies cooperated to fix
prices, consumers would be unjustly hurt. The benefits of cooperation
would be achieved at a significant, undeserved cost to nonparticipants.
(P₁) notwithstanding, the failure of petroleum companies to fix prices
would not be unfair.

Such counter-examples can be avoided if we qualify (P₁) thus:

(P₁') If someone stands to benefit significantly from the participation of others in some cooperative endeavor, then it would be
unfair for him not to participate in it if he can do so *and if the
endeavor would impose no significant, undeserved costs on
nonparticipants.*

Replacing (P₁) by the weaker (P₁') makes the argument invalid. Validity can be restored by adding a new premise:

(P₃) The unionization endeavor would impose no significant, undeserved costs on nonparticipants.

But (P₃) runs afoul of counter-examples: Such benefits as professors
achieved through unionization would be achieved at significant, undeserved costs to others, specifically: unwilling, economically hard-
pressed students, parents, and taxpayers, who would have to pay directly for the increased wages achieved through unionization; those
nonacademic university employees who would suffer from a realloca-
tion of university funds to faculty wages; everyone who would lose such
public and philanthropic beneficences as were shifted to the university
to help meet the demands of unionization; those academics—some of
them unemployed—who would have been hired by the university but
for the increased cost of academic labor, and the consequent decrease in
the number of academic positions, resulting from unionization; those
additional academics who would have been hired by the university but
for the greater job protection, and the consequent drop in the ratio of
open to filled positions, achieved through unionization; students and

other, less direct beneficiaries of education, who would suffer from a drop in the quality of teaching if salary schedules and reappointment criteria were specified in union contracts; the public at large, who, as indirect consumers of research, would suffer similarly from a drop in research quality.

This still does not settle the issue of whether to join the union. A better argument for joining—either a further modification of the above argument or an entirely different one—may yet be found. The norms and techniques presented in this book will not by themselves produce a better argument. What they can do is to help us articulate and evaluate any alternative argument we may produce, thereby helping us to decide whether we have produced a better argument.

Logic alone is limited. It guides reasoning, not by producing reasons, but by providing principles of good reasoning—standards and procedures for articulating and evaluating arguments and explanations. Without topical knowledge or creativity, logic will never lead us anywhere. Without logic, however, topical knowledge and creativity will often lead us astray.

EXERCISES

1. Can you think of *other* arguments—ones different from the *compensation* argument discussed in §12.1—for preferential hiring?

2. Consider the argument, discussed in §12.2, that a restrictive population policy would make our distant descendants better off. Construct a similar argument for a policy of environmental cleanliness, resource conservation, or the preservation of genetic health or variety. Evaluate this argument. Is it open to the objection that afflicted the population argument?

3. Consider the fairness argument for union participation given in §12.4. Construct a similar argument to the effect that we—the present generation—should restrict population growth, preserve our natural environment, conserve scarce resources, or some such thing, in order to serve our shared goal of benefiting our distant descendants. Evaluate this argument.

Evaluate:

4. Unless we institute a policy of preferential hiring, it will be a hundred years before the percentage of good jobs filled by women and minority members equals their percentage of the population.

* 5. We should adopt some sort of well-thought-out national *eugenics* policy. Then future generations would constitute a healthy, creative race of super-men.

   6. We should replace most current urban housing with new luxury housing plus complementary services—living conditions that would attract the affluent back to the city. That's sure to make the urban population much better off. For it will raise the average income of the urban population several-fold.

* 7. If all Democrats vote, a Democrat will probably be elected. So it would be foolish for Democrats not to vote.

   8. Those who voted for Eugene McCarthy in 1976 were foolish, because they threw away votes Carter might well have needed.

* 9. Because they raise the incomes of our lowest-paid workers, federal minimum-wage laws are perforce justified from the point of view of our worst-off workers, even if there be objections to these laws from other points of view.

* 10. What explains the Widget Workers' organizing a union and going on strike, I guess, is that they thought they'd get better wages and greater job protection that way.

  11. A monopoly of the sugar-refining business is beneficial to sugar refiners; and of the corn trade to corn growers; and of silk manufacture to silk weavers, etc., etc.; and thus each class of men are benefited by some restrictions. Now all these classes of men make up the whole community; therefore, a system of restriction is beneficial to the community. (Whately, *Elements of Logic*)

* 12. Well, so we agree that that piece of land was illicitly taken from the Indian tribe in the nineteenth century, the contract of sale having been fraudulent. Thus, while it would admittedly be impracticable to return the land—factories, housing developments, shopping centers, and all—to the tribe, we must at least compensate the tribe. To refuse to do so would compound our injustice against those Indians.

  13. The reason the parsley farmers turned out in such large numbers to vote for Klaghorn is that he promised to fight for an embargo on all imported parsley.

  14. Consider the general argument-form described in §12.3—the form of which the first unionization argument is an example. Compose arguments of the same (bad) form that concern, not unionization, but disarmament, pollution, voting, paying taxes, littering, walking on lawns, keeping promises, and one or two other subjects of your own choosing.

APPENDIX ONE

Procedure for Evaluating Arguments and Explanations: An Outline

Arguments

STEP ONE   *Reconstruct* the argument. This consists of three operations:

▶ *Standardize* the argument, listing its express premises followed by its conclusion, even if the conclusion was tacit. Formulate each step as a fully explicit declarative sentence, expanding ellipses and other abbreviations. Omit all repetition and extraneous matter. Make any strictly stylistic changes needed to obtain a more transparent, more nearly valid logical form.

If the argument is *compound* (if it contains two or more subarguments and therewith one or more intermediate steps, each the conclusion of one subargument and a premise of another), display it as a *tree* in which the express premises occupy the top nodes, the conclusion the bottom node, and the intermediate steps the remaining nodes.

▶ Test the argument as it stands for *validity*.

An argument is *valid* if no argument of the same logical form has true premises along with a false conclusion.

Some *strategies* for ascertaining validity:

Display *logical form.*

Look for *counter-examples.* A counter-example to an argument's logical form is an argument of the same form with obviously true premises and an obviously false conclusion.

Look for a convincing *derivation.*

Apply a *Venn-diagram* test.

▶ If the argument as it stands is not valid, supply reasonable *validating tacit premises* if possible. If this is *not possible*, the argument is *irremediably invalid*, and the procedure stops.

Choose among *alternative validating premises* according to these three criteria:

FIDELITY Add premises that are *faithful to the author's beliefs and intentions*, insofar as these are known and deemed important. So added premises should neither conflict with the stated argument nor make any stated premise gratuitous.

GENEROSITY Be generous to the author by adding premises that are as *plausible* as possible (relative to the argument's intended audience). Added premises should be sufficiently plausible, anyway, to enhance the credibility of the conclusion to some degree.

GENERALITY Add premises that are as *general* as possible, consistent with Fidelity and Generosity.

Some *strategies* for finding validating premises:

Look for the links between terms established by the express premises and the conclusion. Then find new premises that complete the circle of links between terms.

Read validating premises off a Venn diagram by verbalizing some additional diagrammatic feature (usually the shading of some additional area) sufficient to verify the conclusion. Generality calls for shading of the widest possible area, consistent with Fidelity and Generosity.

STEP TWO Check whether the argument depends on any *ambiguity*—whether, that is, the argument contains one or several expressions meeting these three conditions:

(i) The expressions are ambiguous: they have two or more meanings each.

(ii) The argument owes its appeal to interpreting at least one of the expressions more than one way. That is, the combination of plausible premises, valid form, and interesting conclusion requires that at least one of the expressions (it might not matter which one) be taken in two or more senses.

(iii) The argument is valid only if each of the expressions has the same meaning throughout.

STEP THREE   *Evaluate the premises*, looking for premises that are either false or not sufficiently plausible to support the conclusion drawn from them. Use any information you may have. More specifically:

► *Read* each premise *critically*, dwelling on each premise separately, trying to understand every term, looking for partly hidden assumptions, demanding clarity, classifying each premise as general or nongeneral, and further classifying each premise (if possible) as empirical, normative, mathematical, or verbal.

► Check whether the premises are *self-defeating* and whether any of them is *question-begging*.

Self-defeating premises are jointly inconsistent or become so upon the addition of some platitudes.

A *question-begging* premise is about as debatable as the conclusion because it is too close in meaning to the conclusion to enhance the conclusion's credibility to any significant degree.

► Look for *counter-examples* to general premises.

A *counter-example* to a general statement is a concrete case in which what the statement says is false.

Hypothetical counter-examples can refute verbal and most normative generalizations.

Only *actual* counter-examples can refute empirical generalizations.

> Test each premise for *sufficient generality*, asking whether it can reasonably be made more general—whether, in other words, there is any reason for restricting its generality. If it can reasonably be made more general, you may impute the more general version to the argument's author and criticize his argument by criticizing the generalized premise.

Explanations

(including those involved in reverse-explanation arguments)

FIRST THREE STEPS	Same as Steps One, Two, and Three above, except that explanatory premises are not required to be sufficiently plausible to enhance the credibility of the explanatory conclusion drawn from them.
STEP FOUR	Check whether there be any reasonable *alternative explanation*, comparing any you find with the given explanation according to two criteria: PLAUSIBILITY and ECONOMY. The *economy* of an explanation (or explanatory premise) is its *explanatory power* (how much it explains) divided by its *complexity*, the latter being the inverse of *simplicity;* in short, $E = P/C$, where $C = \frac{1}{S}$

Application

ORDER OF APPLICATION	Apply Step One, followed by Steps Two and Three in either order, then Step Four in the case of an explanation. If you find some *objection*, try to *reformulate* the argument or explanation to avoid the objection; then *go back* to Step One. For many explanations, Steps One, Two, and Three are sufficiently unimportant compared with Step Four that they may be omitted to save time and effort.
USES	To help you understand, evaluate, and improve pieces of reasoning (arguments and explanations) with which you are presented, as well as ones you yourself create, hence to write a clear, closely and rigorously reasoned critical, argumentative, or explanatory essay.

APPENDIX TWO

Glossary

AMBIGUOUS EXPRESSION   A word, phrase, sentence, or other expression with two or more meanings.

AMPHIBOLY   Ambiguity (multiple meaning) of the syntactic structure of a sentence or phrase.

ARGUMENT   A piece of discourse that defends or supports some statement by giving reasons for it.

ATOMIC STATEMENT   A statement containing no other statements.

CIRCLE-CLOSING STRATEGY   A strategy for finding an argument's validating tacit premises. It consists in identifying the links between terms established by the express premises and the conclusion, then finding new premises that complete the circle of links between terms.

CLASS   A batch, bunch, set, collection, or totality of things.

COMPOUND ARGUMENT   An argument containing two or more subarguments and therewith one or more intermediate steps, each the conclusion of one subargument and a premise of another.

COMPOUND STATEMENT   A molecular statement, hence a statement containing at least one other, shorter statement.

CONCLUSION   The statement that an argument or explanation is intended to support or explain.

CONNECTIVE   An expression used to form molecular (compound) statements from other, shorter statements.

CONSISTENT STATEMENT OR SET OF STATEMENTS   A statement (or set of statements) for which some statement (or set of statements) of the same logical form is true (or consists wholly of truths).

COUNTER-EXAMPLE TO A GENERAL STATEMENT   A concrete case in which what the statement says is obviously false.

COUNTER-EXAMPLE TO AN ARGUMENT FORM   An argument of that form with obviously true premises and an obviously false conclusion.

DEDUCTIVE ARGUMENT   An argument that purports to be deductively valid, hence one whose conclusion purportedly follows from its premises, hence one whose premises purport not merely to support but to necessitate its conclusion.

DEDUCTIVELY VALID ARGUMENT   *In the loose, broad, nonformal sense:* An argument whose premises necessitate its conclusion, that is, an argument of which it would be impossible for the premises to be true and the conclusion false. *In the strict, narrow, formal sense:* An argument for which every argument of the same logical form that has true premises also has a true conclusion, that is, one for which no argument of the same logical form has both true premises and a false conclusion.

DEPENDENCE ON AN AMBIGUITY   That defect of an argument consisting in the argument's owing its appeal (the appearance of plausible premises plus interesting conclusion plus valid form) to interpreting some expression more than one way, while owing its validity to interpreting the expression uniformly.

DERIVATION   A demonstration of an argument's validity that uses intermediate steps to make evident the connection between premises and conclusion.

ECONOMY   The explanatory power of an explanation or explanatory premise (how much it explains) divided by its complexity (E = P/C), the latter being the inverse of simplicity (C = $\frac{1}{S}$). One of two criteria for comparing alternative explanations, the other being plausibility.

EMPIRICAL STATEMENT   A statement that purports to describe, predict, or explain observable phenomena.

EMPTY CLASS   The (one and only) class that has no members.

EQUIVOCATION   The ambiguity (multiple meaning) of a word.

EXPLANATION   A piece of discourse that states reasons to explain why something is true.

EXPLANATORY CONCLUSION   The conclusion of an explanation.

EXPLANATORY PREMISE   A premise of an explanation.

EXPRESS CONCLUSION   A conclusion that is expressly formulated, not tacit.

EXPRESS PREMISE   A premise that is expressly formulated, not tacit.

FIDELITY   One of three criteria for choosing among alternative validating premises when reconstructing arguments and explanations, the other two being Generosity and Generality. Requires that a premise be faithful to the author's beliefs and intentions, insofar as these are known and deemed important.

GENERALITY   One of three criteria for choosing among alternative validating premises when reconstructing arguments and explanations, the other two being Fidelity and Generosity. Requires that a premise be as general as possible, consistent with Fidelity and Generosity.

GENERAL TERM   A word or phrase (adjectival, verbal, or nominal) used to express some property, feature, type, or trait of things.

GENEROSITY   One of the three criteria for choosing among alternative validating premises when reconstructing arguments and explanations, the other two being Fidelity and Generality. Requires that a premise be as plausible as possible.

HYPOTHESIS   A conjecture or speculation provisionally assumed to see what follows from it. Often explanatory premises are hypotheses.

IMPLICIT GENERAL TERM   A general term foreign to a statement but needed as a label in the statement's Venn diagram.

INCLUSION OF CLASSES   The relation of a class to itself or another when every member of the former also is a member of the latter.

INCONSISTENT STATEMENT OR SET OF STATEMENTS   A statement or set of statements that is not consistent.

INDUCTIVE ARGUMENT   *In the wide sense:* An argument that is not deductive, hence one whose premises purport merely to support, not to necessitate, its conclusion. *In the narrow sense:* An argument whose conclusion generalizes the information contained in its premises.

INTERMEDIATE STEP   A step of an argument (or explanation) that is neither a premise of the whole argument nor the conclusion of the whole argument, but the conclusion of a subargument and a premise of another subargument. Its purpose is to bring out the connection between the premises of the whole argument and the conclusion of the whole argument.

INVALID ARGUMENT   An argument that is not deductively valid.

LEXICAL DEFINITION   A definition that reports an expression's conventional meaning (instead of stipulating a new meaning for it).

LOGICAL EXPRESSION   One of the expressions that determine the logical form of a statement, set of statements, or argument. Just which expressions do this is controversial. According to one prevalent view, the logical expressions are the subject-independent expressions.

LOGICAL FORM   That form, shape, or structure of a statement, a set of statements, or an argument determined by its component logical expressions, hence that form, shape, or structure upon which the validity of arguments, the logical truth of statements, and the consistency of statements and sets of statements depend.

LOGICALLY TRUE STATEMENT   A statement for which every statement of the same logical form is true, hence one for which no statement of the same logical form is false.

MEMBER OF A CLASS   One of those things comprised in, or belonging to, the class.

MOLECULAR STATEMENT   A statement containing one or more other, shorter statements.

NEAR COUNTER-EXAMPLE TO AN ARGUMENT FORM   An argument of that form of which it obviously is (or would have been) possible for the premises to be true and the conclusion false.

NECESSARILY TRUE STATEMENT   A statement that must be true, independently of the way the world happens to be. A statement that could not possibly be false.

NOMINAL DEFINITION   A stipulative definition.

NORMATIVE STATEMENT   A statement that prescribes or evaluates behavior, character, procedures, institutions, artworks, or other things.

OSTENSION   The act of conveying an expression's meaning by pointing to that for which the expression stands.

OVERLAPPING CLASSES   Classes that share at least one member.

PARTIAL DEFINITION   A statement that narrows a locution's meaning without fully defining it.

POPULATION   The class of things described by the conclusion of an inductive argument in the narrow sense, hence the class to which the conclusion generalizes the feature attributed by the premises to some less inclusive class (the sample).

POSSIBLE CASE   A possible world, a possible state of affairs, a complete specification of one way the world might be.

POSSIBLY TRUE STATEMENT   A statement that could be (or could have been) true. A statement that, even if it happens to be false, is not false as a matter of necessity.

PREMISE   An ultimate reason given by an argument or explanation for its conclusion, that is, a reason for which no further reason is given in the argument or explanation in question.

PURE MODIFIER   An adverb or attributive adjective that is not itself a general term but forms part of a complex general term by modifying some simpler general term.

QUESTION-BEGGING PREMISE   A premise that is about as debatable as the conclusion drawn from it because it is too close in meaning to the conclusion to enhance the conclusion's credibility to any significant degree.

REAL DEFINITION   A lexical definition.

RECONSTRUCTION OF AN ARGUMENT   The result of adding reasonable validating tacit premises to the argument's standardization.

RESOLVING AN AMBIGUITY   Specifying which meaning is the intended one. (Often it is context rather than express stipulation that resolves an ambiguity.)

REVERSE-EXPLANATION ARGUMENT   An argument that defends an hypothesis on the ground that it explains something already accepted.

SAMPLE   The class of things described by the premises of an inductive argument in the narrow sense, hence the class of things to which the premises attribute a feature that the conclusion then generalizes to some more inclusive class (the population).

SELF-DEFEATING PREMISES   Premises that are jointly inconsistent or become so upon the addition of some platitude(s).

SIMPLE STATEMENT   An atomic statement.

SINGULAR TERM   A proper name, definite description, singular pronoun, or other word or phase used to designate, to label, to refer to a unique object in order to say something about that object.

SOUND ARGUMENT   An argument that is deductively valid and has true premises.

STANDARDIZATION OF AN ARGUMENT   The argument's express premises followed by its conclusion, formulated as fully explicit declarative sentences devoid of repetition and extraneous matter and with a logical form that is as transparent and as nearly valid as possible.

STEP   One of the statements that constitute an argument or explanation, hence a premise, a conclusion, or an intermediate step.

STIPULATIVE DEFINITION   A definition that stipulates a new meaning (instead of reporting an expression's conventional meaning). Introduces either a new expression or else a new meaning for an old expression.

SUFFICIENT GENERALITY   The test that asks of a premise whether it can reasonably be made more general. If a premise fails this test, a more general version may fairly be regarded as part of the argument and criticized as such.

SUPPOSITION OF A PART OF AN ARGUMENT   A clause that functions as though it were prefixed to every step in the given part of the argument by "If . . . then" (or "Suppose. . . . Then").

TACIT CONCLUSION   A conclusion of an argument or explanation that is not expressly formulated therein, hence a nonexpress conclusion.

TACIT PREMISE   A premise of an argument or explanation that is not expressly formulated therein, hence a nonexpress premise.

TREE DIAGRAM OF A COMPOUND ARGUMENT   A tree diagram in which the express premises of the argument occupy the top nodes, the conclusion the bottom node, and the intermediate steps the remaining nodes, and in which a supposition of any part of the argument may be displayed before a brace spanning that part of the argument.

TRUTH-FUNCTIONAL CONNECTIVE   A connective that always forms a molecular statement from shorter statements in such a way that the truth value of the molecular statement depends entirely on the truth values of the shorter statements.

TRUTH VALUE   Truth or falsity.

UNIVERSE REGION   The entire area of a Venn diagram, including some of the surrounding page. It represents the class of everything.

VALID ARGUMENT   A deductively valid argument.

VENN DIAGRAM   A type of diagram for depicting the contents of statements that express simple class relationships. Areas of such a diagram stand for classes. Overlapping circles or other figures stand for the classes corresponding to simple general terms. Lower-case letters represent singular terms. Shading represents emptiness; fat dots, nonemptiness. Can be used to ascertain validity of many common arguments by representing an argument's premises in one diagram and checking whether the content of the conclusion has automatically been represented thereby.

VERBAL STATEMENT   A statement that purports to be true solely by virtue of its logical form plus the meanings of its component words.

APPENDIX THREE

Suggestions for Further Reading

Each of the following two books contains a philosophically probing discussion of BASIC LOGICAL CONCEPTS that goes beyond Part One above:

Haack, Susan. *Philosophy of Logics*. Cambridge: Cambridge University Press, 1978.

Quine, W. V. *Philosophy of Logic*. Englewood Cliffs, N.J.: Prentice-Hall, 1970.

The former presupposes mastery of a symbolic-logic text such as Quine's *Methods of Logic* or Jeffrey's *Formal Logic: Its Scope and Limits*, cited below.

Although a popular topic among nineteenth-century logicians, LOGIC DIAGRAMS have been little discussed in recent times. For a most entertaining historical survey, see:

Gardner, Martin. *Logic Machines and Diagrams*. New York: McGraw-Hill, 1958.

Many textbooks use the techniques of SYMBOLIC LOGIC to ascertain validity, consistency, and logical truth. These techniques involve translating English sentences into symbolic formulas, then performing certain computation-like operations on those formulas. The following introductions to symbolic logic are especially clear and accurate:

Hacking, Ian. *A Concise Introduction to Logic*. New York: Random House, 1972.

Jeffrey, Richard C. *Formal Logic: Its Scope and Limits*. New York: McGraw-Hill, 1967.

Quine, W. V. *Methods of Logic*, third edition. New York: Holt, Rinehart and Winston, 1972.

Schagrin, Morton L. *The Language of Logic*. New York: Random House, 1979.

The Hacking and Schagrin are brief, easy, and particularly suitable for self-instruction. The Jeffrey and Quine are more challenging and comprehensive. Professor Preston Covey of Carnegie-Mellon University (Pittsburgh, Pa. 15213) has developed a transportable computer-assisted-instruction program that presents the usual techniques of symbolic logic, integrated with the task of argument reconstruction discussed in Chapter Seven above. Often symbolic logic is tied less to the assessment of verbal arguments than to the construction, application, and evaluation of *axiomatic theories*, as in these two classic textbooks:

Suppes, Patrick. *Introduction to Logic*. New York: Van Nostrand, 1957.
Tarski, Alfred. *Introduction to Logic and to the Methodology of the Deductive Sciences*, third edition. New York: Oxford University Press, 1965.

Underlying axiomatic method and the techniques of symbolic logic is a body of mathematical theory, called simply MATHEMATICAL LOGIC, which constitutes one of the great intellectual achievements of the past hundred years. The symbolic-logic texts of Quine and Jeffrey, cited above, present some important elements of mathematical logic. The following is a standard, widely used introduction to this body of theory:

Mendelson, Elliot. *Introduction to Mathematical Logic*. New York: Van Nostrand, 1964.

Written for those who have studied a text of the Jeffrey, Quine, or Suppes variety, this little book gives an introduction to logical theory that is remarkably deep, comprehensive, and accurate for its brevity and readability:

Crossley, J. N., and others. *What is Mathematical Logic?* Oxford: Oxford University Press, 1972.

The less formal side of logic is not much developed compared with the formal side. These three textbooks take different approaches (from the present book as well as from each other) to the NONFORMAL (or not strictly formal) side of LOGIC:

Beardsley, Monroe. *Thinking Straight*, third edition. Englewood Cliffs, N.J.: Prentice-Hall, 1966.
Johnson, Ralph H., and J. Anthony Blair. *Logical Self-Defense*. Toronto: McGraw-Hill Ryerson, 1977.
Scriven, Michael. *Reasoning*. New York: McGraw-Hill, 1976.

Beardsley offers brief, lucid, accurate introductions to a variety of logic-related topics. Johnson and Blair present a taxonomy of fallacies, buttressed by careful attention to the problem of formulating useful criteria of application. Scriven eschews fallacy labels and virtually ignores deductive validity in favor of an emphasis on the macroscopic organization of arguments and criticisms. The most salient differences between these books and mine lies in the starring role I assign to the deductively valid reconstruction of argumentative discourse.

Up-to-date THEORETICAL studies of the NONFORMAL aspects of reasoning are few, and the difference between textbook and treatise is not sharply drawn in this area. The following five pioneering works deserve careful study:

Ennis, Robert H. *Logic in Teaching.* Englewood Cliffs, N.J.: Prentice-Hall, 1969.
Hamblin, C. L. *Fallacies.* London: Methuen, 1970.
Perleman, Chaim, and L. Olbrechts-Tyteca. *The New Rhetoric: A Treatise on Argumentation.* Notre Dame: University of Notre Dame Press, 1969.
Robinson, Richard. *Definition.* Oxford: Oxford University Press, 1954.
Toulmin, Stephen. *The Uses of Argument.* Cambridge: Cambridge University Press, 1958.

The Ennis book, which straddles the textbook-treatise distinction, is especially impressive for its combination of scope, depth, and practicality. Some theoretical discussion also can be found in the journal *Philosophy and Rhetoric* (especially in the series of articles by John Woods and Douglas Walton) and in the stimulating, well-produced *Informal Logic Newsletter* (edited and published by Ralph Johnson and Anthony Blair, Department of Philosophy, University of Windsor, Windsor, Ontario N9B 3P4). Relevant issues occasionally are addressed in books and journal articles on epistemology, philosophy of language, and philosophy of science.

For further EXAMPLES of arguments to reconstruct and criticize, see:

Cornman, James W., and Keith Lehrer. *Philosophical Problems and Arguments: An Introduction,* second edition. New York: Macmillan, 1974.
Pospesel, Howard, and David Marans. *Arguments.* Englewood Cliffs, N.J.: Prentice-Hall, 1978.
Thomas, Stephen N. *Practical Reasoning in Natural Language.* Englewood Cliffs, N.J.: Prentice-Hall, 1977.

See also the *Informal Logic Newsletter,* cited above. Longer stretches of contentious discourse (as opposed to single arguments) may be found in these texts:

Baum, Robert. *Ethical Arguments for Analysis,* second edition. New York: Holt, Rinehart and Winston, 1975.
McKenna, George, and Stanley Feingold. *Taking Sides: Clashing Views on Controversial Issues.* Guilford, Conn.: Dushkin Publishing Group, 1978.

The following books discuss EXPLANATIONS and REVERSE-EXPLANATION ARGUMENTS (including INDUCTIVE arguments):

Campbell, Stephen. *Flaws and Fallacies in Statistical Thinking.* Englewood Cliffs, N.J.: Prentice-Hall, 1974.

Cohen, Morris R., and Ernest Nagel. *An Introduction to Logic and Scientific Method*. New York: Harcourt, Brace, 1934.

Hempel, Carl G. *Philosophy of Natural Science*. Englewood Cliffs, N.J.: Prentice-Hall, 1966.

Lave, Charles A., and James G. March. *An Introduction to Models in the Social Sciences*. New York: Harper and Row, 1975.

Quine, W. V., and J. S. Ullian. *The Web of Belief*, second edition. New York: Random House, 1978.

Salmon, Wesley C. *Foundations of Scientific Inference*. Pittsburgh: University of Pittsburgh Press, 1966.

The Lave and March is the most challenging of the five books. Both it and the Campbell are designed to teach practical skills; the others address philosophic issues. See also Ennis, *Logic in Teaching*, cited earlier. For further study, one should read some of the innumerable textbooks in statistics and in the research methods of the various sciences, natural and social.

This book is the standard survey of the HISTORY OF LOGIC:

Kneale, William K., and Martha Kneale. *The Development of Logic*. Oxford: Clarendon Press, 1964.

Logic shares its interest in argumentative discourse with the ancient subject of RHETORIC. For an authoritative survey, see:

Young, Richard E., Alton L. Becker, and Kenneth L. Pike. *Rhetoric: Discovery and Change*. New York: Harcourt, Brace and World, 1970.

Logic shares its interest in reasoning skills with the new subject of PROBLEM SOLVING, which is grounded largely in cognitive psychology. The following is a stimulating introduction to this fashionable field:

Whimbey, Arthur, and Jack Lockhead. *Problem Solving and Comprehension: A Short Course in Analytic Reasoning*. Philadelphia: Franklin Institute Press, 1979.

=APPENDIX FOUR=
Solutions to Selected Exercises

Here are solutions to the exercises marked with a star.

CHAPTER 1

1. All conservatives are Republicans. (stated premise)
   No Democrat is Republican. (stated premise)
   No Democrat is conservative. (conclusion)

2. No worker is rich. (stated premise)
   Some Democrats are workers. (stated premise)
   Some Democrats are not rich. (conclusion)

4. Example 5:
   Without itches, we wouldn't enjoy scratching. (stated premise)
   Itches are evil. (tacit premise)
   Enjoyment is good. (tacit premise)

   Example 11:
   Homosexual acts involving only consenting adults have no victims. (stated premise)
   All crimes have victims. (tacit premise)

   Example 12:
   If x and y are both odd, then $x - 1$ and $y - 1$ are even. (stated premise)
   A sum of even numbers must itself be even. (stated premise)
   2 is an even number. (tacit premise)
   If x and y are both odd, then $(x - 1) + (y - 1) + 2$ is even. (intermediate step)
   $(x - 1) + (y - 1) + 2 = x + y$. (stated premise)
   If x and y are both odd, $x + y$ is even. (intermediate step)
   A number is odd if, and only if, it is not even. (tacit premise)

5. Most likely *deductive*. As shown in the text, there is a natural, plausible way to supply tacit premises so that the conclusion must be true if the premises are true. This is sufficiently obvious that the author doubtless meant to maintain as much.

In each of the following exercises, the premises precede the conclusion, "S" means "stated premise," and "T" means "tacit premise."

7. Deregulating the price of any good imposes an unfair burden on the poor. (S)
   Natural gas is a good. (T)
   It would be wrong to impose any unfair burden on the poor. (T)
   It would be wrong to deregulate the price of natural gas.

9. Dracula enjoys a great night life. (S)
   Whoever enjoys a great night life is a jet setter. (T)
   Dracula is a jet setter.

11. If we adopt the bill, we're in for trouble. (S)
    If we reject the bill, we're in for trouble. (S)
    Either we adopt the bill, or we reject it. (T)
    We're in for trouble.

13. If personality traits were hereditary, he-men would have he-children. (S)
    He-men do not (always) have he-children. (T)
    Personality traits are not hereditary.

15. If someone can make a rock so big he cannot lift it, then lifting it is something he cannot do. (T)
    If someone cannot make a rock so big he cannot lift it, then making it is something he cannot do. (T)
    God cannot do everything.

17. We all deliberate about alternative courses of action. (S)
    Whoever deliberates about alternative courses of action regards himself as having free will. (T)
    We all regard ourselves as having free will.

18. Societies are subject to the same ethical standards as individuals. (S)
    If X and Y are subject to the same ethical standards, then Y may not do what X may not do. (T)
    Individuals may not kill others except in self-defense. (S)
    To kill others just for the sake of retribution or deterrence is not to kill others in self-defense. (T)
    For society to use capital punishment is for society to kill others just for the sake of retribution or deterrence. (T)
    Society may not use capital punishment.

CHAPTER 2

"V" means "valid." "INV" means "*in*valid" and is always followed by a counter-example.

1. S is a H.
   All H are M.
   ∴ s is M.

   V

2. C A m.
   Some F A m.
   ∴ Some F are C.

   INV

   Lions eat meat.
   Some faculty members eat meat.
   ∴ Some faculty members are lions.

3. Whoever is R is L.
   y are R.
   ∴ y are L.

   V

4. Whoever is R is L.
   y are L.
   ∴ y are R.

   INV

   Whoever is competing in the Olympics is alive.
   You are alive.
   ∴ You are competing in the Olympics.

7. No W is R.
   Some D are W.
   ∴ Some D are not R.

   V

8. No W is R.
   Some G are not R.
   ∴ Some G are not W.

   INV

No pauper is rich.
Some paupers are not rich.
∴ Some paupers are not paupers.

11. If P, Q.
   P.
∴ Q.

   V

14. Whoever is P Ss.
   No B is im-P.
∴ No B fails to S.

   V

15. Some W are S.
   No K are S.
∴ Some K are not W.

   INV

   Some numbers are odd.
   No even numbers are odd.
∴ Some even numbers are not numbers.

CHAPTER 3

Same abbreviations as in Chapter 2.

1. Any P that Ds is J.
   CP Ds.
∴ CP is J.

   V

2. If CP D-ed M, it would be J.
   CP does not D M.
   CP is not J.

   INV

   If capital punishment cured cancer, it would be widely discussed.
   Capital punishment does not cure cancer.
∴ Capital punishment is not widely discussed.

5. If d is a J, then d Hs.
   d Hs.
   d is a J.

   INV

   If Lassie is a man, then Lassie breathes.
   Lassie breathes.
   ∴ Lassie is a man.

7. All Ps R-ed H.
   Some EPs do not H.
   ∴ Some EPs have not been R-ed.

   V

9. Either w O, or w E, or both.
   w O.
   ∴ w not-E.

   INV

   Either we breathe, or we breathe, or both.
   We breathe.
   ∴ We do not breathe.

11. If W F, R.
    If W C, R.
    ∴ R.

    INV

    If we eat the moon, we eat the moon.
    If we eat the moon, we eat the moon.
    ∴ We eat the moon.

13. All K are S.
    Some P are not S.
    ∴ Some P are not K.

    V

15. A H no V.
    Every C Hs a V.
    ∴ A A is no C.

    V

17. T are C B.
Whatever is B is D.
Whatever is D is U to P.
∴ It is U to P T.

V

19. Everybody does not L somebody.
∴ There is somebody everybody does not L.

INV

Everybody does not touch somebody.
∴ There is somebody everybody *(himself included)* does not touch.

21. If something is O-ed, whoever does it is a C.
∴ If G-ing is O-ed, only C will G.

V

24. B-ing amounts to A.
Not B-ing amounts to C.
A is S-er than C.
∴ B-ing is S-er than not B-ing.

V

25. If no-D two things and if one is W, so is the other.
No-D H-ing and T-ing.
It would be W to T.
∴ It would be W to H.

V

26. If a thing does not exist in R, then something G-er than it can be C-ed.
Nothing G-er than any D can be C-ed.
∴ Some D exists in R.

INV

If a thing does not exist in Texas, then something closer to Texas than it can be conceived.
Nothing closer to Texas than any unicorn that was born and has always lived in Austin can be conceived.
∴ Some unicorn that was born and has always lived in Austin exists in Texas.

28. If not-C, W.
    If C, I.
    ∴ If not-I, W.

    V

30. Either W or C.
    If W, then g is not B.
    If C, then g is not O.
    ∴ g is not both B and O.

    V

31. y cannot F all the P all the time.
    ∴ There is some P whom y can never F.

    INV

    You cannot eat all the dishes in your favorite restaurant all the time.
    ∴ There is some dish in your favorite restaurant you can never eat.

32. d exists in I.
    If a thing exists in I but not in R, something G-er than it can be C-ed.
    Nothing G-er than d can be C-ed.
    ∴ d exists in R.

    V

In the following exercises, if a statement is consistent but I cite no true statement of the same logical form, that is because the statement itself is true (so it
may be cited to prove its own consistency). Likewise, if a statement is not
logically true but I cite no false statement of the same logical form, that is
because the statement itself is false. "L" means "logically true," "C" means
"consistent," "N" means "necessarily true," and "P" means "possibly true."

35. P, hence C. Not N, hence not L.
    It is raining water (uttered during rain).

36. L, hence N, hence P, hence C.

37. P, hence C. Not N, hence not L.
    It never rains water.

38. Not C, hence not P, hence not N, hence not L.

39. N, hence P, hence C. Not L.
    Whenever it rains water, it rains wine.

43. N, hence P, hence C. Not L.
    Red is a shape.

45. L, hence N, hence P, hence C.

50. Not C, hence not P, hence not N, hence not L.

51. Not C, hence not P, hence not N, hence not L.

CHAPTER 4

In parentheses after each premise, there is a "•," a lower-case letter, or a particular style of shading (vertical, horizontal, acute), indicating that the premise is represented in the accompanying diagram by a "•" (or chain of connected "•"s), by the given letter (or connected inscriptions thereof), or by the given style of shading. "V" means "valid." "INV" means "invalid."

2. Every H is a D. (≡)
   All D are M. (|||)
   ∴ Each H is a M.

   V

3. Every H is a M. (≡)
   Every H is a D. (|||)
   ∴ All D are M.

   INV

4. No R is a D. (≡)
   Some R is a C. (•)
   ∴ Some C is not a D.

   V

5. All C are A. (≡)
   ∴ All A are C.

   INV

7. Someone is a P. (•)
   Someone is a G. (•)
   ∴ Someone is a GP.

   INV

10. No L is a R. (≡)
    Some R are C. (•)
    ∴ Some L are not C.

    INV

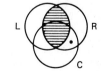

12. Some P have been W. (•)
    k was a P. (k)
    ∴ k was W.

    INV

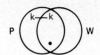

13. All P have been W. (≡)
    l was a P. (l)
    ∴ l was W.

    V

15. All C are R. (≡)
    Every G is R. (|||)
    ∴ Every G is C.

    INV

17. No W are R. (≡)
    Some G are not R. (•)
    ∴ Some G are not W.

    INV

19. Some R C. (•)
    Whatever C is L. (≡)
    ∴ Some R are L.

    V

21. Cs A. (≡)
    Some Fs A. (•)
    ∴ Some Fs are Cs.

    INV

23. d Es. (d)
    Every J Es. (≡)
    ∴ d is a J.

    INV

25. Whoever is R is L. (≡)
    y are R. (y)
    ∴ y are L.

    V

27. A H not-V. (≡)
    Every C V. (|||)
    ∴ A H is no C.

    V

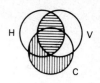

29. All S are M. (≡)
    Some L are M. (●)
    ∴ Some L are S.

    INV

31. Only a C would S. (≡)
    ∴ Any S-er must be a C.

    V

33. No Ps F. (≡)
    All Ps L. (|||)
    There are Ps. (●)
    ∴ Some L-ers do not F.

    V

35. Some A are C. (●)
    Some P are A. (●)
    ∴ Some P are C.

    INV

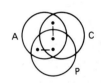

37. E everything. (≡)
    ∴ E everything not-E.

    V

CHAPTER 5

Same notational conventions as in Chapter 4.

2. n R. (n)
   When R, S. (≡)
   ∴ n S.

   V

times at
which R
(it is
raining)

times at
which S
(the
streets
are wet)

3. f cannot both D and be M. (f)
   f is M. (f̷)
   ∴ f cannot D.

   V

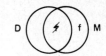

4. All B are I. (≡)
   Nobody is D who M. (|||)
   Whoever is I is D. (///)
   ∴ No B M.

   V

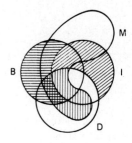

7. Any W who L must be a P. (≡)
   Only MW are P. (|||)
   Every MW is E. (///)
   s is a W who L. (s)
   ∴ s is E.

   V

	WLP	WL̄P	W̄LP	W̄L̄P	WLP̄	WL̄P̄	W̄LP̄	W̄L̄P̄
ME	1 s	1	1	1				
MĒ	1	1	1	1				
M̄E								
M̄Ē								

1 = MW

9. Either d did not H, or d was a J. (d)
   d did H. (f̷)
   ∴ d was a J.

   V

11. Never-W S. (≡)
    t is not S. (t)
    ∴ W t.

    INV

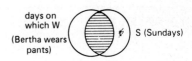

days on
which W
(Bertha wears
pants)   S (Sundays)

13. Either b is both V and H, or else b is S. (b)
    b is not V. (f̷)
    ∴ b is S.

    V

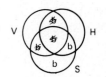

15. Whenever I, T. (≡)
    L only when not-I. (|||)
    J only when not-T but I. (///)
    ∴ L only when un-J.

    V

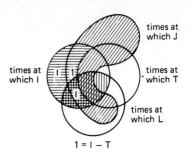

times at
which J

times at
which I

times at
which T

times at
which L

$1 = I - T$

17. Whatever is not I does not B. (≡)
    Ms are I. (|||)
    ∴ Ms B.

    INV

1 = non-I   2 = non-B

19. Some who are R S. (●)
    No one who is R and who Cs would S. (≡)
    ∴ Not all who are R C.

    V

21. Any P that I A. (≡)
    c is a P. (c)
    c I.(⚡)
    ∴ c A.

    V

22. (image of P, c, I, A circles)

23. Whenever I, T. (≡)
    L only when not-I. (|||)
    J only when not-T but I. (///)
    ∴ Whenever un-J, not-I.

    INV

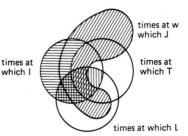

times at w
which J

times at
which I

times at
which T

times at which L

25. An un-J P would not D. (≡)
    c is a P that does not D. (c)
    ∴ c is J.

    INV

1 = P − J, 2 = non-D

27. i is a GV. (i)
    i is a C. (⌁)
    ∴ There is a GC.

    INV

28. Without further qualification, the conclusion does not make proper sense, because "tall" is not a general term; it is a pure modifier.

29. Similar to 28.

31. All C that B F. (≡)
    Any C that Fs Ps. (|||)
    No C that Ps S. (///)
    ∴ No C that Bs S.

    V

	CBF	CBF̄	CB̄F	CB̄F̄	C̄BF	C̄BF̄	C̄B̄F	C̄B̄F̄
PS								
PS̄								
P̄S								
P̄S̄								

33. To D is to C. (≡)
    To R is to B. (|||)
    ∴ C or B.

    INV

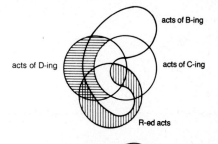

acts of B-ing
acts of D-ing
acts of C-ing
R-ed acts

35. Every C is a D or R. (≡)
    D are B. (|||)
    j is not B. (j)
    Neither is j a R. (⌁)
    ∴ j is not C.

    V

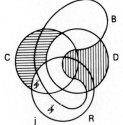

B
C
D
j
R

37. To D is to C. (≡)
    Not to D is to B. (|||)
    ∴ C or B.

    V

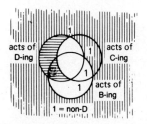

acts of D-ing
acts of C-ing
acts of B-ing
1 = non-D

39. All F are L-ers. (≡)
∴ Whoever Ls a F Ls a L-er.
  (Every Frenchman-lover is a lover-lover.)

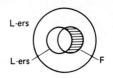

V

41. What is RS is RI. (≡)
  It is not RI to K. (|||)
  c is KS. (c)
∴ c is not R.

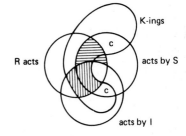

V

43. F all of the P some of the T. (●)
  F some of the P all of the T. (●)
  Not F all of the P all of the T. (≡)
∴ There is some P such that some of the
  T F him and some of the T not F him.

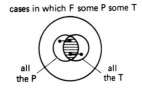

V

CHAPTER 6

Same notational conventions as in Chapter 4.

1. Not both D and M. (ƒ)
  M. (t)
∴ Not D.

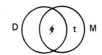

V

2. Either A or B. (t)
  A. (ƒ)
  If A, not C. (ƒ)
∴ D.

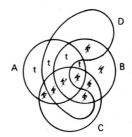

INV

4. Either not W or not P. (t)
   If not W, not B. (⚡)
   If not P, not O. (⚡)
   ∴ Not both B and O.

   V

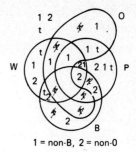

1 = non-B, 2 = non-O

7. If not-C, O. (t)
   If C, I. (t)
   ∴ If not-I, O.

   V

9. If D, J. (⚡)
   Not D. (⚡)
   ∴ Not J.

   INV

11. If not H, then not G unless D. (⚡)
    Not D. (⚡)
    G. (t)
    ∴ H.

    V

1 = non-G-or-D.

13. Not U unless S. (t)
    ∴ If S, U.

    INV

14. R and not R.
    ∴ T.

    V

It is impossible to represent the premise in a diagram. That shows the premise to be inconsistent, hence the argument to be valid.

17. D. (t)
    ∴ R or not R.

    V

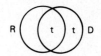

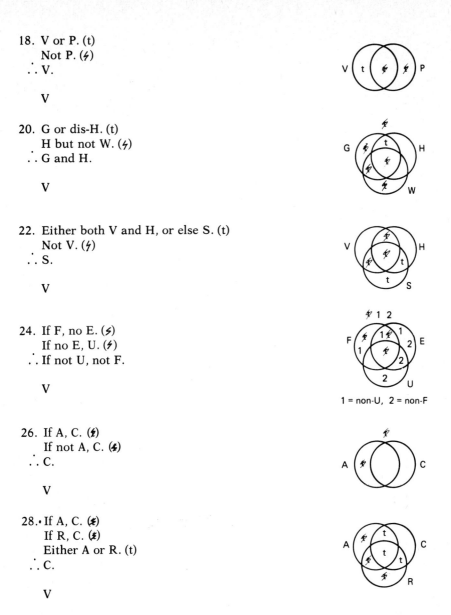

18. V or P. (t)
    Not P. (⚡)
    ∴ V.

    V

20. G or dis-H. (t)
    H but not W. (⚡)
    ∴ G and H.

    V

22. Either both V and H, or else S. (t)
    Not V. (⚡)
    ∴ S.

    V

24. If F, no E. (⚡)
    If no E, U. (⚡)
    ∴ If not U, not F.

    V

26. If A, C. (⚡)
    If not A, C. (⚡)
    ∴ C.

    V

28. If A, C. (⚡)
    If R, C. (⚡)
    Either A or R. (t)
    ∴ C.

    V

In the following exercises, a multiple-diagram test is used only if needed, that is, only if the argument in question contains connectives, its connective structure is invalid, and its atomic components are structurally related. When a multiple-diagram test is used, the *first diagram* depicts the argument's *connective structure;* the first set of statements to be tested for consistency is marked by a brace and accompanied by a diagram (used to ascertain consistency); and any other such set is given in a similar way *only if the first proves inconsistent.* For an inconsistent set of statements, the statement not representable in the accompanying diagram is so marked.

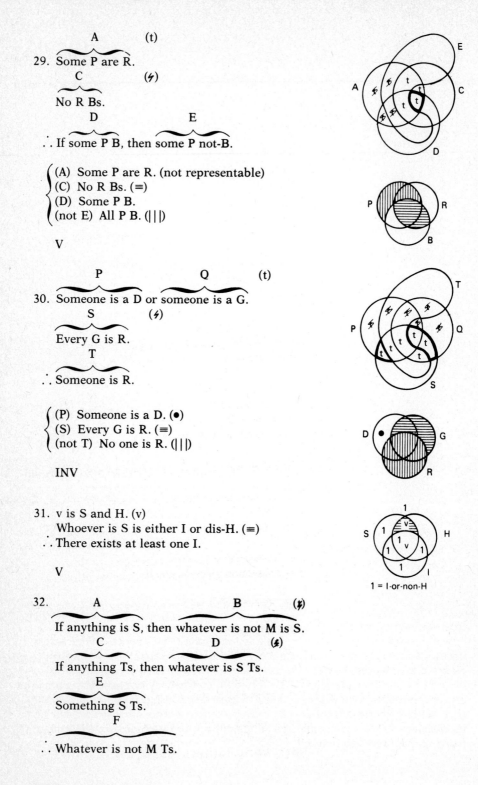

$$\overbrace{A}^{} \qquad (t)$$

29. Some $\overbrace{P}$ are $\overbrace{R}$.

$$\overbrace{C}^{} \qquad (\not{4})$$

No $\overbrace{R}$ Bs.

$$\overbrace{D}^{} \qquad\qquad \overbrace{E}^{}$$

$\therefore$ If some $\overbrace{P\ B}$, then some $\overbrace{P\ not\text{-}B}$.

$\left\{\begin{array}{l}\text{(A) Some P are R. (not representable)}\\ \text{(C) No R Bs. } (\equiv)\\ \text{(D) Some P B.}\\ \text{(not E) All P B. } (|\,|\,|)\end{array}\right.$

V

$$\overbrace{P}^{} \qquad\qquad \overbrace{Q}^{} \qquad (t)$$

30. Someone is a D or someone is a G.

$$\overbrace{S}^{} \qquad (\not{4})$$

Every $\overbrace{G}$ is R.

$$\overbrace{T}^{}$$

$\therefore$ Someone is R.

$\left\{\begin{array}{l}\text{(P) Someone is a D. } (\bullet)\\ \text{(S) Every G is R. } (\equiv)\\ \text{(not T) No one is R. } (|\,|\,|)\end{array}\right.$

INV

31. v is S and H. (v)

Whoever is S is either I or dis-H. ($\equiv$)

$\therefore$ There exists at least one I.

V

32.

$$\overbrace{A}^{} \qquad\qquad\qquad \overbrace{B}^{} \qquad (\not{4})$$

If anything is S, then whatever is not M is S.

$$\overbrace{C}^{} \qquad\qquad \overbrace{D}^{} \qquad (\not{4})$$

If anything Ts, then whatever is S Ts.

$$\overbrace{E}^{}$$

Something S Ts.

$$\overbrace{F}^{}$$

$\therefore$ Whatever is not M Ts.

	EF	EF̄	ĒF	ĒF̄
ABCD	t	t		
ABCD̄	~~t~~	~~t~~	~~t~~	~~t~~
ABC̄D	t	t		
ABC̄D̄	t	t		
AB̄CD	~~t~~	~~t~~	~~t~~	~~t~~
AB̄CD̄	~~t~~	~~t~~	~~t~~	~~t~~
AB̄C̄D	~~t~~	~~t~~	~~t~~	~~t~~
AB̄C̄D̄	~~t~~	~~t~~	~~t~~	~~t~~
ĀBCD	t	t		
ĀBCD̄	~~t~~	~~t~~	~~t~~	~~t~~
ĀBC̄D	t	t		
ĀB̄CD	t	t		
ĀB̄C̄D	t	t		
ĀB̄C̄D̄	~~t~~	~~t~~	~~t~~	~~t~~
ĀB̄C̄D	t	t		
ĀB̄C̄D̄	t	t		

To verify conclusion, "t" must be excluded from all heavily outlined areas. First plus third constitute EF̄BCD region; second plus fourth constitute EF̄BC̄ region; fifth is EFABCB region; sixth is EFABC region. Hence, four combinations to test for consistency:

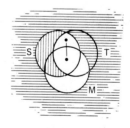

{
(E) Something S Ts. (●)
(not F) Some non-M does not T.
            (not representable)
(B) Whatever is not M is S. (≡)
(C) Something Ts.
(D) Whatever is S Ts. (|||)
}

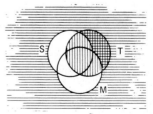

{
(E) Something S Ts. (not representable)
(not F) Some non-M does not T.
(B) Whatever is not M is S. (≡)
(not C) Nothing Ts. (|||)
}

{
(E) Something S Ts. (not representable)
(not F) Some non-M does not T.
(not A) Nothing is S. (≡)
(not B) Some non-M is not S.
(not C) Nothing Ts. (|||)
}

V

39. All P R M. (≡)
   Some E P not-M. (●)
∴ Some E P were not R.

V

             P
40. Supposing ‿‿‿‿‿‿‿‿‿‿ there will be a C if
     not-Q   S
   ‿‿‿‿‿   ‿‿‿‿‿
   p does not R, then r will have A
        T   (t)
   ‿‿‿‿‿
   and (r will have) M.
     T   (≢)
   ‿‿‿‿‿
   r does M.
     not-Q
   ‿‿‿‿‿
∴ p does not R.

1 = P-if-not-Q = Q-or-P; 2 = S-and-T.

{
(Q) p Rs. (p)
(S) r will have A. (r)
(T) r will have M. (≢)
}

INV

       P   Q   (≢)
42. If any M K, all M K.
           not-Q   not-P
∴ If some M do not K, then no M Ks.

V

1 = non-Q, 2 = non-P

$$\overbrace{\hspace{2cm}}^{A} \quad \overbrace{\hspace{1.5cm}}^{B} \quad (\natural)$$

44. If every M is a L or a S, then no M is a N.

$$\overbrace{\hspace{2cm}}^{C} \quad (t)$$

Some M are L N.

$$\underbrace{\text{not-A}}$$

∴ Some M are neither L nor S.

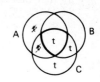

$$\begin{cases} \text{(A) Every M is a L or a S. } (\equiv) \\ \text{(B) No M is a N. } (|||) \\ \text{(C) Some M are L N. (not representable)} \end{cases}$$

V

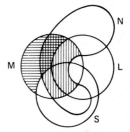

$$\overbrace{\hspace{1cm}}^{C} \quad (t)$$

46. M IS AN A.

$$\overbrace{\text{not-D}} \quad (\ )$$

m will not B.

$$\overbrace{\hspace{1cm}}^{E} \qquad \overbrace{\hspace{1cm}}^{D}$$

∴ Some A Ps if m Bs.

V

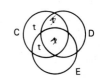

$$\overbrace{\hspace{2cm}}^{A} \qquad \overbrace{\hspace{1.5cm}}^{B} \quad (t)$$

48. Either every M is R, or no M is R.

$$\overbrace{\hspace{2cm}}^{C} \quad (\not{5})$$

Some M are L.

$$\overbrace{\hspace{1.5cm}}^{D} \quad (\not{5})$$

No R are L.

$$\overbrace{\hspace{2cm}}^{B}$$

∴ No M is R.

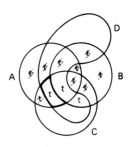

$$\begin{cases} \text{(A) Every M is R. } (\equiv) \\ \text{(not B) Some M is R. } (\bullet) \\ \text{(C) Some M are L. (not representable)} \\ \text{(D) No R are L. } (|||) \end{cases}$$

V

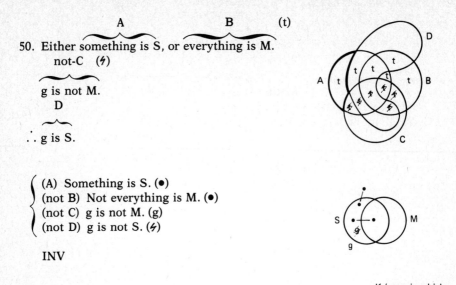

50. Either something is S, or everything is M. **A B (t)**

    not-C (↯)

    g is not M.
       D

∴ g is S.

    { (A) Something is S. (●)
      (not B) Not everything is M. (●)
      (not C) g is not M. (g)
      (not D) g is not S. (↯)

    INV

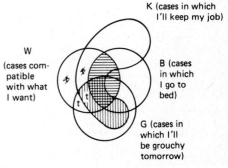

54. Not W B. (≡)
    Whatever W comes true. (t)
    If not B, G. (↯)
    It is not possible for both
      G and K. (|||)
∴ Not K.

    V

56. Only those who L the Q are R
      by the K. (≡)
    The Q is a B. (|||)
    No one who Ls a B is R by
      anyone. (///)
∴ No one L the Q.

    INV

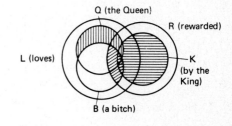

CHAPTER 7

"E" means "*express* premise"; "T" means "*tacit* premise." It is possible for you to have a correct answer that does not exactly match mine.

1. Girlie magazines debase women. (E)
    Whatever debases women is bad. (T)
  ∴ Girlie magazines are bad.

3. Capital punishment deters crime. (E)
   Any punishment that deters crime is justified. (T)
   ∴ Capital punishment is justified.

5. Some Ugandans are Christian. (E)
   No Christian loves Idi Amin. (T)
   ∴ Not all Ugandans love Idi Amin.

7. Whoever has an Albanian accent cannot have a proper Irish brogue. (E)
   Every Albanian has an Albanian accent. (T)
   ∴ Those who have proper Irish brogues are not Albanians.

9. Someone is a politician. (E)
   Someone is greedy. (E)
   ∴ Someone is a greedy politician.
   Irremediably invalid.

11. God prevents every catastrophe He knows of and can prevent. (E)
    God knows of every catastrophe. (E)
    God can prevent any catastrophe. (E)
    Whatever is prevented does not exist. (T)
    ∴ There are no catastrophes.

13. Someone is enamored of Red China. (E)
    No one enamored of Red China is unhappy about breaking relations with Taiwan. (T)
    ∴ Not everyone is unhappy about breaking relations with Taiwan.

15. To outlaw prostitution is to legislate morality. (E)
    We should not legislate morality. (T)
    ∴ We should not outlaw prostitution.

17. Pornography serves no purpose but to stimulate lust. (E)
    Whatever serves no purpose but to stimulate lust is wrong. (T)
    ∴ Pornography is wrong.

19. Everyone has the right to publish whatever information he wishes to publish. (E)
    The *Pentagon Papers* is information. (T)
    The *New York Times* wished to publish the *Pentagon Papers*. (T)
    ∴ The *New York Times* had the right to publish the *Pentagon Papers*.

21. Cheating on school assignments by students who use term-paper mills is entirely the fault of those students. (E)
    Anything illicit done by term-paper mills consists in contributing to cheating on school assignments by students who use the term-paper mills. (T)
    If it is illicit for X to contribute to Y, then contributing to Y is X's fault. (T)

The term-paper mills are not (the same entities as) the students who use them. (T)
Whatever is entirely someone's fault is no one else's fault. (T)
∴ Term-paper mills do nothing illicit.

23. Pornography does no psychological harm. (E)
Naked bodies per se are not evil. (E)
Whatever is seriously wrong with pornography is either psychological harm done by pornography or the evil of naked bodies per se. (T)
Pornography should be outlawed only if something is seriously wrong with it. (T)
∴ Pornography should not be outlawed.

25.

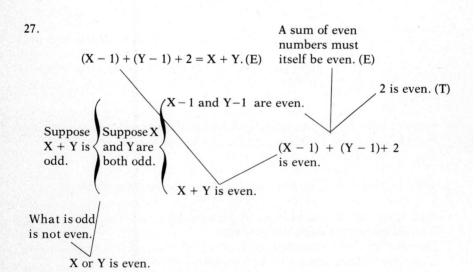

27.

29.
If X needs a Y and if all but one Y conflicts with other things X needs, then X needs that particular Y. (T)	Bosworth's course is another American History course. (T)	There are just two American History courses I can take besides Bosworth's: One conflicts with Sex Education, the other with Basket Weaving. (E)	One who needs a course had better take it. (T)

Suppose
I am
going
to
graduate.
}

I'll need another American History
course plus Sex Education
and Basket Weaving. (E)

I'd better take Bosworth's course.

31. People may not kill people just for the sake of retribution or deterrence. (E)
Society may do only what people may do. (T)
Capital punishment is society's killing people just for the sake of retribution or deterrence. (T)
What may not be done is wrong. (T)
∴ Capital punishment is wrong.

33. Some evil exists. (E)
Whoever is omnibenevolent wants to prevent any evil. (T)
Whoever is omnipotent can prevent any evil. (T)
Whoever both wants to do something and can do it does it. (T)
What is prevented does not exist. (T)
∴ God is not both omnibenevolent and omnipotent.

35. Prohibitionists and antipornography crusaders propose to impose restrictions on others. (T)
Prohibitionists and antipornography crusaders do not propose to impose upon others restrictions they would not gladly have imposed upon themselves. (E)
Those who propose to impose restrictions on others are being unfair only if they would not gladly have those restrictions imposed upon themselves. (T)
∴ Prohibitionists and antipornography crusaders are not being unfair.

37. If I hadn't bought the stolen fur coat, someone else would have bought it. (E)
If someone else had bought the stolen fur coat, the harm (if any) would have been the same as the harm from my having bought it. (E)
If the harm from not doing something would be the same as the harm from doing it, then there is nothing wrong with my doing it. (T)
∴ There was nothing wrong with my buying the stolen fur coat.

38. There is no difference between allowing congenitally deformed infants to die and terminating the lives of ill, unwanted elderly people. (E)

If there is no difference between two things and one is all right, so is the other. (T)

If it is all right to allow congenitally deformed infants to die, it is all right to terminate the lives of ill, unwanted elderly people.

It is not all right to terminate the lives of ill, unwanted elderly people. (T)

It is not all right to allow congenitally deformed infants to die.

39. Many people don't believe that homosexuality is wrong. (E)
Those who favor antihomosexuality laws are just trying to foist their own controversial religious beliefs on others. (E)
If those who favor anti-X laws are just trying to foist their own controversial religious beliefs on others, and if some people do not believe that X is wrong, then adopting anti-X laws violates the wall of separation between church and state. (T)
∴ Adopting antihomosexuality laws violates the wall of separation between church and state.

CHAPTER 8

1. line of printed matter
straight mark
policy

3. concern
heed
protection

5. the thing on your shoulders
chief
top
title
foam at top of glass of beer

7. container
argument
situation

9. power
   right to do something
   he who exercises legitimate control
   source of support for a statement

11. motive
    explanation
    justification
    rational faculties

13. "Frequently" modifies either "talked" or "fishing."

15. Means either "You will save time and you will *avoid* cutting your fingers
    . . ." or "You will save time and you will *cut* your fingers. . . ."

17. Means either that no greater contribution (than this book) has been made
    between the Second World War and now, or that the *last* contribution of
    equal or greater merit was the War itself.

19. "Normally" modifies either "eats" or "don't get."

21. Means either "(3 × 2) + 1 = 9 " or "3(2 + 1) = 9."

23. Means either a *large bone* belonging to a dog, or a bone belonging to a *large
    dog;* and in either case "belonging to" means either "that is *part* of" or "that
    is the *property* of."

25. Circular.

27. Definiens and definiendum are not grammatically similar. Compare "He
    aims to preach a sermon" with "He aims what clergymen do when they give
    uplifting speeches during church services a sermon."

28. Loaded. Makes empirical statement instead of giving meaning.

In each of the examples to follow, I cite an ambiguous expression and note how
the argument depends for its appeal on the expression's multiple meaning. In
each case, validity requires a uniform interpretation. Although I do not bother
to point this out separately (having just done so generally), *you* must do so.

31. Feathers are light. (E)
    Whatever is light dispels darkness. (T)
∴ Feathers dispel darkness.

   First premise true only if "light" means "not heavy"; second true only if
   "light" means "opposite of dark."

33. All angles of a triangle are equal to two right angles. (E)
ABC is an angle of a triangle. (E)
∴ ABC is equal to two right angles.

First premise true only if "all angles" means "all the angles, taken together as a unit"; but argument valid only if "all angles———are" means "each angle———is."

35. It is the government's job to care for national resources. (E)
People's health is a national resource. (E)
∴ It is the government's job to care for people's health.

First premise most plausible only if "national resources" is narrowly construed to cover seacoasts, park lands, and so on. But second premise true only if "national resources" is construed more broadly than this—much more broadly than usual.

37. Daniel Ellsberg aided the enemy. (E)
Whoever aids the enemy is a traitor. (T)
∴ Daniel Ellsberg is a traitor.

Second premise plausible only if "aids the enemy" is construed so narrowly as to make first premise questionable.

39. Senator Klaghorn represents his constituents. (E)
Whoever represents someone has feelings much like the latter's. (T)
∴ Senator Klaghorn has feelings much like those of his constituents.

First premise not highly plausible unless "represents" means "is the elected representative (deputy) of." But second premise plausible only if "represents" means "typifies."

41. A miser doesn't have enough money. (E)
Whoever is rich has enough money. (T)
∴ A miser is not rich.

First premise plausible only if "enough money" means "enough money so that one has no strong need or desire for more." But second premise plausible only if "enough money" means "enough money to secure a high standard of living."

43. Analyzed in detail in §12.1.

45. Everyone does only what he thinks will give him the most satisfaction in the end. (E)
To do only what one thinks will give one the most satisfaction in the end is to be a pleasure-seeker. (T)
∴ Everyone is a pleasure-seeker.

First premise plausible only if "satisfaction" is interpreted broadly, so that it includes the satisfaction of the ascetic and the pursuer of noble causes as well as that of the sensualist. But then, second premise implausible unless "pleasure" is given a similarly broad (and nonstandard) construction, in which case conclusion is not terribly interesting.

47. Young women who dress provocatively invite rape (of themselves) to happen. (E)
 Whoever invites a thing to happen has only himself to blame when it happens. (T)
∴ Young women who dress provocatively have only themselves to blame when rape (of themselves) happens.

First premise plausible only if "invite" means something like "increase the likelihood of," or "provocatively" means "in a manner exceeding established norms of permissible sexual suggestiveness," or both. But with "invite" interpreted that way, second premise implausible (else I should have only myself to blame for getting mugged because I "invited" it by leaving my house). And with "provocatively" interpreted that way, conclusion is less interesting than it seemed at first to be.

CHAPTER 9

1. To outlaw prostitution is to legislate morality. (E)
 We should not legislate morality. (T)
∴ We should not outlaw prostitution.

First premise is maximally plausible only if "morality" is interpreted broadly, as something like "the general norms of right and wrong." In that case, second premise is implausible, a law against murder being a counter-example. Second premise is plausible only if "morality" is interpreted much more narrowly, as "private values" or some such thing. Argument is valid only if "morality" is interpreted uniformly.

3. Pornography serves no purpose but to stimulate lust. (E)
 Anything that serves no purpose but to stimulate lust is wrong. (T)
∴ Pornography is wrong.

Counter-example to the first premise: Pornography also serves the purpose of entertainment. The second premise, too, is questionable.

5. It is highly conducive to the interests of the community that each person should enjoy a liberty, perfectly unlimited, of expressing his sentiments. (E)
 What is highly conducive to the interests of the community is, on the whole, advantageous to the state. (T)
 To allow a person unbounded freedom of speech is for it to be the case that he enjoys a liberty, perfectly unlimited, of expressing his sentiments. (T)
∴ To allow every person unbounded freedom of speech is always, on the whole, advantageous to the state.

First premise is question-begging.

7. Democratic governments are popularly elected. (E)
Popularly elected governments are more popular than other governments. (T)
∴ Democratic governments are more popular than other governments.

Second premise is true only if "more popular" means "staffed by leaders more likely to win elections," in which case conclusion is relatively uninteresting.

9. Standardization:
No evil should be allowed that good may come of it.
∴ Punishment should be abolished.

Ignore tacit premises for the moment. Express premise is not sufficiently general. Equally plausible generalization:

No evil should be allowed.

If even those evils that have good consequences should not be allowed, then surely *no* evil should be allowed. Reconstruction based on generalized premise:

No evil should be allowed.
Punishment is an evil.
Punishment has been instituted.
Anything that should not be allowed but has been instituted should be abolished.
∴ Punishment should be abolished.

Validity requires a uniform interpretation of "evil." If "evil" is so interpreted that an evil thing can have compensating virtues on top of its evil aspects, then first premise is false, necessary though painful dental treatment being a counter-example. If, on the other hand, "evil" means "evil *on balance* (evil without compensating virtues)," then second premise is question-begging.

11. It is not possible for everyone to be right in his private judgment in religious matters. (E)
One who is not right in his private judgment in some matters has no right of private judgment in those matters. (T)
∴ Not everyone has the right of private judgment in religious matters.

The suggested tacit premise is preferable, according to Generality, to this one:

One who is not right in his private judgment in *religious* matters has no right of private judgment in *religious* matters.

Counter-example to second premise: You have the *right* to make *wrong* private judgments about political candidates, about which restaurant will serve you the tastiest meal, about who will win the Miss America contest, and so on.

13. Laws against "abnormal" sexual practices prevent people from leading their lives as they please. (E)

Any law that prevents people from leading their lives as they please is unjustified. (T)

∴ Laws against "abnormal" sexual practices are unjustified.

Counter-example to second premise: Laws against murder, theft, rape, or whatever, justifiably prevent murderers, thieves, rapists, and whomever from leading their lives as they please. (Can also say argument depends on ambiguity of "leading their lives as they please.")

15. In a democracy like ours, the government should do whatever a majority want. (E)

∴ In a democracy like ours, if a majority want the institution of prayer in the public schools, the government should institute prayer in the public schools.

If the premise is supposed to hold in a reasonable range of possible cases, not just actual ones, there are numerous counter-examples to it: The government should not suppress the Jehovah's Witnesses, incarcerate Negroes in concentration camps, or any such thing, even if a majority want the government to do so. If the premise is supposed to hold only in actual cases, such decisive counter-examples are harder to find, since it is not clear just what majorities prefer, and actual majority preferences probably are not as outrageous as those in the hypothetical cases just cited. Still, owing to those cases, the premise is at least questionable.

17. If people are allowed to allocate their Social Security contributions to the retirement program they think is best, many will make poor choices of how to allocate their Social Security contributions. (E)
People should not be allowed to do something if many would make poor choices of how to do it. (T)

∴ People should not be allowed to allocate their Social Security contributions to the retirement program they think is best.

Counter-examples to second premise: Many people make poor choices of what car to buy, of what movie to see, of what dish to order from a menu, of what hypothesis to try in some piece of research, of what company to invest in, and so forth. Yet (within broad limits) people should be allowed to do these things.

19. Everyone has the right to perform private actions. (E)
Private actions are (defined as) actions affecting the legitimate interests of no one but the actor. (E)
To have an abortion is to perform an action affecting the legitimate interests of no one but the actor. (T)

∴ A woman has the right to have an abortion.

Third premise is question-begging. It says, in effect, that the fetus is not someone with a legitimate interest in staying alive.

21. For reconstruction, see Chapter 7, Exercise 40. This argument is not too bad. You must interpret "the same" to mean "morally similar." One might ques-

tion first premise on ground that Hindus object to *killing* beef cattle whereas Moslems do not object to *killing* swine.

23. Hitler did what he thought was morally right. (E)
Whoever does what he thinks is morally right is a moral person in a way. (T)
∴ In a way, Hitler was a moral person.

Conclusion is not maximally interesting (although it still is somewhat interesting) if "moral person" is interpreted according to second premise. Yet validity requires uniform interpretation.

25. We cannot allow each citizen to decide for himself which laws he'll obey. (E)
To allow civil disobedience is to allow each citizen to decide for himself which laws he'll obey. (T)
Not to allow something is to crack down on it. (T)
∴ We have got to crack down on civil disobedience.

Depends on ambiguity of "civil disobedience." If this term is used in the standard way, it does not apply to *all* law violations, but only to certain nonviolent, symbolic, or protest-type law violations, so second premise is false. If the term is used broadly enough to make the second premise true, the conclusion is relatively uninteresting. The term must be used uniformly for the argument to be valid. (Also depends on ambiguity of "crack down.")

27. A crackdown by management on employee theft would likely be more costly than the theft itself. (E)
Not to crack down on something is to allow it. (T)
If cracking down on X would be more costly than X, then it also would be more costly than allowing X. (T)
If doing something would be more costly than not doing it, then it would be better not to do it than to do it. (T)
∴ It would be better for management to allow employee theft than to crack down on it.

Only if "better" means something like "preferable from the point of view of all relevant considerations, including ethics" is the conclusion maximally interesting; only then is it a real recommendation or prescription. But then the fourth premise is questionable, witness this arguable counter-example: I borrow your car, promising to return it, but find that it would be more costly, on balance, to return it than to keep it, because I can profit from its use more than you can. But you demand its return. Surely it would be better (even though more costly) to return it. Validity requires that "better" be construed uniformly.

29. For reconstruction, see Chapter 7, Exercise 34. Criticism given in §12.1.

CHAPTER 10

For each exercise, I cite the explanatory conclusion, labeled C; the express explanatory premise, labeled P; and one or more alternative explanatory premises, labeled A, A_1, A_2, or A_3.

1. (C) When Ignatz opened the door of his house, I saw a woman disappear into the bedroom.
   (P) Bertha was at Ignatz's house.
   (A) Some other woman was at Ignatz's house.

Whether A is plausible enough to diminish P's plausibility depends on context.

3. (C) I saw her coming out of the firehouse with a license plate on her bicycle.
   (P) She just got her license plate at the firehouse, and it is the Fire Department that registers bicycles and gives out license plates.
   (A_1) She went to the firehouse to visit a fireman, having previously gotten her license plate.
   (A_2) She went to the firehouse to report a fire, having previously gotten her license plate.

Barring further information, A_1 and A_2 are plausible enough to detract somewhat from P.

5. (C) The alarm rang.
   (P) Someone pulled a fire-alarm switch somewhere in the city.
   (A) There was a fire somewhere in the city.

P is slightly more plausible than A. But A is significantly *more economical*. It is about equally simple but *more powerful*, since it explains P along with C.

7. (C) Female students often go to see Professor Chalkdust, to whom they talk in a sweet, sexually suggestive way.
   (P) Professor Chalkdust is irresistible to women.
   (A_1) Female students try to use their feminine charms to get good grades from Professor Chalkdust.
   (A_2) People try to use readily available, relatively costless means to gain personal advantage.

Barring further information, A_1 is as plausible as P. A_2 is much more economical.

9. (C) The fire started in his bedroom.
   (P) He was smoking in bed.
   (A_1) An electric device in his bedroom had faulty wiring.
   (A_2) He kept highly inflammable substances in his bedroom.

A_1 and A_2 are plausible enough to weaken P somewhat, but not to refute P (barring further information).

11. (C) Once a staunch segregationist, Senator Julep recently voted to give the predominantly black District of Columbia Congressional representation.
    (P) Senator Julep has had a change of heart regarding black people.
    (A_1) Blacks recently began voting in large numbers in Senator Julep's state.
    (A_2) Elected officials try to maximize their electoral support.

A_1 is arguably more plausible than P, and it clearly is more economical. A_2 is more economical still.

13. (C)   Those who use seat belts have a lower automobile fatality rate than nonusers.
    (P)   Seat belts save lives.
    (A)   Those who are safety-conscious enough to use seat belts also tend to drive more safely than others.

It is hard to say whether A is more plausible than P. It is plausible enough, though, to weaken P.

15. (C)   A trail of crumbs leads from the living room to the front porch, where the cookie box lies crumpled under the rocking chair.
    (P)   The cookie box was opened in the living room, then carried to the porch.
    (A)   The cookie box was opened on the porch by someone who then walked to the living room.

Perhaps not quite as plausible as P (barring further information), A is plausible enough to detract from P somewhat.

17. (C)   The car moved.
    (P)   The gas pedal was depressed.
    (A)   The driver wanted to move the car and knew that the easiest way was to depress the pedal.

A is more economical than P because it is more powerful, and it is more powerful because it explains P along with C.

19. (C)   Most letters received by legislators concerning the Equal Rights Amendment support passage.
    (P)   A majority of citizens support passage.
    (A)   Among those citizens who feel strongly enough about the ERA to write their legislators about it, a majority support passage.

A is more plausible than P.

21. (C)   In a recent election, a majority opposed a law forbidding discrimination against homosexuals in employment.
    (P)   A majority of citizens oppose equal employment opportunities for gays.
    (A_1)   A majority of citizens believe that equal employment opportunities for gays should not be *legally mandated*.
    (A_2)   A majority of citizens oppose new laws governing whom one can hire.
    (A_3)   Among those citizens who felt strongly enough about the issue to vote, a majority opposed equal employment opportunities for gays.

A_1-A_3 are easily as plausible as P. A_2 is more economical than the others.

23. (C)   Klaghorn got 53 percent of the vote.
    (P)   Fifty-three percent of his constituents favor Klaghorn.

(A)   Fifty-three percent of those of his constituents who cared enough to vote favor Klaghorn.

A is more plausible than P, but P is more economical (because simpler). Whether or not A is strictly better, it is a reasonable enough alternative to weaken P.

25. (C)   The average car in the United States is traded in every 3¼ years; in Sweden, Volvos last an average of 11 years; and more than 95 percent of all Volvos sold in the United States in the last 11 years are still on the road.
    (P)   Volvos tend to last longer than American cars.
    (A)   Americans tend to trade in their cars while they are still in good condition, and most Volvos sold in the United States in the last 11 years were in fact sold in the last *few* years.

Obviously A is more plausible. It also is arguably more economical because more powerful.

27. (C)   The customer attests to having cured his warts with his genuine Swiss Army knife.
    (P)   A genuine Swiss Army knife is good enough for minor surgery, like cutting off warts.
    (A)   Any decent pocket knife is good enough for minor surgery, like cutting off warts.

About as plausible as P, A is more economical because more powerful.

CHAPTER 11

6. Capital punishment has been shown to be an effective deterrent. (E)
   Any punishment that has been shown to be an effective deterrent is just. (T)
   ∴ Capital punishment is just.

   Counter-example to second premise: Boiling in oil would not be a just punishment for overparking, even if shown to be an effective deterrent.

7. It is unjust for anyone ever to take a human life except when necessary to defend another human life. (E)
   Every case of capital punishment is a case of someone's taking a human life. (T)
   Never is capital punishment necessary to defend a human life. (T)
   ∴ Capital punishment is unjust.

   There are arguable counter-examples to the first premise: To defend oneself against serious injury (not death), one might have to kill an attacker. Soldiers kill each other even when that is not necessary to protect their *lives*. Some such actions are arguably just.

8. People should be legally allowed to do anything they want so long as they do not harm others. (E)
Every case of abortion is a case of someone doing what she wants without harming others. (T)
∴ Abortion should be legally allowed.

If killing a fetus who would otherwise survive delivery counts as "harming others," then almost every case of abortion is a counter-example to the second premise. If killing such a fetus does *not* count as "harming others," then the first premise is as questionable as the very practice it is being used to defend. Validity requires a uniform interpretation of "harming others."

9. Infanticide is morally wrong. (E)
There is no relevant difference between abortion and infanticide. (E)
If there is no relevant difference between two things and one is morally wrong, so is the other. (T)
∴ Abortion is morally wrong.

Some people would disagree with the first premise, some with the second. Both are plausible. A strong criticism would be an arguable counter-example to the second premise. I have found none. Although not conclusive (the first two premises being debatable), the argument is pretty good.

11. The objective of the Civil War was to prevent both the dissolution of the Union and a few more years of slavery. (T)
Dissolution of the Union and a few more years of slavery would not have been bad enough to justify killing hundreds of thousands of people, including conscripts and noncombatants. (E)
The Civil War killed hundreds of thousands of people, including conscripts and noncombatants. (T)
If (doing) X did A, if the objective of X was to prevent B, and if B would not have been bad enough to justify A, then X was not worth the cost. (T)
∴ The Civil War was not worth the cost.

When you send ten soldiers into battle and two die, have you killed those two, or have you merely risked the lives of all ten so that each had a one-in-five chance of dying? The verb phrase:

(K)   to kill hundreds of thousands of people

can be interpreted two ways:

(K₁) to kill each of hundreds of thousands of people directly,
(K₂) to risk the lives of sufficiently many people to a sufficient degree so that hundreds of thousands end up dying.

For the conclusion to be maximally interesting, "the Civil War" must refer to the actions of Lincoln and others who chose to wage war, in which case, to ensure validity, we must interpret "the Civil War" the same way in the third premise. But then, the third premise is plausible only if (K) means (K₂). To preserve validity, we must interpret (K) the same way in the second premise, in which case that premise is somewhat less plausible than it seemed at first to be. Not strikingly implausible, though. So this criticism weakens the argument without destroying it.

13. Capital punishment discriminates against the poor. (E)
Whatever discriminates against the poor is unjust. (T)
∴ Capital punishment is unjust.

The conclusion is maximally interesting only if calling a practice unjust is taken to mean that it is unjustifiable or unacceptable, not merely that its administration could be fairer. But then, to ensure validity, we must interpret "unjust" the same way in the second premise, in which case the latter is less plausible than it seemed at first to be. For our entire criminal justice system discriminates against the poor, in a weak sense of "discriminate." And if we interpret "discriminate" strongly enough to make the second premise plausible, then validity demands the same strong interpretation in the first premise as well. But that would diminish the plausibility of the first premise.

15. This is a reverse-explanation argument. Explanatory conclusion:

Countries that do not use capital punishment have fewer murders per population than do countries that use it.

Explanatory hypothesis (and conclusion of argument):

Capital punishment does not work (as a deterrent to murder).

Alternative, equally plausible hypothesis:

The less a country's need to deter a particular type of action, the less likely it is to adopt any given purported deterrent, especially a severe one.

17. Everyone has the moral right—and ought to have the legal right—of free speech and association. (E)
The right of free speech and association is the right to organize and voice one's beliefs. (T)
Whoever has the moral right—and ought to have the legal right—to do something should not be prevented from doing it (T)
∴ Organizations that purvey hate—the Nazis, the K.K.K., and so on— should not be prevented from organizing and voicing their beliefs.

Just by making the second premise explicit, we see that it is at best questionable: The right of free speech and association is the right to organize and voice one's beliefs *within certain limits,* such as the prohibitions against slander, against inciting riots, and so forth. Perhaps the activities of the Nazis, K.K.K., etc., are within these limits. But that is *another argument.* The *given* argument says nothing about these limits.

19. Standardization:
To abort a fetus is to let it die, not to kill it.
∴ To abort a fetus is not morally wrong.

Two candidate tacit premises:

(T₁) Letting *a fetus* die, without killing it, never is morally wrong.
(T₂) Letting *a thing* die, without killing it, never is morally wrong.

(T₂) is preferable according to Generality. Counter-example to (T₂): I can perform a simple, virtually costless procedure to save an accident victim's life. In failing to perform it, I let the victim die; I don't kill him. But my *omission* is morally wrong.

CHAPTER 12

5. Under a well-thought-out national eugenics policy, future people would constitute a healthy, creative race of supermen. (E)
   Future people would not be nearly as well off in the absence of a well-thought-out national eugenics policy than they would be if they constituted a healthy, creative race of supermen. (T)
   The cost to us of adopting a well-thought-out national eugenics policy would be small. (T)
   We are far less numerous than future people. (T)
   If we are far less numerous than X's, if X's would not be nearly as well off in the absence of a certain policy as they would be under that policy, and if the cost to us of adopting the policy would be small, then we should adopt it. (T)
   ∴ We should adopt a well-thought-out national eugenics policy.

   This depends on an ambiguity of the form of words:

   (*) ——s would not be nearly as well off in the absence of . . . as they would be under. . . .

   The second premise is plausible only if (*) means:

   those who would be ——s in the absence of . . . would not be nearly as well off in the absence of . . . as those who would be ——s under . . . would be under. . . .

   But validity requires that (*) have the same meaning in the fifth premise, in which case that premise is not as plausible as it seemed.

7. If all Democrats vote, a Democrat probably will be elected. (E)
   If many Democrats do not vote, a Democrat probably will not be elected. (T)
   Every Democrat would be much happier if he voted and a Democrat were elected than he would be if he did not vote and a Democrat were not elected. (T)
   Assuming each soandso probably would be much happier if all soandsos did a certain thing than he would be if many—himself included—did not do it, then each soandso probably would be much happier if he did it than he would be if he did not do it. (T)
   Assuming somebody probably would be much happier if he did a certain

thing than he would be if he did not do it, then it would be foolish for him not to do it. (T)

∴ It would be foolish for Democrats not to vote.

The disarmament and pollution examples of §12.3 are counter-examples to the fourth premise.

9. Federal minimum-wage laws raise the incomes of our worst-off workers. (E)
Whatever raises the incomes of soandsos is justified from the point of view of soandsos. (T)

∴ Federal minimum-wage laws are justified from the point of view of our worst-off workers.

The second premise is most plausible only if the form of words:

    X raises the income of Y

means:

    X makes those who would have been Ys in the absence of X better off than those very same individuals would have been in the absence of X.

But validity requires the same meaning in the first premise, and that decreases the plausibility of the first premise: when the minimum wage rises by law, some erstwhile minimum-wage earners get raises, but some lose their jobs, dropping out of the class of minimum-wage earners.

10. This is an explanation. Reconstruction:

    All Widget Workers thought they'd get better wages and greater job protection if they all took part in organizing a union and going on strike than they'd get if many did not take part. (E)
    Each Widget Worker preferred his taking part in organizing a union and going on strike and getting better wages and greater job protection to his not taking part and not getting these things. (T)
    If someone prefers doing X and getting Y to not doing X and not getting Y, and if he thinks he will get Y if he does X but not if he does not do X, then he will do X. (T)

∴ The Widget Workers each took part in organizing a union and going on strike.

Valid only if "*they'd* get better wages and greater job protection if they all took part . . ." means "*each* of them would get better wages and greater job protection if *he* took part . . .," in which case the first premise is implausible. Or you can drop the last tacit premise above in favor of these:

    Assuming each soandso prefers all soandsos' doing X to many soandsos' not doing X, then each soandso prefers his doing X to his not doing X.
    Whoever prefers doing something to not doing it will do it.

This ensures validity. But the first of the two new premises is open to the disarmament and pollution counter-examples.

12. We took the piece of land from the Indian tribe by means of a fraudulent contract of sale. (E)

To take something by means of fraudulent contract is to take it illicitly. (T)

We illicitly took the piece of land from the Indian tribe.

If X illicitly took something from Y, then for X to refuse to compensate Y for it would be for X to compound the injustice against Y. (T)

For us to refuse to compensate the Indian tribe for the piece of land would be for us to compound the injustice against the tribe.

We must not compound any injustice. (T)

Not to refuse to do something is to do it. (T)

We must compensate the Indian tribe for the piece of land.

If "we" and "the Indian tribe" refer to *institutions* (broadly conceived) rather than *people*, the conclusion is somewhat less interesting (since it does not then clearly impose any obligation on anyone), and the third premise ("If X . . .") is somewhat less plausible. Suppose, on the other hand, that we interpret "we" and "the Indian tribe" as referring to *people*. Then for the conclusion to be interesting (to say anything about current policy), "we" and "the Indian tribe" must refer to people who are *now* we and who *now* belong to the tribe. But the first premise is plausible only if "we" and "the Indian tribe" refer to our ancestors and those of the present-day tribesmen. In that case, validity requires that the third premise mean the following:

If *erstwhile* Xs illicitly took something from *erstwhile* Ys, then for *present* Xs to refuse to compensate *present* Ys for it would be for present Xs to compound the injustice against *present* Ys.

But this is implausible.

Index

About the Author

Thomas Schwartz received his A.B. in philosophy from Brandeis in 1965 and his Ph.D. in philosophy from the University of Pittsburgh in 1969. From 1969 to 1973 he was Assistant Professor of Philosophy at Stanford, where he held a joint appointment in Human Biology. He moved to Carnegie-Mellon in 1973 as Associate Professor of Philosophy and Urban and Public Affairs and chairman of the Philosophy Program. Since 1976 he has been Associate Professor of Government at the University of Texas at Austin, where he currently chairs the Formal Theory, Methodology, and Honors programs. He has held visiting appointments in philosophy at the University of Pittsburgh and in political science at the University of California, Irvine. Best known for his work in social-choice theory—the abstract, mathematical study of political and economic processes—he has also contributed to moral and political philosophy and to logic. His publications have appeared in journals of economics, political science, philosophy, and formal logic.